Complete
Handyman
do-it-yourself
Annual

Complete Handyman do-it-yourself Annual

A COMPILATION OF SPECIAL INTEREST PROJECTS
FOR THE MODERNIZING AND CARE OF HOMES AND
FURNISHINGS, INDOORS AND OUTDOORS
Prepared by the Editors of POPULAR SCIENCE
Also published under the title,
POPULAR SCIENCE 1986 DO-IT-YOURSELF YEARBOOK

1986

H. S. STUTTMAN CO., INC. *publishers*   Westport, CT.   06889

Copyright © 1985 by Popular Science Books

Published by

Popular Science Books
Times Mirror Magazines, Inc.
380 Madison Avenue
New York, NY 10017

Distributed to the trade by

Rodale Press, Inc.
33 East Minor Street
Emmaus, PA 18049

ISBN: 0-943822-61-0

Manufactured in the United States of America

introduction

This fourth *Popular Science Do-it-Yourself Yearbook* is both traditional and unprecedented. It includes the kind of step-by-step projects and techniques you have come to expect in the series; yet in many ways it is unlike any Yearbook that has come before.

As always, the editors have singled out the very best do-it-yourself articles from *Popular Science* magazine. You'll find chapters that span the range of DIY areas, from the latest technology in homebuilding and remodeling to indoor and outdoor woodworking projects at every skill level. You'll also find original contributions from the best free-lance technical and how-to writers in the field, in areas that appear for the first time in this Yearbook.

New for 1986

New this year is a detailed, fully illustrated Car Care section. It takes you from trouble-shooting complex new electronic ignition systems to applying a professional-looking paint job. Another first for 1986 is an original series of heirloom-furniture projects by master woodworker and writer Nick Engler. Featured in this section are plans for an ornate cherry grandfather clock your family will cherish for generations to come. Four-color illustrations in all sections of the Yearbook constitute yet another first.

How about adding on an energy-efficient, all-seasons room? The details are inside, along with 14 other chapters covering home improvements, repairs, maintenance, and remodeling. You can even build your own version of today's most popular catamaran with tips from Peter and Susanne Stevenson, beginning on page 121.

Trends in DIY

The DIY field is growing fast, as you can probably tell from the increasing number of hardware stores and home centers. Folks who once wouldn't have picked up a hammer are now avid do-it-yourselfers. Annual increases of at least 10 percent in tool and material sales will probably continue. And analysts predict the DIY industry will grow from the huge $15 billion it already was back in 1980 to more than $60 billion by 1995.

Reasons for this growth include more and more people entering the active DIY years. The increasing number of women do-it-yourselfers also plays a part, as do rising costs of professionally done work, an improved economy, and an ongoing move to the sunbelt, where DIY is ever-popular.

Plumbing manufacturers are fast devising better materials that are easier to use—such as CPVC and PB water-supply tubing—and proving them safe. The special female adapter shown in my plastic-plumbing chapter (page 146) didn't exist when my original article first appeared in *Popular Science* just a few months ago. And have you seen the selection of tubular-fixture drain traps and other tubular goods on store racks? Now you can do anything you want with fixture drains. Simple solvent-welding plastic pipes and fittings have replaced lead-and-oakum-joined cast iron and silver- or sweat-soldered copper. Coming on strong are fist-size automatic vent valves that replace through-the-roof vent stacks in drain-waste-vent plumbing.

Electrical wiring products are becoming easier to use, too—and safer. Once unknown, the ground-fault circuit interrupter is now a code requirement for certain household locations. It protects against dangerous shocks from a faulty appliance. Newly introduced plastic outlet boxes and flexible plastic conduit let any home electrician install protected wiring behind the walls. Also, supplies and instructions for surface raceway wiring are now readily available in stores—including the huge warehouse home centers that have developed into a major market force.

Energy-saving is also high on the do-it-yourselfer's priority list. Check out the chapter on heating-system add-ons beginning on page 39.

Wood has always been a satisfying medium. That's why more than a third of this Yearbook is devoted solely to indoor and outdoor woodworking projects. Now a new breed of high-tech, electronic power tools is making this attractive DIY area easier and more rewarding for both experienced and beginning woodworkers. Further developments in this area include useful new fasteners such as the drywall screw. Originally developed for hanging plasterboard, the screw serves as a nail replacement in many woodworking and around-the-house uses. It's double-threaded for quick, easy driving.

The ultimate do-it-yourself project is building a house. While most do-it-yourselfers don't get that involved, an increasing number do become owner-builders. "Two Unique Homes You Can Build Yourself" (page 11) can help you do the same. Other chapters detail features you may want in your next home, whether or not you build it yourself. You'll also find creative techniques for working with the new solid-color laminates, solid-wood strip paneling, and more of the latest materials.

Possibly the fastest-growing DIY area is auto care and repair. Maybe you've noticed the new auto-parts supermarkets sprouting up. Even established DIY retailers are setting aside space for auto-care items. A problem for the do-it-yourselfer, however, is the automobile's increasing complexity. Rigid fuel-mileage requirements and emissions regulations have brought high-tech to the family car. Instead of getting easier to fix, cars are getting downright tough to work on. Nevertheless, this year's new auto section covers areas you can still handle yourself—and includes how to trouble-shoot a myriad of sophisticated emission-control gadgetry that could hold the key to better driveability and gas mileage from your car.

And still more

Many of the Yearbook chapters I've described so far were provided by free-lance writers. This year, you'll also find an unprecedented number of excellent contributions from the editorial staffs of *Popular Science* magazine and the Times Mirror Book Division. Projects such as the beautiful multilevel deck (page 22) by W. David Houser, who also built the all-seasons room it surrounds. Or the space-saving swinging-bookcase room divider by John Sill, beginning on page 68. All of which combine to make this fourth, *1986 Popular Science Do-it-Yourself Yearbook* a truly exciting and varied package for the year of Halley's comet. Enjoy!

RICHARD DAY
Consulting Editor for Home and Shop
Popular Science

the authors

Below is an alphabetical sampling of the authors for this issue. They include freelancers as well as members of the *Popular Science* New York and field staff.

Mark Bittman is a full-time freelance writer who lives in New Haven, Connecticut. His hobbies are carpentry and cooking, and those are also the subjects about which he most likes to write. His work appears regularly in *Popular Science*. His food articles are published in newspapers on both coasts (and in between), and he also writes for magazines such as *Business Week* and *Advertising Age*.

Paul and Marya Butler have been building boats for over 20 years. The 8-foot Norwegian pram shown in their "Wood-epoxy Construction" chapter is but one example of their craft. The husband-and-wife team also contribute to a number of publications—Paul doing the writing, Marya the illustrating. They are currently working on a book on wood-epoxy dory construction.

Bob Cerullo has over 25 years' experience as a line mechanic, service manager, and as a technical writer for such magazines as *Popular Science* and *Motor*. Owner and operator of a 23-bay auto repair shop, Bob wrote the chapter on trouble-shooting front disc brakes beginning on page 162. He is also vice-president of the International Motor Press Association, a member of the Society of Automotive Engineers, and a frequent guest on radio programs dealing with automotive subjects.

Richard Day, consulting editor for home and shop at *Popular Science,* has been writing in the how-to field for some 30 years. Specializing in home plumbing, concrete and masonry, and electrical wiring, he has written numerous magazine DIY articles and over a dozen related books. These include *How to Build Patios and Decks* and *How to Service and Repair Your Own Car.* He is also a director and past-president of the National Association of Home and Workshop Writers.

R. J. DeCristoforo has long been one of the leading woodworking writers. Besides serving as consulting editor for tools and techniques for *Popular Science,* he is the author of countless how-to articles—five of which are incorporated in this Yearbook. He has also written over two dozen books, including *How to Build Your Own Furniture, DeCristoforo's Housebuilding Illustrated,* and his classic, *The Complete Book of Stationary Power Tool Techniques.*

Carl De Groote, author of the chapter "Install these Skylights from Indoors," is a prolific architect and illustrator for the major DIY publications. Renowned for his knowl-

edge of construction and attention to detail, Carl is often asked to produce intricate drawings from mere snapshots. You'll see his drawings throughout this Yearbook; they are easily recognizable by their distinctive style and "CDG" monogram.

Amy L. Delson is president of her own full-service architecture firm in Warren, New Jersey. The firm's work includes health facility planning and design, as well as commercial and residential projects—the latter of which includes the high-rise planter deck beginning on page 102. An alumnus of the Harvard University Graduate School of Design, Ms. Delson is a registered architect in New York and New Jersey and is NCARB-certified.

Nick Engler founded the how-to magazine, *HANDS ON!* and managed Shopsmith's publishing department for over three years. During that time, he helped produce not only the magazine, but over 100 project plans, books, manuals, and a syndicated newspaper column for woodworkers. Today he writes freelance for various publications on the subjects of how-to, science, and technology. Nick also provided three of the four heirloom-furniture projects you'll find in this Yearbook.

Don Geary is a free-lance writer living in Salt Lake City, Utah. A home-computer enthusiast who also enjoys woodworking, Don designed and built the veneered-stand computer carrel shown on page 65. In all, he has written 17 books and hundreds of magazine articles for the home and outdoor do-it-yourselfer.

Gene and Katie Hamilton are a writing-and-photography team that specializes in the home and workshop field. They are the authors of *Build It Together* as well as DIY consultants for the Minwax Wood Finish Company and Reader's Digest General Books. They also contribute regularly to *The Family Handyman, Popular Mechanics, Home Mechanix,* and *Popular Science.*

A. J. Hand began preparing for a career as a writer-photographer at the age of six by assisting his writer-father, the late Jackson Hand, with photo setups. A. J. later served on the *Popular Science* staff, winding up in 1975 as the magazine's home workshop editor before he began freelancing full-time. His photos have appeared on many magazine covers, and his articles appear in magazines and in his syndicated newspaper column, "Hand Around the House." He is the author of *Home Energy How-to,* as well as five of the chapters in this Yearbook.

William J. Hawkins worked for five years at RCA before joining *Popular Science* as electronics editor in 1970. While still at RCA, he won an electronics contest sponsored by *PS* and Allstate Insurance to find better auto anti-theft devices. Besides his editorial duties, Hawkins has also been responsible for installing and maintaining the magazine's computer system. He has appeared on network shows such as "Good Morning America," "Today," and "Omni." He also covers the home how-to area, as his chapter on replacing patio doors attests.

W. David Houser, art director for *Popular Science,* often writes up his home projects for the magazine. You'll find two of them side by side in this Yearbook's house remodeling section. In addition to woodworking, he also restores old MGs.

Jack Keebler heads up this year's new car-care section with his chapter, "Beginner's Guide to Auto Repainting." His varied automotive background includes writing and editing for Hearst's Motor Manuals, as well as hands-on experience as a BMW mechanic. Currently associate automotive editor for *Popular Science,* Jack lives in Oakland, New Jersey, with his wife, Wendy.

Alfred W. Lees, *Popular Science* group editor for reader activities, is in charge of all DIY instruction. He built the Lockbox leisure home as the focus of 19 feature articles during the 1970s. He also created the *PS* "Leisure-Home" and "Storage from Scratch" series, as well as the national design competition for plywood projects, which he judges. His books include *Popular Science Leisure Home* (with Ernest V. Heyn) and *67 Prizewinning Plywood Projects.*

Donald Maxwell is a past first-prize winner in the *Popular Science/*American Plywood Association plywood projects competition. He and his wife Carol have taught in colleges all over the world, most recently in central China. Don currently teaches English at a college in Virginia, where he also operates a telecommunications service for faculty and handicapped students. He has also written poetry, fiction, and essays on education and computers. His unique chapter on inside-out house siding begins on page 138.

Jim McCann, whose original grandfather clock design begins on page 42, has a background that includes not only woodworking, but metalworking, electronics, power mechanics, and industrial design. As a former project plans specialist for Shopsmith, Inc.—a power-tools manufacturer in Ohio—Jim helped design and build over 100 projects for the firm's publishing department. He also spent several years advising woodworkers in the "Ask Smitty" column in *HANDS ON!* magazine. Today Jim works in Shopsmith's engineering laboratory, helping to design power tools for home shops.

Bernard W. Powell has worked across a broad range of American industry. Currently a business writer specializing in management-level articles, he has a working knowledge that includes chemicals, plastics, packaging, wastewater treatment, mining, and metallurgy—to name a few areas. Bernie's "Easy-Access Woodshed" chapter represents one of his many how-to articles that have appeared in mass-media publications. In addition to woodworking, he enjoys traditional blacksmithing in an old-time blacksmith shop he reconstructed on his property in Redding Ridge, Connecticut.

Susan Renner-Smith, a senior editor at Popular Science, writes and edits articles on all topics covered by the magazine, ranging from space stations and electronic home banking to tiling bathrooms. She lives—with her husband, Norman Smith, and son, Eric—in a 60-year-old house that serves as a proving ground for the products and projects she reports on.

George Sears is a seasoned free-lance writer who has long covered the automotive servicing scene for *Popular Science* magazine. His chapters on trouble-shooting auto emissions systems and electronic ignition represent but two of his many contributions in this sought-after area of information.

John Sill is vice-president and editorial director of Popular Science Books. As the chapter on the swinging-bookcase room divider attests, John's spare-time interest turns to woodworking, a prime love of his life since he picked up a spokeshave in a fifth-grade manual training class. He particularly enjoys designing and building his own furniture for articles appearing in magazines such as *Popular Science* and *Workbench.*

Neil Soderstrom is a partner in Zambory & Soderstrom Designs Inc., which offers furniture plans by mail. He is also an independent book producer specializing in heavily illustrated how-to and nature books. A board member of the National Association of Home and Workshop Writers, he has written for numerous periodicals. His own books include *Chainsaw Savvy, Heating Your Home with Wood,* and—with E. D. Fales—*How to Drive to Prevent Accidents.*

Peter and Susanne Stevenson are the husband-and-wife team behind Stevenson Projects, a California company that supplies do-it-yourself plans for scores of projects ranging from furniture to sailboats. Pete's the designer-builder-writer. Susie's the business manager and publications director. Many of their projects have been featured in national magazines such as *Popular Science;* you'll find two of these projects in the section on outdoor woodworking projects.

contents

I. House Design and Construction   2

Stilt Houses **2**
The House that Computers Built **4**
Energy-saving Two-faced House **8**
Two Unique Homes You Can Build
     Yourself **11**

II. House Remodeling   14

Easy-to-Install Mirrored Wall **14**
11 Fresh Ideas to Transform Your
     Bathroom **16**
Passive-solar All-seasons Room **19**
Multilevel-deck Outdoor Entertainment
     Area **22**
Solid-wood Strip Paneling for Your
     Home **26**
Double-frame Window Stretches View
     —Saves Energy **30**
Install these Skylights from
     Indoors **33**

III. Energy-saving Techniques   36

Keep the Heat Inside with Outside
     Insulation **36**
Eight Heating-system Add-ons **39**

IV. Woodworking Projects   42

INDOORS
Grandfather Clock **42**
Revolutionary Lowboy **50**
Queen Anne Drop-leaf Dining
     Table **55**
Storage Wall for Home Electronics **60**
Double-duty Room **62**
Two Computer Carrels **65**
Swinging-bookcase Room Divider **68**
Two-faced Bed/Wardrobe Divider **72**
Queen Anne Secretary **76**
Make Your Own Tambour Doors **83**
Organize Your Garage with
     Waferboard **86**
Nine Do-it-Yourself Safety Devices for
     Power Tools **89**
Flip-top Bench for Compact Tools **93**

OUTDOORS
Fanciful Functional Fences **98**
High-rise Planter Deck **102**
Butcher-block Patio Stool **105**
Compact Patio Sports Center **106**
All-season Skylight Gazebo **110**
Easy-access Woodshed **113**
Elevated Deck with Spa **115**
Parquet Deck **118**
Cocky Catamaran **121**

Woodworking Techniques and
Materials   124

Wood-epoxy Construction **124**
Solid-color Laminates **128**
Biscuit Joinery **132**
14 Clever Fasteners **134**

Home Repairs and Maintenance   138

Hide Peeling Paint with Inside-out
    Siding **138**
Pave a Patio with Ceramic Tile **140**
Replace Your Old Patio Doors **142**
Installing Plastic Plumbing **145**
How to Check for Wrong-way
    Polarity **148**

Car Care   152

Beginner's Guide to Auto
    Repainting **152**
How to Check Your Emissions
    Systems **155**
Trouble-shooting Electronic
    Ignition **158**
Trouble-shooting Front Disc
    Brakes **162**
Curing Preignition and
    Detonation **165**

Latest in Tools and Tool
Techniques   168

Electronic Table and Radial Saws **168**
Compact Four-in-One Tool **171**
Glue-gun Shoot-out **172**
How to Choose and Store
    Carbide Cutters **176**

Index **180**

stilt houses

In this living-dining room, track lights are attached to tensioning rod, part of structural system of Archimède home. Right: Eureka home.

If you drove through the tiny village of St. Frédéric in the Beauce region south of Quebec City, you'd be most impressed by its large stone church. But inside an unremarkable-looking steel building at the edge of town, something revolutionary takes place. There, in the factory of Les Systèmes Archimède, a pair of 50-ton presses squeeze out unique prefabricated building components designed by architect Jacques Poirier: base, roof, and wall panels, each filled with polyurethane-foam insulation and with doors and windows molded in place. A galvanized-steel frame, split along 99 percent of its length to minimize heat transfer, forms the perimeter of each panel. Exterior-finish materials can be applied at the factory or installed on site. What is truly unusual about the panels, however, is their shape: Because of Archimède's unique hexagonal modules, the four-sided components have no right angles.

The variety and styles of homes possible with this system are essentially unlimited. From three to ten 183-square-foot hexagonal modules can be assembled to create homes from 550 to almost 2,000 square feet. They can be one or two stories high and be built on columns or on conventional foundations. Archimède (Box 100, St. Frédéric, Beauce, Que., Canada G0N 1P0) offers three series of homes designed by Poirier: the Delta series, built entirely on stilts; Alpha, built on a slab or full basement; and Eureka, a hybrid built primarily on stilts but with a small ground-level entry on a slab.

On a high-speed tour of southern Quebec with Archimède general manager Serge Maheux, I saw a two-story, 57-unit condominium project near Montreal; a home on steel columns in another suburb, which, on its heavily wooded site, looked like a tree house for adults; a four-unit condominium under construction on a sloping site at a ski area; a cottage on stilts on a cliff overlooking a lake; and a two-story home built on a conventional foundation. Maheux told me that since the company began operation in 1980, more than 200 Archimède homes have been built

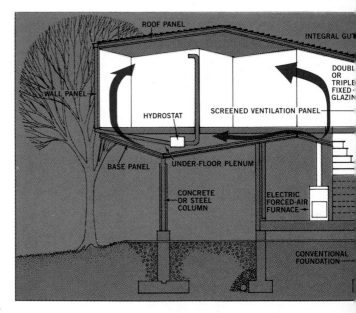

throughout Quebec and on the island of St. Martin in the Caribbean. "A 40-foot container holds an entire home, including appliances," says Maheux.

The company has even built two houses 15 miles from the nearest road on the Gaspé Peninsula. "They're emergency shelters for skiers in Gaspésie Park," explains Maheux, "so our crews lived in tents, and helicopters brought in the panels two or three at a time."

Normally, the finished shell of an Archimède home is ready for interior work in less than a week. The panels are lifted into place by crane and quickly bolted together.

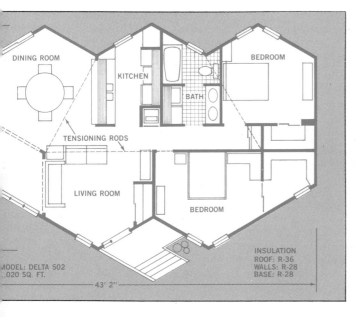

DINING ROOM

KITCHEN

BATH

BEDROOM

TENSIONING RODS

LIVING ROOM

BEDROOM

INSULATION
ROOF: R-36
WALLS: R-28
BASE: R-28

MODEL: DELTA 502
,020 SQ. FT.

←——— 43' 2" ———→

Welder assembles galvanized-steel frame: It's split along 99 percent of its length to cut thermal conduction. Above right: polyurethane foam is injected into panel inside 50-ton press. It takes 20 minutes for foam to harden.

Joints are sealed by on-site foaming equipment. With the shell complete, owners either finish the interior themselves or hire subcontractors.

Heating bills typically run one-half to one-third those of homes with conventional construction. "It costs me $300 a year to heat," says Ben Cyr, owner of the lakeside cottage I visited. "If anything, it's too warm. And because of the shape, it's not boring like an ordinary house." Cyr was referring to the angled walls that provide most rooms with at least two exposures. Cathedral ceilings with 10½-foot peaks contribute to the spacious interiors.

Prices? "The primary saving for us is labor," says Maheux. "The building trades average $23 an hour, but our factory workers average only $6.50 an hour." The 930-square-foot "tree house" I saw cost, in Canadian dollars, $27,947 for the shell plus $438 for transportation and $9,400 for erection. Maheux estimates interior finishing at $16,000. The 1,600-square-foot condos near Montreal sell for $58,000, ready to move in—*by Richard Stepler. Drawings by Adolph Brotman.*

the house that computers built

Imagine a prefabricated home that adapts to any site or climate. A home that expands or contracts to suit your family's needs for space, has interior partitions that can be moved or modified to provide for growing children, has computerized environmental controls, and includes robots that cook your food, wash your clothes, and vacuum your floors. Best of all, it costs less than the price of a conventionally built home. A dream of the distant future?

Not so, says Professor Charles Owen. He and a team of students and faculty at IIT's Institute of Design in Chicago used powerful minicomputers to design this "House of the Future." Although the house exists only in plans and scale models—and in the memory of the team's DEC and Hewlett-Packard computers—Owen says it could be built within a few years using existing or near-term technology.

What the IIT team has developed is not merely one house of the future but a versatile system of building components that can be used for high-rise apartments, two- or three-story townhouses, and single-family homes. "The system's interior components could even be used to renovate older buildings," says Owen.

Key to the cost-saving in the IIT design, like other manufactured-housing projects of the past, is industrial production and prefabrication of its components.

The IIT team used computers extensively, both to help organize their research and identify problem areas, as well as to design the project's components. In fact, computers were essential to efficiently manage a com-

plex project created by a large team: 24 students and five faculty from the product-design, architecture, planning, and engineering programs at IIT. Computers also helped speed the work. The entire project, from basic research through detailed concepts and models, took just 24 weeks.

The final design shows meticulous attention to detail and ingenious solutions to household problems. The structural system is a steel post-and-beam frame based on a 1.2-by-1.2-meter (3.9-by-3.9-foot) grid. A basic module is 3.6 meters (11.8 feet) long, but variations are possible in 1.2-meter increments to permit modules up to 7.2 meters (23.6 feet) long. The prefabricated frames can be stacked up to three or four stories high. (Higher structures would require extra supporting frames.) Deep floors (or ceilings), prefabricated in 3.6-meter-square modules, come with flexible systems of electric wiring, plumbing, and ductwork for heating, cooling, and ventilation already in place. Removable panels allow easy access to utilities.

Exterior enclosure components permit a variety of architectural styles: Bay windows or greenhouses, gabled

or flat roofs, and decks or porches are all possible. Theoretically, you could build a saltbox for New England or an adobe-style house for the Southwest. "Finish materials can be anything," says Owen. "You could use stucco in Florida or cedar shakes where that was popular. More likely, you would go to completely modern materials: interior foams and aluminum skins with vinyl over that for a really low-maintenance house."

All components are designed to be easy to install and remove. As a result, you could start with a small house and then add to it if your need for space increased. Interior partitions also contribute to flexibility: All of them are movable. You can even relocate kitchen and baths.

Automated household functions

A distributed computer network with a powerful central microprocessor monitors the performance of household functions such as environmental control, fire detection, food preparation, and security. These functions are, in turn, controlled by their own microprocessors.

A predictive climate-control system

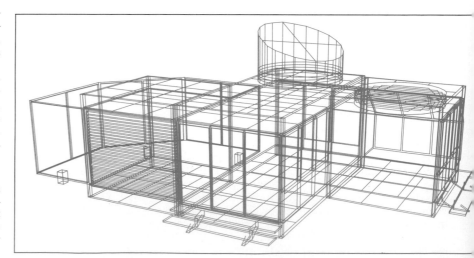

Computer-generated drawing shows one possible configuration of IIT's innovative House of the Future. The project won the 10-million-yen grand prize in Japan's first International Design Competition, held in Osaka.

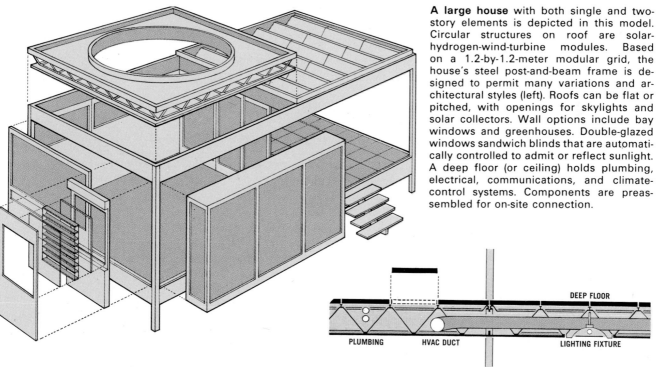

A large house with both single and two-story elements is depicted in this model. Circular structures on roof are solar-hydrogen-wind-turbine modules. Based on a 1.2-by-1.2-meter modular grid, the house's steel post-and-beam frame is designed to permit many variations and architectural styles (left). Roofs can be flat or pitched, with openings for skylights and solar collectors. Wall options include bay windows and greenhouses. Double-glazed windows sandwich blinds that are automatically controlled to admit or reflect sunlight. A deep floor (or ceiling) holds plumbing, electrical, communications, and climate-control systems. Components are preassembled for on-site connection.

DEEP FLOOR

PLUMBING　　**HVAC DUCT**　　**LIGHTING FIXTURE**

coordinates the operation of equipment such as heat pumps, humidifiers/dehumidifiers, and solar collectors. Indoor and outdoor sensors, including temperature, humidity, barometric pressure, and wind speed and direction, provide some of the inputs to help the system maintain a comfortable interior climate.

Independent energy sources supplement power drawn from the utility grid. These include:

● Solar-hydrogen-and-wind-turbine modules: These produce electricity by using solar heat to break down an electrolytic solution of hydrogen bromide. The wind turbine generates electricity directly.

● Biomass system: Bath and kitchen waste fed to a biomass tank produces methane gas, which is compressed and stored for later use.

● Thermal-energy-storage system: This includes six components: gas furnace fired with gas from the biomass system, auxiliary electric furnace, heat-storage pile, an air-conditioning

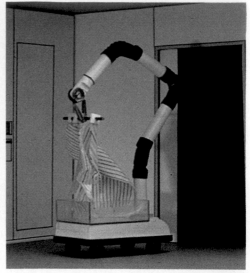

Entertainment center (above) includes a holographic TV set, admittedly the only technology in the scheme that's not "near term." Mobile service unit (above, right) sorts the laundry; it vacuums, too. The kitchen (right) has a "food wall" that stores, prepares, and cooks food via a robot chef.

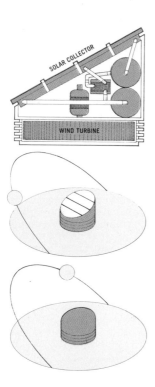

Solar-wind module (above) tracks the sun; solar heat breaks down hydrogen bromide into hydrogen and bromine. These are recombined as needed to produce electricity. Wind turbine provides additional power. The home's robot can be programmed to perform a variety of household tasks using MIMIC (right). To set a table, for example, you'd first instruct the computer by voice command to go into MIMIC mode. Then, after placing IR or radio emitters on your hands and arms, you'd perform the task you wanted the robot to mimic. Sensors would note position, speed, and direction of movement; with this in its memory, the robot could perform the task on command.

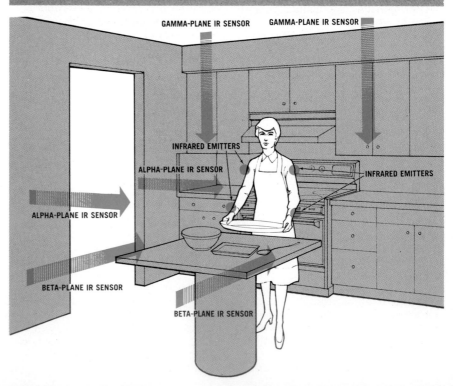

For sleeping, studying, etc., spaces can be enclosed by folding walls (shown open, above). Bath (right): Open spa allows space for exercise. Wash basin, toilet, bidet, shower, and tub can stand alone or be enclosed for privacy.

unit, and, of course, a microprocessor for control.

The climate-control system coordinates the operation of all of these systems, using the most economical source (or combination) to heat and cool the home. For example, if the system determines that wind speed is more than sufficient to meet the home's power needs, it sends surplus power back to the utility grid, reducing the electric bill.

Fire protection is handled by ceiling-mounted, heat-seeking extinguishing systems. If the home control system detect as fire (using sensors in the air ducts), pop-down nozzles in the area scan it with infrared sensors. If a fire is located, the nozzles spray it with Halon gas, smothering the fire without damaging property. While fighting the fire, the home control system also alerts occupants as well as the fire department.

The home control system also provides security:
● A perimeter "fence"—actually a buried cable—sets up an electromagnetic field that is monitored by sensors. The control system is alerted if someone passes through the field.
● Voice-activated locks in exterior sliding doors recognize only occupants of the house or those who are given temporary passes.
● Pressure-sensitive windows have sensors that alert the control system if broken.
● Heat-sensing detection is the final defense if an intruder gains entrance. Using the IR sensors of the fire-extinguishing nozzles, the control system

can inform police of the intruder's location, alert occupants, or even attempt to frighten him.

A robot that moves on flat surfaces and communicates with the home control system vacuums the floors and shampoos the rugs. (Yes, the robot does windows.)

A robot can also do vacuuming, and it could wash clothes "if you help it out by clipping things you want cleaned on hangers," says Owen. "A bar code on a tag attached to an article of clothing could indicate how it's to be washed, and the robot could locate and sort the clothes by finding the clips."

In the kitchen, a robot could be taught to set the table using IIT's MIMIC programming system (see drawing). It could also serve food "in the sense of bringing in foods that are placed on a serving cart," says Owen.

Nothing should ever get lost in the closets of the House of the Future. These are "storage cores"—dustproof enclosures with automated systems of

rotating shelves or tracks with hangers for clothing (similar to those you see in dry cleaners' shops). If you want an item, you'd ask the home control system to find it for you. It would direct you to the appropriate storage core and rotate the shelf the item is on to the access door.

In a child's room, the access door would be placed lower. Modular replaceable partitions allow interior spaces to change as children grow, and features such as wash basins that can be relocated closer to the floor via flexible plumbing solve problems of scale.

What company could produce such an all-encompassing housing scheme? "A company like Sears," says Owen, "or another multiservice company that could supply all the internals, even the electronics. Or a consortium of companies could do it." Whether or not IIT's House of the Future is ever built, it represents an impressive achievement—*by Richard Stepler. Drawings by Adolph Brotman.*

energy-saving two-faced house

As you drive along the road east of the house, you catch glimpses of it through the trees. It's a strange sight indeed: The curving white north face is abruptly halted by the straight cedar-clad south face. "From that side it looks as if half the house was cut off," volunteered Beverly Chu. It is an accurate, if irreverent, description. Mrs. Chu and her husband, Wilson, are the owners of this unique house in the town of West Chester, Pennsylvania, where they live with their small daughter, Jessica. While most owners tend to speak of their innovative houses in almost sacred terms, Mrs. Chu often talks of hers with refreshing humor and objectivity. But then she proceeds to tick off its salient features with relish:

● The north face is superinsulated and curved to deflect winter winds. Its few small windows are strategically located for daylighting and effective cross ventilation.

● The south face has abundant windows to admit solar energy in winter. A roof overhang protects the windows from the high summer sun.

● The house is elongated on the east-west axis so that every room has daylight and a view—as well as solar gain in winter.

● There are no east or west sides, and no east- or west-facing windows—they are difficult to shade in summer.

The house is the creation of Robert Bennett, an architect who practices in nearby Bala-Cynwyd. Wilson wanted a solar house. "Other architects we talked to had some ideas for energy efficiency, but Bob was really a solar purist," said Mrs. Chu, "and we were impressed with his credentials."

Bennett has degrees in mechanical engineering and space physics as well as architecture, and is the author of a solar reference book, *Sun Angles for Design*. A native of Texas, he was the

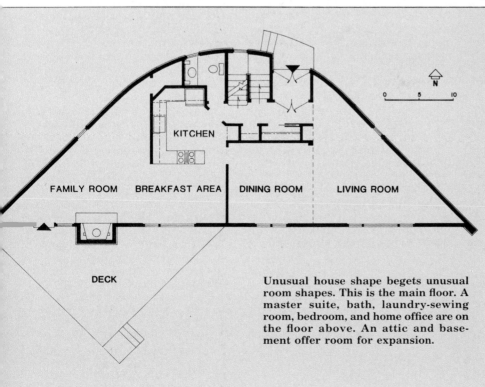

FAMILY ROOM   BREAKFAST AREA   DINING ROOM   LIVING ROOM

KITCHEN

DECK

0   5   10

N

The front of the Solar Biangle (facing page, top), is vaguely castlelike with its curving face and slender, recessed windows. Living room (facing page, bottom) has black slate floor to absorb solar heat. Most windows are on the south side (above); insulated drapes reduce heat loss on winter nights. An awning over the window in the breakfast area keeps out summer sun; others are shaded by the roof overhang. The deck, on which architect Bennett and the author talk while Jessica Chu plays, was expanded.

Unusual house shape begets unusual room shapes. This is the main floor. A master suite, bath, laundry-sewing room, bedroom, and home office are on the floor above. An attic and basement offer room for expansion.

national coordinator for the American Solar Energy Society in 1977 and '78. In that capacity he spent six months touring the country, meeting the key people involved in the then-nascent field of passive-solar design. He returned to the Philadelphia area (where he had worked as an engineer and got his architectural degree) to establish a practice, specializing in passive-solar residential and commercial design.

Solar hybrid

The Chus' house—Bennett calls it the Solar Biangle—is Bennett's first venture into hybrid design, combining passive-solar features and superinsulation. "Originally I was considering a direct-gain solar house for them," he said, "but economics made me turn to superinsulation. A direct-gain house requires a lot of glass, and once you have that much glass, you need a lot of thermal mass to keep the house from overheating and to store the heat for use at night."

Most passive-solar houses are built of masonry, which also acts as thermal mass, or they contain drums of water or have rock beds beneath. "But when you put in more glass and more mass, you start to push up the construction costs," Bennett noted. Instead, he put in more insulation, so the Chu house loses very little heat. That means it doesn't need to gain or store as much heat as does a purely passive-solar house. Consequently, he could reduce the glass and mass—as well as cost.

But why the unusual shape? "One of my rules of thumb is that if a house is the same on each face, it's probably not very energy efficient," Bennett replied. "The northern exposure is so different from the southern. And east and west are different from either north or south. The fact that it is an unusual form means it's responding to those considerations.

"Typically, passive-solar houses are elongated along the east-west axis to get the maximum southern exposure. But then you also get a long northern exposure in a conventional rectangular house" (something Bennett admits he has never designed). The Solar Biangle evolved from a triangular house he designed for an Atlantic City, New Jersey, client. For the Chu house he reduced the triangle's three faces to two—with the igloo as his inspiration. "It's one of my favorite examples of

environmentally designed buildings," said Bennett. "It responds to cold winds by having the minimum surface area for maximum volume inside, and the curved shape helps to deflect the wind."

After the startling appearance of the house when you see it from the east side, when you approach it from the front, the north side, it looks surprisingly conventional. It sits at the end of a cul-de-sac in an area of large lots and large houses. The white stucco of its facade echoes other houses in the neighborhood. The front door opens into an air-lock entry, which leads to a narrow entry hall.

Inside, the sense of conventionality disappears once more. To the left is the living room, a triangle, or more accurately a trapezoid: The apex of the triangle is sliced off to form a wall about 18 inches wide. Three other major rooms (the family room at the west end of the main floor and the master bedroom and Mrs. Chu's office on the second floor) are similar trapezoids. In fact, the only square room in the house is Jessica's bedroom. "We didn't want her to grow up with strange complexes," Mrs. Chu quipped humorously.

All rooms but a small powder room near the entrance have a view to the south across a lawn and an adjacent farm. The south glass equals 9 percent of the house's 2,100 square feet of floor space. Had the house been a pure direct-gain solar design, Bennett would have had to increase the south glass to equal 25 percent of the floor space to enable it to achieve the same energy-saving performance.

The long, narrow slits of windows on the north are strategically placed so the house has effective cross ventilation. And they're recessed into the thick wall. That screens the northeast and northwest windows from the low morning and evening sun. All windows are double glazed.

Building it

Despite the unconventional appearance of the house, its construction was fairly standard, according to Bennett. The walls have 6-inch fiberglass batts between 2 × 6 studs. ("When the studs for the north wall went up, the neighbors thought we were building a circus tent," said Mrs. Chu.) A polyethylene vapor barrier isolates the insulation from the wallboard on the inside, and 2-inch-thick rigid insula-

tion board was tacked to the outside of the studs. Finally, the north wall was finished with stucco and the south with cedar siding. The insulation value of the walls and attic is R-30; that's less than in some superinsulated houses but far more than the R-11 or R-12 walls of standard houses with 2 × 4 framing. Basement walls have 2-inch-thick insulation board (Thermax) on the outside.

The only thermal mass Bennett added in the house is the black Pennsylvania slate floor tile in the living room and dining room; it is laid over a 1-inch-thick concrete slab. The largest windows are in that area, and the winter sun shines in brightly, warming the masonry.

Though the house has more south-facing glass than most, the total window area is about standard. Despite its extra insulation and energy-saving features, the cost of the house was also standard for large, custom houses in the area.

Performance

The Chus' house has not been independently monitored for energy use, but they did keep track of their energy bills for the first one and a half years. The first winter, they spent $275 (at seven cents a kilowatt-hour) to operate their electric air-to-air heat pump and a kerosene heater. Their average cost for air conditioning during each of two summers was $85. Superinsulation contributes to the low cooling as well as heating cost. And on summer nights the Chus open the windows and turn on their whole-house fan to cool the house. "We don't usually turn on the air conditioner until it's in the 90s," Mrs. Chu informed me.

Total cost of heating and cooling while they kept records came to $360 annually—roughly 66% less than for a conventional new house in the region. The Chus further reduced their energy bills by installing a passive-solar, batch-type water heater. But they do not know how much it contributes. In addition, Bennett's careful attention to providing daylight for every room reduces lighting costs.

"It's a comfortable house, laid out for the way we live," said Mrs. Chu. And energy bills 66 percent below par make the two-faced house very appealing—any way you look at it—*by V. Elaine Smay. Photos by Greg Sharko.*

two unique homes you can build yourself

Here are two unusual and appealing homes that make the latest architectural styles accessible to the do-it-yourselfer. One is a redwood kit house, while the other is from a set of plans that grew out of masonry research. Either house would be at home on any vacation site—and can be finished by a novice.

The first home is an energy-efficient precut package house designed by architect William Bruner for Pacific Frontier Homes. It sports a custom look as it thrusts its glazed sunspace forward onto the deck, with an upper walkway cutting behind the separate shed roof to connect two upper terraces. Yet the Eagle's Nest is a manufactured home that shouldn't be much more expensive than an architect-designed home you'd build from scratch—especially if you exercise the options for owner participation in building and finishing.

Annual heating bills of $130 in the upper Midwest is the goal of this 1,280-square-foot home, one of the Day-Star Collection.

Dubbed "Eagle's Nest" by its creator, Pacific Frontier Homes, handsome precut shown on previous page and in three interiors (surrounding photos) has multiple skylights for maximum solar gain.

Loft bedroom (above), tucked under parallel ridge beams at the top of the house, is suffused with light from large clerestory windows and skylights at left, as well as from the glazed wall at the stairwell.

Living room has cozy wood-stove corner despite open floor plan. View at upper right is from beneath loft toward skylighted solarium. Kitchen can be seen beyond. Stair (lower right) mounts to loft.

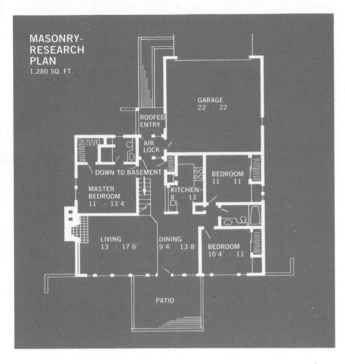

MASONRY-RESEARCH PLAN
1,280 SQ. FT.

GARAGE 22' · 22'

ROOFED ENTRY

AIR LOCK

DOWN TO BASEMENT

BEDROOM 11' · 11'

MASTER BEDROOM 11' · 13'4"

KITCHEN 8' · 13'

LIVING 13' · 17'6"

DINING 9'4" · 13'8"

BEDROOM 10'4" · 11'

PATIO

PRECUT PLAN
LOFT: 379 SQ. FT.
MAIN FLOOR: 836 SQ. FT.

26'

3' · 13' · 10'

CL

5'9"

LOFT

6'6"

16'

20'

3'9"

REDWOOD DECK

4'

36'

10' · 3' · 13' · 10'

AIR LOCK   LAUNDRY

5'9"

WOOD STOVE

EATING BAR

KITCHEN

22'   14'

BEDROOM   LIVING

14'3"   26'

SOLARIUM

6'

10' · 16' · 10'

The open floor plan packs a lot of living into compact space—1,215 square feet here. Sunspace, living room, kitchen, laundry, and one bedroom and bath are located on the ground floor. The second floor offers a loft bedroom with bath plus those two pocket redwood decks. The rustic interior features 4 × 4 redwood posts (it's a post-and-beam house), 1 × 6 redwood tongue-and-groove paneling, fir rafters, and pine-ceiling decking. The kitchen has custom redwood cabinetry and Sears appliances.

The exterior siding is 1 × 8 clear, tung-and-groove redwood with a resawed face. The multiple skylights might be impractical for a more severe climate, but they do wonders in capturing maximum solar gain and light in the foggy north-coast area of California where this prototype was built. The wood stove (from Vermont Castings) furnishes all the heat required. The backup heating system has never been turned on.

Frontier Homes specializes in redwood post-and-beam structures. The posts and rafters are cut, notched, drilled, stained, and numbered—keyed to the construction drawings. The framing can thus be assembled in a day or two by three or four workers (there are no rafters that two people can't handle). The construction process is somewhat labor intensive because there are many individual pieces to install, but the skills required are well within the realm of most do-it-yourselfers. Moreover, the company can also advise you on how much DIY is practical for your location and experience.

The second home is one of several passive-solar designs known as the Day-Star Collection, based on three years of energy research funded by the Wisconsin Concrete and Products Association. Space-saving open floor plans are designed to collect the sun's heat, store it in masonry-mass walls, and preserve it successfully within a heavily insulated building envelope.

After the research was completed, architect Dale Kolbeck was commissioned to design three model homes, including this "ranch plan." All three plans include all-glass southern walls, earth-bermed north walls, air-lock entries, and double walls to create an envelope.

The ranch plan optimizes its 1,280 square feet with a flexible living-dining room; the glass wall and the cathedral ceiling soaring up to clerestory windows give this space an expansive feeling. Solid masonry heat-storage walls join the masonry fireplace to stabilize temperatures. The sun provides 63 percent of the home's heat, leaving the owner with greatly reduced annual costs for natural gas—*by Al Lees.*

How to get further data on both homes
Construction drawings for the masonry ranch house are available from Day-Star Collection, Anders, Inc., 21420 W. Greenfield, New Berlin, WI 53151. Send $300 for one set, $325 for ten sets. Also available for $400: the plans on plastic sepias that can be erased, redrafted, and printed to meet local codes. For data on the Eagle's Nest kit, write Pacific Frontier Homes, Inc., Box 1247, Fort Bragg, CA 95437, or phone John Bailey, president, at (707) 964-0204.

easy-to-install mirrored wall

Have you got a room tucked away somewhere that doesn't get sufficient sunlight? Or a drab room that doesn't encourage lingering? Now's your chance to work a little magic—and you can do it all with mirrors.

In just a few hours you can add style, light, and a sense of space to a room by mirroring a wall—without using adhesives.

With a new wall-to-wall mirror system from Mechanical Mirror Works, Inc. (41 Madison Ave., New York, NY 10010), screws and tape replace adhesives. And to make mirroring a wall even easier, the system also replaces large, unwieldy pieces of custom-made glass with easy-to-handle beveled panels and 6-inch-wide beveled strips.

Each panel has two 1/4-inch tabs on each side for screws that fasten the panel to the wall. On the face of each panel are two strips of tape that run from top to bottom. The tape is for attaching the beveled strips, which overlap the panels to cover screw heads and drill holes. In the corners, one side of the strip is fastened to a panel, and the other side is anchored by double-faced tape to wooden risers, which are nailed to the wall.

The mirrored panels come in 24-, 30-, and 36-inch widths, all at a standard 84-inch height. The various sizes, combined with the 6-inch strip —which can overlap an area of up to 5 inches—make it easy to mirror a wall of almost any expanse. Any wall between 50 and 62 inches wide, for example, is taken care of by two 24-inch panels and three beveled strips.

Six 36-inch panels and seven strips can cover a wall 228 to 244 inches wide, for little over $1,000.

For installation, panels must be plumb and evenly spaced along the wall. Make sure you hang the end panels 1 to 5 inches away from the adjoining walls. This leaves enough space for the wooden pieces to be nailed and for the strips to overlap. Remember, the area to be overlapped cannot exceed 5 inches.

Although I hung the panels on standard drywall using toggle bolts (supplied), there are other ways to secure them. If the tabs of the panels correspond with the location of wall studs, drill 1/16-inch holes for panhead screws. If the wall is masonry, use anchors.

Once the mirrors are in place, nail the wood strips into the corners. Now

all that remain for installation are the 6-inch strips, which will be anchored by tape. Peel away the tape covering on the panel and wooden strips; then line up the beveled strips, and press them into place—*by Charles A. Miller. Photos by Greg Sharko.*

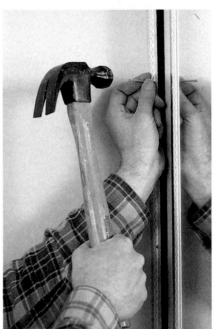

Before and after photos (left) tell the story: A mirrored wall enhances this room. To install mirrors, begin by spacing mirrored panels equally along the wall, leaving 2 to 4 inches between corners and end panels (above). Use a plumb bob to establish vertical lines on both sides of each panel, and pencil in lines. Position panels, starting at one end, and mark location of tabs. Drill holes, and insert screws through tabs; don't overtighten (top right). Nail wooden strips supplied into the corners (above right). Be sure double-sided adhesive tape faces out. Wipe the back of the mirror strips, and line up each one with the top of the panels (right). Press strips firmly into position, being careful not to touch tape.

11 fresh ideas to transform your bathroom

My bathroom was a mess—broken and missing tiles, chipped fixtures, leaky faucets, peeling walls. And then there was the shower —or lack thereof.

The builder had installed an angled five-foot-square tub intended for space-saving corner installation, then boxed in the gap at the foot to create a ledge and a planter. This assembly ate up floor space—and trapped water. Also, there was no way to enclose the tub for use as a shower. (In desperation I hung a custom-cut shower curtain from a ceiling track, but it never kept the bathroom dry.) I couldn't simply tear out the planter and put up a wall on which to hang a tub enclosure—the installation would intersect the large

3-by-6-foot window that stretched across the back wall.

Finally, storage space was tight. The unstructured space under the sink in a functional but inelegant vanity just wasn't sufficient for my family.

The solution? My wife and I sat down and sketched out the improvements we wanted, as shown in the drawing. The remodeling was built around a compact whirlpool tub 5 feet long, 32 inches wide, and 16 inches deep with a tuck-under motor—a real space-saver. Access to this motor would be in a linen closet at the foot of the tub.

Your bathroom may not be in the dire straits that ours was. But by picking and choosing from our 11 tips,

you'll be able to transform your bathroom into an attractive—and more useful—space.

You may want to build the vanity first and have it waiting. To expedite matters I had Styline Products of Massapequa, New York, build our vanity.

Start construction by framing the linen closet after the new tub is installed. If your whirlpool has a motor that doesn't tuck under its foot, the space beneath the shelves can store this mechanism. The full-height linen closet also provides a wall on which to hang a shower enclosure.

To separate the bath area from the rest of the room—and increase the feeling of space—I nailed a 2 × 8 valance board in front of the tub and

Where to start? This cramped and unattractive bathroom—dominated by a battleship of a tub and unattractive planter —needed light, storage space, an enclosed bath, and a new floor and walls— all in a 7-by-10-foot space.

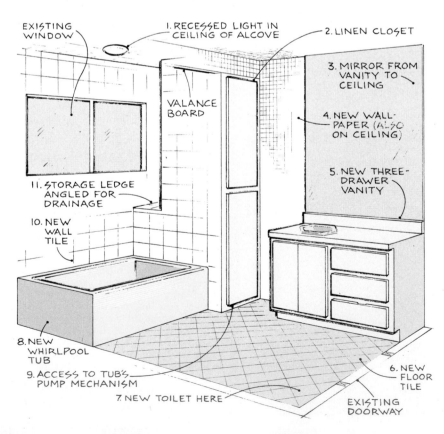

EXISTING WINDOW

1. RECESSED LIGHT IN CEILING OF ALCOVE

2. LINEN CLOSET

VALANCE BOARD

3. MIRROR FROM VANITY TO CEILING

4. NEW WALL-PAPER (ALSO ON CEILING)

5. NEW THREE-DRAWER VANITY

11. STORAGE LEDGE ANGLED FOR DRAINAGE

10. NEW WALL TILE

8. NEW WHIRLPOOL TUB

9. ACCESS TO TUB'S PUMP MECHANISM

7. NEW TOILET HERE

6. NEW FLOOR TILE

EXISTING DOORWAY

A bathroom transformed! Linen closet holds plenty of towels, and backsplash-to-ceiling mirror enhances feeling of space (top right). Wallpaper on back of door also adds sense of spaciousness, and San Miguel toilet (bottom right) fits in with room's contemporary look. Note unobstructed window and tilted bath shelf (middle right). Recessed light over tub and patterned doors (above) provide luxury (recessed ceiling light over vanity not shown).

linen closet. If you follow my lead, make sure you adjust the height of the linen closet's top door accordingly.

Next, after making sure that the plumbing was in place for the tub, I covered the walls, ceiling, and linen closet with Wonder-Board, a concrete-core wallboard reinforced with fiberglass (Modulars Inc., Box 216, Hamilton, OH 45012). Allow access to electrical wires for the recessed light and tub motor through the closet.

Wonder-Board is ideal for bathroom installations. Unlike gypsum products, this cement-surfaced panel isn't affected by moisture and has very low coefficients of expansion and contraction in a wet environment. Water that seeps under tile won't decay, delaminate, or disintegrate this material.

The next step, tiling over Wonder-Board, is different from the usual installation procedure. First, insert pre-sanded dry-set or latex portland cement mortar in joints between panels. Cover the joints and corners with 2-inch-wide fiberglass tape coated with mortar. Spread a thin layer—it should be as shallow as $3/32$ inch after tiles are pressed in—of the mortar, and rake it with a notched trowel. Then lay the tiles. I used 6-inch-square tiles here and on the floor of the linen closet.

Install the tub, then mount the

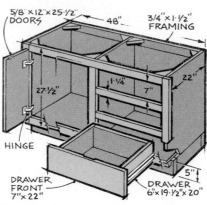

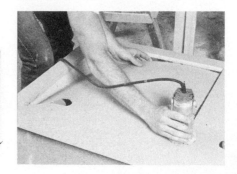

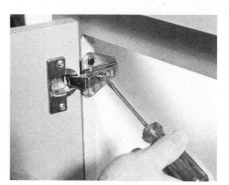

Single-sink, triple-drawer vanity offers plenty of storage space—and sleek design. Frame unit with 1 × 2 pine, and enclose with ⅝-inch particleboard; fasten with glue and screws for added strength. Brush contact cement on ⅛-inch plastic-laminate sheet and all wood surfaces, including framework around doors and drawers. Allow adhesive to dry—5 to 10 minutes—then attach, using paper slip sheet under laminate. Punch starter holes, and use router to cut open-

ings for doors and drawers (above, far right). Jigsaw makes fast work of hexagonal-shaped opening in 1-inch-thick particleboard counter top before laminate is applied. Attach splashboard; fill seam with bead of waterproof caulk. Fasten drawer runners to inside framing. Cap drawers' side panels with plastic edging for finished appearance. Use concealed hinges (right) to attach doors with finger recess routed into top edge.

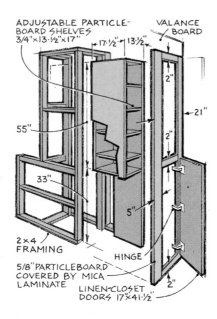

Frame linen closet with 2 × 4s; leave space in front of window for shelf. Use level to check verticals.

Sink 1½-inch (minimum) galvanized roofing nails ½ inch from edge to secure ⁷⁄₁₆-inch Wonder-Board panels.

bypass (two-door) tub enclosure. The easy-to-install stainless-steel unit comes with all necessary hardware.

Start by cutting the bottom track ¼ to ⅜ inch shorter than the tub rail (exact border size varies with model). Caulk the bottom of the track, and lay it down on the rail—no screws are needed. Then mark the screw holes for the wall jambs (tracks come with predrilled holes) and use a carbide-tipped bit to drill into the tile. Snap the wall tracks into place, and fasten them with plastic anchors and screws. Measure—very few walls are plumb—and cut the top track, and snap it into place. Attach the rollers to the door panels with screws, and lift the

door panels onto the track. Install the J-hooks for the door-glide system in the bottom track. Use the pressure-sensitive tape to secure the aluminum handles. Finally, caulk around all tracks.

To finish off the tub area, slide the separately built cabinet (see drawing), with attached floor-to-ceiling laminate facing, into the linen-closet frame, and secure from the inside with 2-inch-long screws.

Now you can add pizazz to the rest of the room. I recommend a bright, colorful wallpaper—mine is custom-colored with a gray-and-raspberry pattern.

This is the time to install recessed

lighting and other new fixtures. For the floor, I used 4-inch-square tiles that matched those in the bath area. But for contrast, and to enhance the feeling of separation and space, I installed the floor tiles diagonally—*by Marc Brett. Drawings by Gerhard Richter.*

MANUFACTURERS' ADDRESSES

The following manufacturers were selected by POPULAR SCIENCE for participation in this project:
American Olean Tile, Lansdale, PA 19446 (Matte wall tile, Crystalline floor tile; both in Sterling Silver); **Kohler,** Kohler, WI 53044 (Guardian cast-iron whirlpool tub, San Miguel toilet, Hexsign basin; all in Raspberry); **Levolor Lorentzen, Inc.,** 1280 Wall St. W., Lyndhurst, NJ 07071 (mini-blinds); **Morton-Jonap Wallpapers,** 12 Midland Ave., Hicksville, NY 11801 (Palate pattern); **U.S. Gypsum, Kinkead Div.,** 101 S. Wacker Dr., Chicago, IL 60606 (Vista-Glide shower enclosure).

passive-solar all-seasons room

To make our home better match our outdoor living style, my wife, Rita, and I undertook an ambitious building project. The spacious, airy all-seasons room shown is the centerpiece of our outdoor renovation. Encircled by multilevel decking, the room links the house with the landscaped pool area. In summer the room serves as a low-maintenance passageway for swimmers and as an inviting refuge from the rain. In winter the new wing becomes a cozy retreat.

Our design strategies apply to anyone who wants to add an outdoor-oriented room. They include:
● Planning skylight placement for winter solar gain.
● Building an open, Belgian truss-roof system with an exposed-beam cathedral ceiling.
● Using oversize sliding glass doors to provide an immediate visual link with the outdoors.
● Facing inner walls with rough-sawn redwood siding.
● Installing a low-maintenance vinyl-tile floor.
● Installing security wiring during construction.

Spacious light-filled room forms the new wing. It has four 8-foot-wide glass doors—one framing the mountains to the northeast, two on the southwest wall below the skylights, and one on the fireplace wall (above). A soaring asymmetric ceiling faced with tongue-and-groove redwood emphasizes the wide-open feeling of the room. The walls, paneled with redwood siding, match the house's exterior, efficiently enhancing the illusion of being outside.

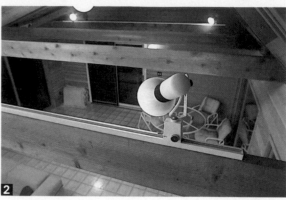

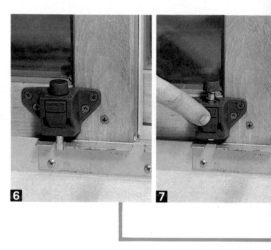

Massive double rafters sandwich collar beams, forming rugged roof truss (1) that creates built-in frame for skylights with ultraviolet-resistant double-pane tempered glass. Ceiling fan provides ample air movements for summer ventilation, thanks to giant shade tree outside (visible through skylights). Track lights atop collar beams (2) swivel 360 degrees for variety of dramatic lighting effects not possible with conventional concealed lighting. Sears programmable security system (3) inside main house remotely controls seven pole-mounted outdoor spotlights. Lights, divided into three zones, can also be controlled by switches in new wing (4). (For safety around swimming pool, even indoor electric circuits are protected by ground-fault interrupters.) Pop-out security switch in a door frame (5) triggers alarm when door is opened. Switch can be wired to any type of alarm—author chose siren. Sturdy plunger-type lock on Caradco glass doors (6, 7) allows doors to remain slightly open for ventilation.

For maximum solar gain in winter, we designed four skylights into the southwest-facing roof. A large tree shades the skylights in summer, so we don't need the more costly venting types; a ceiling fan works fine. In winter the asymmetric roof encourages snow dumping, an important concern for this site in New York state.

Trusty truss

We designed the asymmetric roof for architectural distinction as well as solar practicality. But the dual-pitch roof made careful construction even more critical. For adequate strength, we chose a Belgian open-truss design with two sets of collar beams sandwiched between massive four-beam rafters (see drawing).

Doubling up on either side of the collar beams disperses the roof load (which would normally require supports 16 inches on center) while creating the soaring cathedral ceiling. For roof strength as well as good looks, we

bridged the trusses with a redwood tongue-and-groove ceiling. Thermax rigid-board insulation topped by plywood decking, building paper, and asphalt shingles complete the roof. To prevent rot in the dead-air space where the new wing ties into the old roof, we installed a 10-foot length of ridge vent.

The truss roof allowed us to conceal a track-lighting system atop the collar beams instead of mounting the tracks on ceiling or walls. We ran the wiring directly down into the wall. The effect is elegant—the light appears to be floating up on top.

We planned the truss to create a built-in frame for the 4-foot-square double-pane Caradco skylights, saving one step in installation. But the unconventional roofing system made it impractical to install the windows from inside. To ease placement from the outside, we nailed temporary pegs of wood to the top corners of the opening. These pegs projected no more

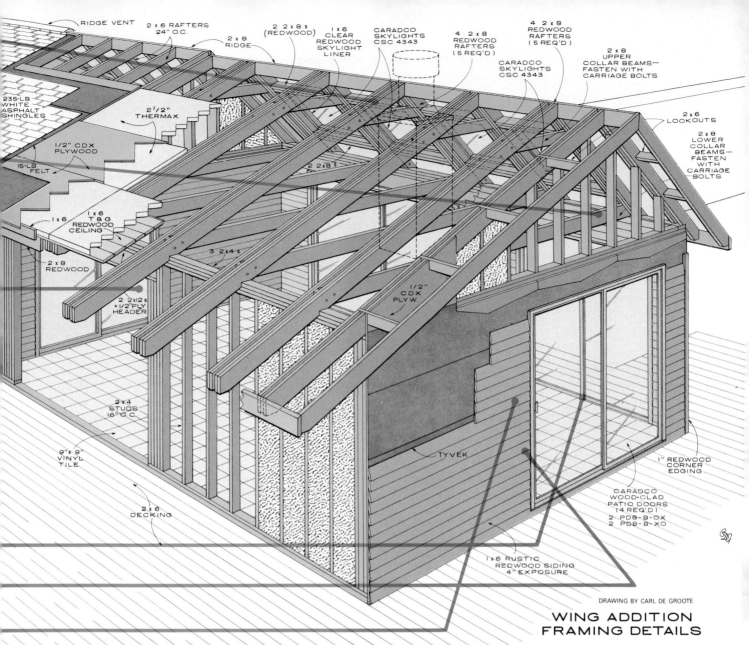

RIDGE VENT

2 x 6 RAFTERS 24" O.C.

2 x 8 RIDGE

2 2x8s (REDWOOD)

1 x 6 CLEAR REDWOOD SKYLIGHT LINER

CARADCO SKYLIGHTS CSC 4343

4 2 x 8 REDWOOD RAFTERS (5 REQ'D)

4 2 x 8 REDWOOD RAFTERS (5 REQ'D)

CARADCO SKYLIGHTS CSC 4343

2 x 8 UPPER COLLAR BEAMS—FASTEN WITH CARRIAGE BOLTS

2 x 6 LOOKOUTS

2 x 8 LOWER COLLAR BEAMS—FASTEN WITH CARRIAGE BOLTS

235-LB WHITE ASPHALT SHINGLES

2½" THERMAX

1/2" CDX PLYWOOD

15-LB FELT

1 x 6 T & G REDWOOD CEILING

1 x 6 REDWOOD CEILING

2 x 8 REDWOOD

3 2 x 4 s

1/2" CDX PLYW

1/2" CDX PLYW

2 2x12s + 1/2" PLY HEADER

2 x 4 STUDS 16" O.C.

9" x 9" VINYL TILE

2 x 6 DECKING

TYVEK

1" REDWOOD CORNER EDGING

CARADCO WOOD-CLAD PATIO DOORS (4 REQ'D) 2-PD8-8-OX 2 PD8-8-XO

1 x 6 RUSTIC REDWOOD SIDING 4" EXPOSURE

DRAWING BY CARL DE GROOTE

WING ADDITION
FRAMING DETAILS

than 1½ inches from the opening, just enough to hook the skylight frame (without touching the glass) as we lifted the window into position.

A light-splashed room

The dramatic high ceiling punctuated by light streaming in from the skylights is just part of the open, airy look so essential to our design. To give the room more of the outdoor feeling we craved, we installed four oversize 8-foot-wide sliding glass doors with a total of 20 percent more glass than standard 6-foot doors. The door frames came unassembled, but Caradco supplied a detailed 25-step installation booklet, which we followed with no trouble.

After we mounted the doors, we wired a security-alarm button into the frame. We also installed a computer-controlled security-lighting system—see captions for details.

To enhance the outdoor illusion, we finished the walls with the same rustic sequoia siding used on the outside. The unfinished rough-sawn texture visually links indoors with out—and requires no maintenance.

Before we put up the outside siding, we wrapped the house with Tyvek, an air-infiltration barrier made of spun-bonded olefin. Neither film nor paper, this sheet of high-density polyethylene fiber keeps cold air from penetrating seams and cracks while allowing free moisture flow, preventing condensation problems.

Finally, we installed a rugged, low-maintenance Armstrong Glazecraft vinyl-tile floor. Because the wing is built over soil, we used ¾-inch pressure-treated plywood as an underlayment with ¼-inch Luan plywood on top. After snapping intersecting chalk lines and dry-laying the tiles for fit, we applied mastic to a quarter of the room at a time, then laid the tiles alternately along the two chalk lines.

We also installed a one-piece heat-circulating fireplace to make the room as inviting on cold winter nights as it is by day. The unit was conveniently located behind a tile-faced wall with hidden storage cabinets—*by W. David Houser. Photos by Greg Sharko. Drawing by Carl de Groote.*

The following manufacturers were selected by POPULAR SCIENCE for participation in this project. For further information, write directly to the source.

Source	Item
American Olean Tile Lansdale, PA 19446	Caribbean II glazed tile
Armstrong World Ind. Box 3001 Lancaster, PA 17604	Glazecraft dry-back floor tiles
California Redwood Assn. 591 Redwood Hwy.—3100 Mill Valley, CA 94941	Tongue-and-groove ceiling and rustic siding
Caradco Corp. Box 920, Rantoul, IL 61866	Cladwood sliding doors and skylights
Heatilator Inc. 1915 W. Saunders Rd. Mount Pleasant, IA 52641	Zero-clearance BH42 fireplace
Samsonite Furniture Samsonite Blvd. Murfreesboro, TN 37130	Table, Z-frame chairs

multilevel-deck outdoor entertainment area

My wife, Rita, and I spend as much time outside as inside our house. But despite a swimming pool and a large piece of property, our backyard was not really set up for outdoor living.

A small raised deck, our main outdoor dining area, was cramped with four people on it. Steep, narrow stairs made a lower-level deck practically useless for entertaining (see "before" photo). Railroad ties, dug into a steep slope, led up to the pool. Some visitors found the climb difficult—and poolside entertaining was inconvenient.

To unify the house and pool area, we decided to build an all-seasons room—shown in the preceding chapter—encircled by easy-access decks. In the process we developed design and construction tricks adaptable to many outdoor-living projects. They include:

- A concrete-pier foundation.
- A knee-wall building support.
- Multilevel decking.
- Low-rise steps.
- Under-deck storage.
- A kitchen pass-through.

BEFORE

Both wing and deck foundations (1) rest on concrete piers topped with galvanized Teco post bases (2). Beveled wood spacers adapt the fasteners to fit the double beams (see diagram, opposite), which are attached with galvanized nails. Galvanized joist hangers (3) anchor the joists to the end beams; where the joists *cross* a beam, they're toenailed in place (use only galvanized fasteners). Stringers for the stairs (4) are notched over the deck frame.

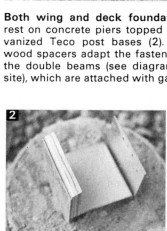

PHOTOS BY RITA HOUSER

AFTER

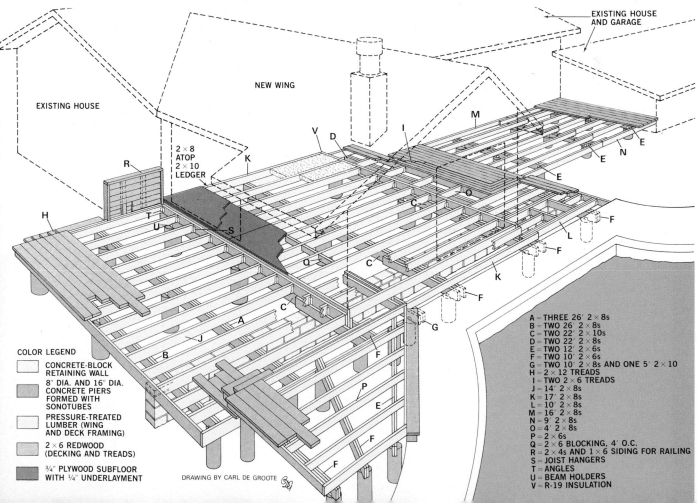

EXISTING HOUSE AND GARAGE

NEW WING

EXISTING HOUSE

2 × 8
ATOP
2 × 10
LEDGER

COLOR LEGEND

CONCRETE-BLOCK
RETAINING WALL

8″ DIA. AND 16″ DIA.
CONCRETE PIERS
FORMED WITH
SONOTUBES

PRESSURE-TREATED
LUMBER (WING
AND DECK FRAMING)

2 × 6 REDWOOD
(DECKING AND TREADS)

¾″ PLYWOOD SUBFLOOR
WITH ¼″ UNDERLAYMENT

DRAWING BY CARL DE GROOTE

A = THREE 26′ 2 × 8s
B = TWO 26′ 2 × 8s
C = TWO 22′ 2 × 10s
D = TWO 22′ 2 × 8s
E = TWO 12′ 2 × 6s
F = TWO 10′ 2 × 6s
G = TWO 10′ 2 × 8s AND ONE 5′ 2 × 10
H = 2 × 12 TREADS
I = TWO 2 × 6 TREADS
J = 14′ 2 × 8s
K = 17′ 2 × 8s
L = 10′ 2 × 8s
M = 16′ 2 × 8s
N = 9′ 2 × 8s
O = 4′ 2 × 8s
P = 2 × 6s
Q = 2 × 6 BLOCKING, 4′ O.C.
R = 2 × 4s AND 1 × 6 SIDING FOR RAILING
S = JOIST HANGERS
T = ANGLES
U = BEAM HOLDERS
V = R-19 INSULATION

The first step was planning. After discussing how we wanted to use our property, we decided to replace the old raised deck with a new wing to bridge the dip between house and pool. We also built a large deck linking house and garage. This serves as the main outdoor dining area and the entry to the multilevel deck complex.

A set of L-shape steps lead from the ground-level deck to the new wing and a wraparound deck facing the pool. For easy climbing, the stairs have low risers and broad treads.

At the far side of the pool a raised trapezoid-shape deck allows sunning away from the crowd. The sun deck is stepped down to a secluded cabana deck on the far side of the new room.

Raised deck at poolside (above) is stepped down to spacious cabana deck (1) on far side of new wing. Cantilevered roof will shade future built-in bar. Large storage area below deck railing (2) is camouflaged by a flush-fitting redwood door that hangs on a special joint (see 4b). Shallow depth of pass-through window (3) creates a deep sill that's handy for food placement. Duckboard for summer hose storage is tucked in niche between upper and lower decks (4a). Flush-fitting door to second under-deck storage space (behind hose) pulls up and out for easy access. The top of a 1×4 ripped in half at a 45-deg. angle forms the top rail of the door (4b). The rail hooks over the mating bottom piece mounted to the deck joist above the storage compartment. Oil-tank fill pipe (5) is hidden in hatch framed by beams and joists, with removable deck section. An electronic bug killer mounted on the nearby work shed (6) lures insects away from the grill, shown on the main deck by the re-sided garage.

DRAWING BY EUGENE THOMPSON

We wanted to avoid extensive excavation, and we wanted a structural link between the new wing and decking. So we built a concrete-pier foundation using Sonotubes, the cylindrical cardboard forms that are usually sunk in the ground before pouring the concrete footings.

The building method was simple. Using a backhoe and post-hole digger, we dug holes below the frost line and inserted the forms. After pouring in a layer of stones for drainage, we filled the forms with concrete (using a wheelbarrow and ramp as needed) and inserted anchor bolts. When the concrete cured, we attached U-shaped fasteners to hold the beams that support both deck and wing subframing.

Framing for the new wing rests on only six concrete piers. For extra stability, the wing sits atop a concrete-block retaining wall, which extends the width of the upper decking (see drawing). This 3-foot-high knee wall provides firm anchorage for both room and decking, with far less work than that required for a conventional foundation. The wall also greatly simplified framing of both deck and wing because all beams are installed on the same level. (Note in the framing sketch that the floor joists for the enclosed room sit 1½ inches higher than the deck joists. Decking planks are 1½ inches thick.)

Building the stairs was simple once we determined the dimensions of treads (two 2×6s) and risers (6 inches). Using two boards for each tread aids drainage while visially blending the stairs with the decking.

To store equipment and outdoor furniture, I designed two under-deck storage areas and a pull-up hatch for the oil-tank fill pipe (see photos). To wed the redwood add-ons to the existing house, we re-sided it and installed new windows, including a sliding window for passing food from kitchen to deck. The window is shorter and shallower than the old double-hung one, so we had to reframe the opening—*by W. David Houser. Color photos by Greg Sharko. Drawings by Carl De Groote and Eugene Thompson.*

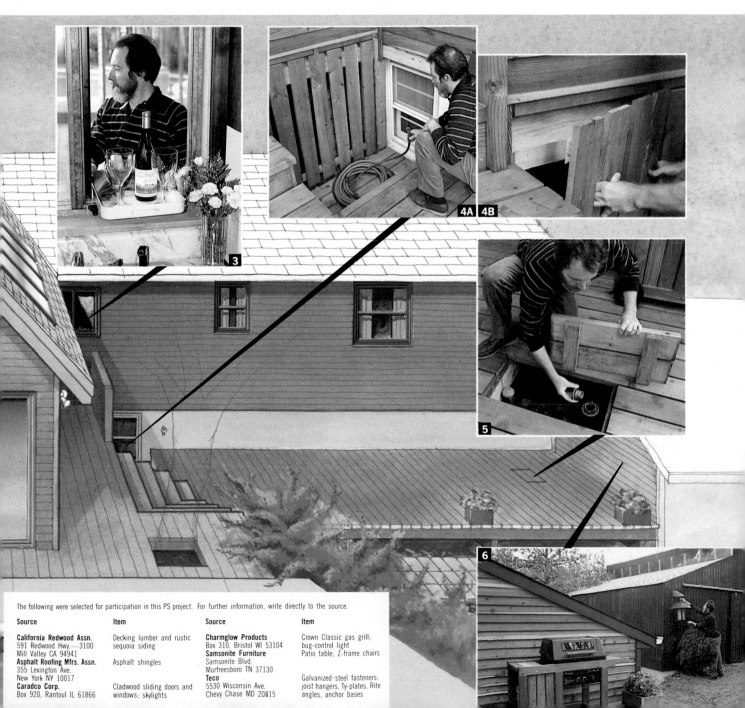

The following were selected for participation in this PS project. For further information, write directly to the source.

Source	Item	Source	Item
California Redwood Assn. 591 Redwood Hwy.—3100 Mill Valley CA 94941	Decking lumber and rustic sequoia siding	**Charmglow Products** Box 310, Bristol WI 53104	Crown Classic gas grill; bug-control light
Asphalt Roofing Mfrs. Assn. 355 Lexington Ave. New York NY 10017	Asphalt shingles	**Samsonite Furniture** Samsonite Blvd. Murfreesboro TN 37130	Patio table; Z-frame chairs
Caradco Corp. Box 920, Rantoul IL 61866	Cladwood sliding doors and windows; skylights	**Teco** 5530 Wisconsin Ave. Chevy Chase MD 20815	Galvanized-steel fasteners; joist hangers, Ty-plates, Rite angles, anchor bases

solid-wood strip paneling for your home

Those ubiquitous 4-by-8-foot sheets of stimulated-wood-grain or veneer-faced plywood paneling are facing a growing competitor: strip, or plank, paneling.

Why the shift to planks? Because they look so good. Why live with imitation wood when you can have a room—or an accent wall or bar alcove —paneled in genuine cedar or rich oak? And planks offer a lot more freedom of expression: You can create handsome herringbone, chevron, and diagonal layouts, for example.

Almost a score of plank-paneling manufacturers (see table) now produce strips made from a wide variety of tree species, and many of them offer the woods prefinished. The companies have also devised convenient packaging aimed at do-it-yourselfers.

Today's plank panelings can be sorted into four piles: hardwoods; mostly unfinished softwoods; thicker

PS COMPARISON TABLE: SHOPPING FOR STRIP PANELING

Brand	SIZE Thick. (in.)	SIZE Width (in.)	Species	Approx. price per sq. ft. ($)	Comments— special features
ABEDA WOOD PRODUCTS					
Rembrandt	5/16	3½	Clear western red cedar	1	
			Knotty western cedar	0.77	
		4, 6	Knotty pine	0.70	
Rembrandt Ultra-Thin	1/64	3½	Clear western red cedar	0.90	"Peel & Stick" pressure-sensitive back
Country Accents Wainscot	5/16	3½	Knotty pine, knotty cedar, clear western red cedar	0.90–1	Package includes matching beaded chair rail and baseboard
ARBOR WOOD PRODUCTS					
Arbor	5/16	3⅝	Clear western red cedar	n.a.	
			Knotty western red cedar	n.a.	
			Lodgepole pine	n.a.	
ASPEN VALLEY LUMBER CO.					
Ash-Lok Aspen-Lok Cedar-Lok Pine-Lok	⅜	4, 6	Ash Aspen Cedar Pine	1.09 0.74–0.80	End-matched; trim moldings available
Aspen Valley	⅝	3½ 5½	Knotty pine	0.62–0.82	Surface is textured to reveal grain; matching trim moldings available
Nor-Wood Beachcomber Nor-Wood Candlelight		Pkg. is 3½, 4½, 5½	Pine	1.25	
Norwood Olde Mill		5½			
Nor-Wood Designer Planks		3½			
Nor-Wood Wainscot		5½		3.95 per pkg.	Matching prefinished cap molding available
BARCLAY MFG. CO.					
Thunder Mountain	5/16	3½	Lodgepole pine	0.81	Installation clips available
			Western red cedar, knotty cedar	1.19	
Country Planking	⅝	6	Pine	0.88	
Real Oak	⅜	2⅜, 3⅜, 4⅜	Oak	2.15 unfinished 2.51 finished	Available light- or dark-toned; has random simulated end-matched V-joints

Brand	SIZE Thick. (in.)	SIZE Width (in.)	Species	Approx. price per sq. ft. ($)	Comments— special features
BARCLAY MFG. CO.					
Barclay	¾	6, 8	Pine	1.04	Simulates wormy chestnut, pecky cypress, barn wood, walnut, beveled planks, rustic cedar, rustic oak, or rustic walnut; matching moldings available
GEORGE C. BROWN CO.					
SuperCedar	⅜	2½, 3, 3½, 4	Aromatic red cedar	1.15–1.25	End-matched
BUSINESS SERVICES INTL.					
GPL Diffusion Le Clad	⅜	2¾	Oak	3.90	End-matched or butt-jointed t&g
		2 5/16– 5¼	Chestnut	1.96	End-matched
			Pine, clear and knotty	Prefinished, about 1.40	End-matched or butt-jointed t&g; finger-jointed available; moldings and installation clips available.
CHAMPION INTL. CORP.					
Pine Brook 4 Pine Crest 2 Pine Valley 4	½	4	Knotty pine	0.74	
GREENWOOD FOREST PRODUCTS					
Penticton	5/16	3¾	Lodgepole pine	0.75	
			Clear western red cedar, knotty western red cedar	1.05	
LEWIS HYMAN					
Luan E-Z Strips	⅛	3½	Luan mahogany	0.28–0.30	Apply with manufacturer's adhesive
KAKABEKA TIMBER					
Kakabeka	½	4, 5, 6	Red oak	2.55	End-matched; moldings available on special order
			Black ash	2.40	
			Maple	2.40	
			White birch	1.39	
			White pine	1.03	
			Knotty cedar	1.39	
		4	Jack pine	0.70	

| Brand | SIZE | | Species | Approx. price per sq. ft. ($) | Comments— special features |
	Thick. (in.)	Width (in.)			
OSAGE PRODUCTS					
Osage	5/16	3½	Aromatic red cedar	1	End-matched; 42-in. length ideal for use as wainscoting
OSTERMANN & SCHEIWE, U.S.A.					
Profilewood	7/16	4	Western red cedar, Douglas fir, western hemlock, California redwood	From 1 for thin knotty pine to 3 for redwood	Supplied with clips for installation
	3/8	3½	Lodgepole knotty pine		
Woodwise	5/16	4	Hemlock, clear cedar, knotty cedar, knotty pine		
Beadwood	3/8	4	Western hemlock		
JC PENNEY CO.					
Penney's	—	4	Wood and mirror strip set	3–6	Price depends on style of mirror strips chosen
	1/10	3 7/16	Western red cedar	0.59	Apply with adhesive
	—	—	Luan mahogany and mirror strip set	2.58	Apply wood with adhesive; mirrors use double-faced tape (included)
	5/16	3½	Pine	1.70	Kit includes matching top rail and baseboard
	3/8	3 5/8	Aromatic red cedar	1.56	

Clear western red-cedar strips are applied diagonally in a contemporary living room (above). In the installation shown below, redwood exterior siding is carried right through a window wall.

In keeping with its sharp looks, plank paneling carries a steeper price tag. Pine plank paneling costs 75 cents to $1 per square foot; the fancy hardwood plankings can cost three to seven times that much. And unless the paneling is prefinished, you will also have the expense of finishing it. By comparison, veneer rosewood or walnut on ¼-inch-thick 4-by-8-foot panels sells for $1 to $1.25 per square foot. Printed-grain bargain-grade chipboard costs only 20 cents per square foot in 4-by-8 sheets.

It pays to shop around

There are good reasons to visit a few suppliers before you buy:

● You may find a special price on irregular planks.

● Descriptions and pictures of wood species won't always live up to your expectations. It's a good idea to see the wood firsthand.

● Compare available thicknesses. Thicker planking will work better on unsupported stud walls. On the other hand, you might want to buy thinner and generally less-expensive planking if you're going to apply it directly over drywall or another smooth, flat surface.

● Understand trim options. Many of the plank-paneling suppliers don't offer matching moldings and trims for their products. What you need may be available as standard millwork, but if not, you can make your own trim from matching lumber or by having someone cut it for you.

● Not all planks are created equal. Inspect the planking carefully to be sure it is smooth surfaced—unless you want a rough-sawn texture.

● Compare end-joining options. I like planking that is end-matched—with tongue-and-groove end joints. This feature practically eliminates the possibility of making mistakes when you're cutting and butting square-cut planking ends—*by Mack Philips.*

Pine plank paneling applied horizontally frames the fireplace above. Strip paneling in prefinished oak is shown at right in a vertical application.

pine planks toned and textured to simulate other woods; and thin specialty planks.

Hardwood plank-paneling suppliers offer a great range of species, including burley pecan, cherry, oak, birch, and black ash. The hardwoods are somewhat more expensive than softwoods, of course, but they're worth it because of their rich and elegant appearance.

The softwood plank-panel offerings range from aspen to redwood and even aromatic red cedar, which has long been used as a closet-lining material. Now this showy wood is being applied to accent walls and is also being used as wainscoting.

Several companies also market softwood plankings that are stationed and textured to stimulate other wood species or the natural effects of the sun and weathering.

The thin planks—generally about ⅛ inch thick—are relatively inexpensive and easy to use. Flexible and able to conform to curved surfaces, they go up with adhesive. They also require a backing that is solid and smooth. J.C. Penney sells kits combining mirror strips with wood.

The planks are easier to handle than 4-by-8-foot sheets of paneling, and there is practically no waste because leftover strips can usually be fitted in somewhere during the course of a project. Similarly, the risk of miscalculating angles, jogs, and outlet boxes is less than when working with large sheets of paneling.

Plank paneling has also become lighter and easier to apply since manufacturers, to reduce costs, have skinned down the thickness of many types to ½ inch or less. (Most plank paneling had been ¾ inch thick.)

SOME MANUFACTURERS OF STRIP PANELING
Abeda Wood Products, Winfield, B. C., Canada VOH 2CO; **Arbor Wood Products Ltd.,** 5820 Byrne Rd., Burnaby, B. C., Canada V5J 315; **Aspen Valley Lumber Co.,** Box 209, Land O'Lakes, WI 54540; **Barclay Mfg. Co., Inc.,** Box 954, Westbury, NY 11590; **George C. Brown Co., Inc.,** P.O. Drawer B, Greensboro, NC 27402; **Business Services Intl.,** 1 Newbury St., Peabody, MA 01960; **Champion Intl. Corp.,** 1 Champion Plaza, Stamford, CT 06921; **Greenwood Forest Products Ltd.,** Box 9, Penticton, B.C., Canada V2A 6J9; **Lewis Hyman, Inc.,** 12824 S. Cerise Ave., Hawthorne, CA 90250; **Kakabeka Timber Ltd.,** Box 78, Kakabeka Falls, Ont., Canada POT 1WO; **Osage Products Co.,** Box 314, Eldon, MO 65026; **Ostermann & Scheiwe, U.S.A.,** Box 668, Spanaway, WA 98446; **JC Penney Co., Inc.,** Box 1270, Milwaukee, WI 53201; **Ply-Gem Mfg. Corp.,** 919 Third Ave., New York, NY 10022; **P&M Cedar Products Inc.,** Box 7349, Stockton, CA 95207; **Potlatch Corp., Townsend Unit,** Box 916, Stuttgart, AR 72160; **Real Wood Products,** 90 Foch St., Eugene, OR 97402; **Sears, Roebuck and Co.,** Sears Tower, Chicago, IL 60684; **Simpson Timber Co.,** Drawer V, Arcata, CA 95521.

installing strip paneling

A variety of plank-paneling profiles are available (left). Even the same pattern can vary considerably in appearance, depending on the width and the thickness you choose. Some planks are reversible, but others have an anticupping groove pattern on backside.

Before they go up, solid-wood planks need the right choice of finish. In some cases—such as areas exposed to heavy traffic or direct sunlight—no finish at all may be best, so a fading or scratched finish won't be a problem later on.

When stain is used before finishing, the semitransparent varieties are best because they let the natural grain show through. The easiest way to get a good-looking finish is to use a stain wax or penetrating oil, coating the entire plank before installation. Harder finishes such as varnish and shellac can hamper the natural expansion and contraction of wood; they'll also give it a yellow tone that will deepen with age. If the planking is to be used in a high-moisture area, first give it an all-over coating with a water-repellent preservative.

Experiment with finishes to see how they look. Test-finish the back of a plank, sanding it first if necessary— *Mack Phillips*

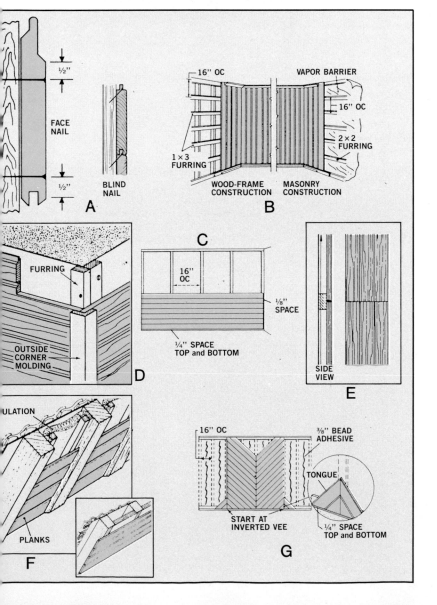

When nailing strip paneling in place, either the face-nail or blind-nail method (A) can be used. With hardwood planks you must first drill small holes for the nails. To glue planks, use 3/8-inch beads of good-quality panel adhesive. This isn't recommended over old lath and plaster, old paneling (the adhesive may not stick to the finish), or in high-moisture areas. Some suppliers suggest you use surfaced furring strips (B) at least 3/4-inch thick by 2 or 3 inches wide behind planks rather than applying them directly to existing wall surfaces. Thinner planks will need closer-spaced furring strips. In humid areas, furring should be notched on the wall side to allow air circulation. A polyethylene vapor barrier is strongly recommended for masonry walls. Leave an expansion gap (C) at the edges of the wall, and use a level as you install each plank. Corners can be supported and trimmed as shown (D). Furring should also support butt joints (E), while end-jointed butts in heavier stock may not need it. Ceilings are paneled much the same as walls—except for cathedral types (F). Insulation is behind planking used on exposed beam ceiling (far left) or pitched attic (inset). Basic technique for installing planking on a slant or herringbone pattern (G) is to start at the bottom at a 45-degree angle in the case of a slant pattern or with an inverted "V" for a herringbone design.

double-frame window stretches view – saves energy

A spectacular view was being wasted. The backyard stretched all the way to the Delaware Water Gap, but from the existing window it was all but invisible. And the double-hung window itself was old and leaked heat badly.

The owner of the house in rural New Jersey remedied both drawbacks in one move—he installed a double wood-frame insulated-glass window that was equipped with efficient, tight-fitting jam liners. The result?

Both his room and his energy outlook brightened.

You can double a small window, too. Here are suggestions for doing the job from the National Woodwork Manufacturers Association, sponsor of the New Jersey project. The room shown has a sheathed wood-frame wall covered with conventional siding and an interior finished with wall-board. The replacement window is a preassembled unit.

Your first task is to locate the wall

Dramatic change in small room (inset), which was saddled with a tiny double-hung window, came about thanks to new 6-foot window and updated decor.

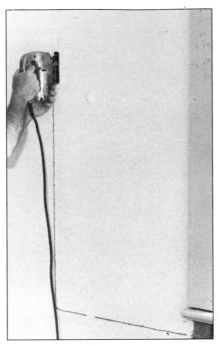

Replacement of old window starts with removal of interior casing to expose the wall. Height matches the sliding door.

A jigsaw is used to cut the rough opening in interior wall. Cut wallboard through on all sides, bypassing studs.

A circular saw is used for the outside cuts. The saw cuts partway through the studs so less hand-cutting is required.

Wall section, complete with old window, is lifted out and lowered to the ground. It can easily be dismantled.

Using a ladder for support, raise window into position—ease it up one step at a time. Once it's in place, check for level.

studs at either side of the planned opening. Measure the width of the opening, and mark cutting lines on either side—but be sure that the cuts will be at least 1½ inches away from existing studs. Use a level so that the lines are perfectly vertical.

Measure down from the ceiling to establish the new window height. To make room for a new header and longer sill, add 6 inches to the measurement at the window top and 1½ inches to the bottom. With a

level, mark the horizontal cuts at top and bottom. Be sure there are no wires or plumbing runs in the way—relocate them if necessary.

To indicate the outside cut, drill a ¼-inch hole through the wall at each corner of the box you've drawn inside. Go outside and remove the shingles or siding to expose the sheathing in the area to be cut, and draw cutting lines from hole to hole.

Now return to the inside. Use a portable jigsaw to cut the opening in the

wallboard (if the windowsill or casing at the top interferes with the rough opening cuts, remove it before cutting). When making the horizontal cuts, skip over the studs—you can cut them later with a handsaw.

Remove the wallboard carefully and save the pieces for reuse. Remove any insulation from between the studs and set it aside, too.

Now go outside and, with a portable circular saw, cut the rough opening in the wall sheathing, following the lines carefully. Again, skip over the studs. If the ceiling joists are supported by the wall you're working on, support the ceiling temporarily by propping it with 2 × 4s—before you begin cutting the wall studs.

To install the new structural sill, cut a 2 × 4 at least 6 inches longer than the width of the opening (assuming that the existing studs do not frame the new opening), and center it over the ends of the existing cripple (trimmed short) studs along the bottom of the opening. Add cripple studs, if necessary, to support the ends. Be sure the sill is level, and then nail it into place.

To form a header, cut two 2 × 6s to the required length, sandwich a piece of ½-inch plywood between them as a spacer, and nail them together. Hold the header in place so that it bears against the cripple studs at the top of the opening, and measure down to the sill to determine the length of the trimmer studs you'll need on either side. Cut the trimmer studs to the proper length.

If, as is likely, the window does not fit directly between the existing studs, measure for new trimmer studs at the sides of the rough opening. After the rough opening has been cut, measure the distance to the nearest existing wall studs at either side, deduct ½ inch, and cut blocks of 2 × 4s to this length. Nail these blocks to one side of the trimmer studs. The blocks will bear against the existing studs when the trimmer studs are set into the wall. Push the header into position at the top of the opening, and tap the trimmer studs into position—stuff insulation into the wall space behind them. Toenail the trimmer studs to the sill and header, and nail sheathing to the sides of the new frame.

With a helper, lift the new window unit into the opening from the outside. Make sure the unit is plumb, level, and square. Use shims if necessary, then nail it into position with three-inch galvanized finishing nails. Put a drip cap over the top of the window to keep rain out. Now sheathe the wall at the top and bottom of the window, and put on the siding. Caulk around the entire unit.

Stuff insulation into any gaps from the inside, then cut pieces of wallboard to cover the header and sill, and nail into place.

Now trim, add a windowsill if desired, and paint or stain to suit. You're now ready to step back and enjoy your doubled view—*by Charles A. Miller. Drawing by Carl De Groote.*

Interior trim is nailed in place after sanding the wall smooth. Wood can be painted or stained to match decor.

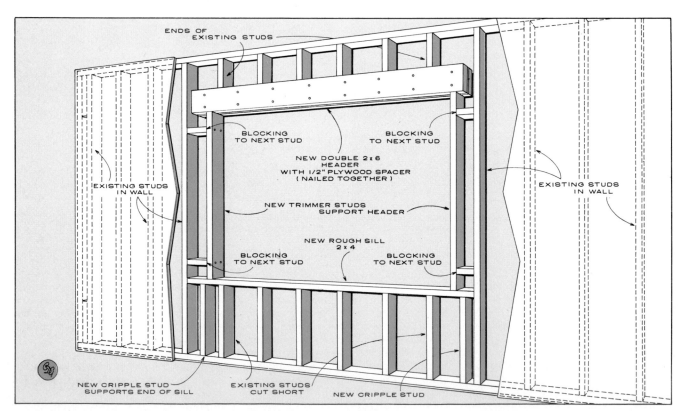

Replacing an old window with a larger unit means that you have to cut a new rough opening in the existing wall. Diagram is for the wall pictured on the preceding pages—that is, one without heavy ceiling and roof loads.

install these skylights from indoors

Bringing the sunlight indoors through a skylight is an idea with inescapable appeal: It brightens up a room during the daylight hours without using energy and may offer passive solar heat gain as well. Just as important, glimpses of sky or trees through openings in the ceiling can provide a decorative touch that brings a room to life.

Yes, you say, but clambering around on the roof isn't your idea of a safe and sane project. Now there's a better way: skylights you install from indoors, without ever setting foot on the roof.

These new skylights (made by Caradco Corp., Box 920, Rantoul, IL 61866) are designed with the do-it-yourselfer in mind. They are made in two sections for easier handling during installation. A receiving rim mounts around a rectangular hole cut through the underside of the roof, and the separate double-glazed skylight panel slips into place after the rim has been tightly sealed where it meets the roof shingles. During installation, both the receiving rim and the skylight panel are hoisted through the

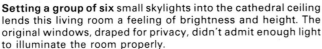

Setting a group of six small skylights into the cathedral ceiling lends this living room a feeling of brightness and height. The original windows, draped for privacy, didn't admit enough light to illuminate the room properly.

hole in the roof from the room below. And because the units are spaced to fit within standard rafter spacing, you can do the job with minimal structural change, whether you install one unit or a cluster of six, as I did.

Skylights aren't limited to places like my cathedral-ceiling living room. If you have a house with a flat ceiling below an attic, you can bring in the sunshine by constructing a light well. With this type of house, you install the skylight (or skylights) in the roof, but you work from the attic floor. Then you drop a plumb line from the corners of the skylight to the floor and cut out this section of the room ceiling below. Build the light well by framing and boxing-in the area from the room ceiling to the roof, adding insulation to the outside of this box. For a multiple-skylight light well, leave the attic-floor joists in place, painting them white to downplay their visibility as they cross the well.

When you peel the shingles back 2½ inches from the top and sides of the receiving-rim opening, you can roll 1-inch dowels underneath the shingles to keep them out of the way. Leave the roofing felt around the hole intact.

Set the receiving rim in place, and trace its inner border onto the felt paper. Remove the rim, and apply a thick bead of sealant around the opening, ¼ inch inside the outline. Then screw the rim to the roof, trimming the shingles so they overlap it by one inch at the top and sides. Seal all screw heads and the edges of all shingles before attaching the skylight panel—*by Carl J. De Groote. Photos by Greg Sharko.*

First step in installing skylights is to cut openings in ceiling (photo above), working from sturdy scaffold. Use stud finder before cutting to make sure holes are between rafters. Rough openings for these skylights are 14½ inches by 27½ inches. After removing insulation, cut out this area of roof, starting from drilled holes at corners. Box-in opening for skylight (center photo) at top and bottom with double headers the same size as your rafters. Standing up through opening in roof (top), peel back shingles, and lay bead of sealant before popping back down to push rim out hole ahead of you. Bottom should overlap shingles by 1 inch, but top and sides must slip under shingles and be sealed (drawing).

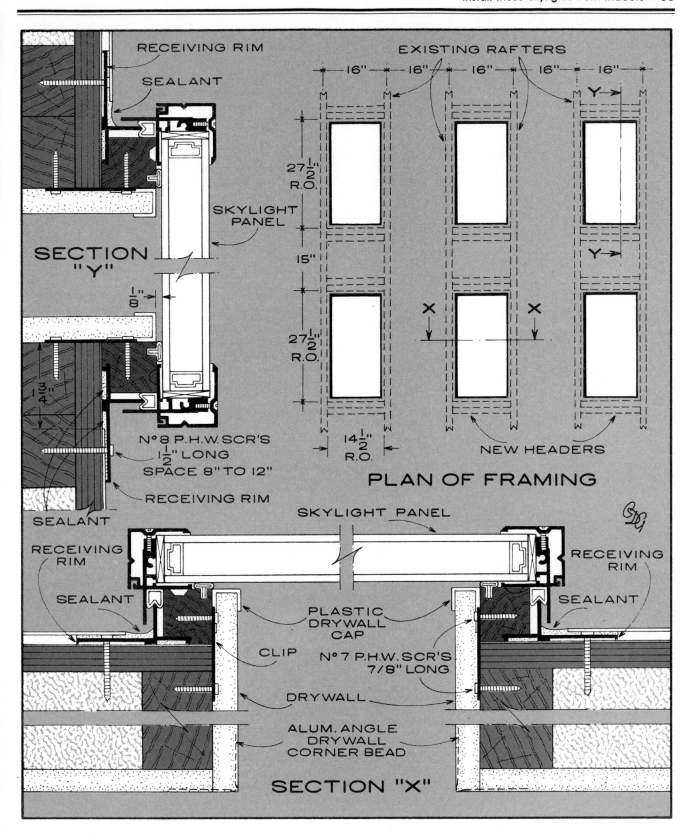

RECEIVING RIM

SEALANT

EXISTING RAFTERS

16" 16" 16" 16" 16"

Y

27½" R.O.

SECTION "Y"

⅛"

SKYLIGHT PANEL

1¾"

15"

27½" R.O.

Y

N°8 P.H.W. SCR'S 1½" LONG SPACE 8" TO 12"

RECEIVING RIM

SEALANT

14½" R.O.

X   X

NEW HEADERS

PLAN OF FRAMING

RECEIVING RIM

RECEIVING RIM

SEALANT

SEALANT

SKYLIGHT PANEL

PLASTIC DRYWALL CAP

CLIP

N°7 P.H.W. SCR'S 7/8" LONG

DRYWALL

ALUM. ANGLE DRYWALL CORNER BEAD

SECTION "X"

keep the heat inside with outside insulation

It makes sense: Wrap your home in plastic, and you're bound to keep heat in and drafts and cold air out. A new idea? Well, not really.

Exterior insulation has been used for some time on commercial buildings: the tall white hotel with the rough finish; the newly stuccoed office building; and the bank with the "sculptured" look. They may all have been insulated with a layer of polystyrene. Although exterior insulation has had a reputation for being expensive, more recently the cost of materials has made it competitive with brick and stucco for use on concrete structures. (It's not economical for use over wood.) And now some two dozen manufacturers offer it for residential use.

Exterior insulation typically consists of four basic component layers:

● *Insulation board.* Made of expanded or extruded polystyrene, the 2-by-4-foot-by-1-inch-thick (or more) board is the primary material. It is glued or nailed directly to the shell of the house. Some boards have tongue-and-groove edges; with others, the joints between the boards are covered with adhesive tape. Extruded polystyrene has a slightly higher R-value and costs more than expanded polystyrene, but either works well.

● *Reinforcing mesh.* Made of woven fabric or fiberglass, the "chicken wire" mesh adds strength to the insulation-board base to prevent surface cracks.

● *Adhesive coat.* Typically, it's a mixture of portland cement and an acrylic or acrylic-latex bonding agent used to bond the mesh to the polystyrene board.

● *Finish coat.* This is a stuccolike coating, which protects the polystyrene from the elements and ultraviolet rays. The finish may be precolored or painted.

The result is "outsulation": a clean, modern-looking covering that offers enormous energy savings for a whole variety of reasons.

Conventional cavity insulation has inherent problems: Studs (and bridges between them), corner posts, sills, electric boxes, floors, ceilings, settled insulation, and missed areas can allow heat to escape from your house. And any large temperature difference in a poorly insulated interior wall can be harmful to its finish as well. Though a careful job of cavity insulation can plug most of these problem areas, it will not insulate as well as wrapping with polystyrene board.

Just an inch of polystyrene gives about ten times the R-value of conventional structural sheathing. And according to tests by Dow, makers of Styrofoam boards, the tongue-and-groove polystyrene sheets can reduce air infiltration by as much as 25 percent. This, of course, means lower thermostat settings, fewer drafts, and greater comfort. But there's more.

"When you wrap a house in polystyrene, any concrete-block or foundation material becomes a thermal mass," says Steve Day of Conproco, a company that uses exterior insulation on masonry structures. "Concrete and similar materials are awful insulators, but they store heat magnificently when moved inside."

Exterior insulation covers the entire external wall space, including the foundation, a tremendous siphon of heat. That makes it a particularly appealing option for any concrete-block structure in which cavity insulation is difficult to install or requires a great deal of preliminary framing. Such buildings benefit greatly by moving the thermal mass of their walls into the living space. And by adding south-facing glass, the house can become a passive-solar showcase.

Friedrich Goeman of W. R. Bonsal, makers of the Sure-wall system, points out that exterior insulation also "reduces the dangers of fire-related smoke inhalation by placing combustible insulation materials on the house's exterior." Also, because the interior of the building remains undisturbed, no interior floor space is lost. A retrofit can even be done while the house is occupied.

The tough and permanent finish coat of exterior insulation protects the building from the elements and essentially waterproofs the structure. Many of the finishes are "self-cleaning" as well; they are easily hosed down or even rinsed clean by rain. But there are some differences.

Flexibility

All polystyrene expands and contracts significantly due to temperature swings. To prevent cracking, manufacturers deal with the problem in two ways. One way is to make the top coating flexible enough to tolerate the changes. The other is to make it so tough that it limits them.

The coating used to limit the movement is typically a mixture of portland cement reinforced with fiberglass and an acrylic or acrylic-latex bonding agent. This coating is hard enough to withstand hammer blows, but because the panels still move, expansion joints are needed about every 12 feet. The advantage of this system is that it is relatively easy to install (it can be done by a do-it-yourselfer, but that is not usually recommended by the makers). It's also lower in cost—about one-quarter the cost of lath-stucco.

The more flexible systems usually have a fiberglass mesh that is held in place by the coating compound. The

Covered with Dryvit exterior insulation, homes such as these have a tough, newly stuccoed appearance. "Outsulation" is ten times more energy efficient than conventional sheathing, and it's claimed to last 25 years or more without maintenance. Dryvit offers 21 colors in four types of finish coats.

37

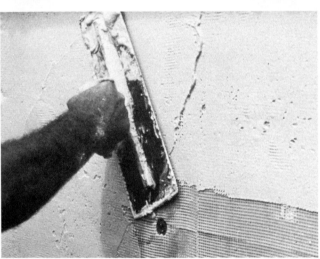

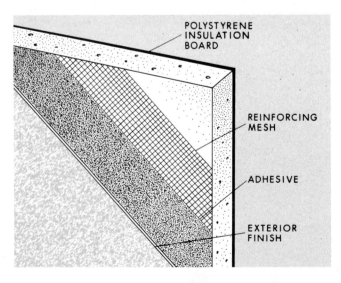

coatings often contain a higher percentage of acrylics—making them more expensive—and may require two applications. They may also need a backing board between the polystyrene and the studs. Until recently, these systems had the disadvantage of providing less impact resistance. But Dryvit, STO, and other makers have since introduced flexible coatings that have a rock-hard surface.

"We went with the flexible system because we felt that the one-piece look and real insulation advantages of exterior insulation without expansion joints are far more attractive," says Ray Di Giacomo of Dryvit. "And there are now no real disadvantages." STO's Buck Buchanan adds that the systems with more acrylics in the cover coat give "greater crack resistance and better color consistency."

Which is the one to choose? Stuart White, a Hanover, New Hampshire, architect who has worked extensively with both types of systems in northern New England feels that neither is truly superior. And, of course, some companies offer both.

Costs

"Exterior insulation combines perfectly with mortarless cement-block construction," says Conproco's Day. "The same compound used on the surface of the cement blocks can be used—with the addition of a latex-acrylic modifier—as a mastic for applying the polystyrene boards and as a coating for the boards as well. That makes building, insulating, waterproofing, and finishing a home a much more compact, cost-efficient operation."

But owners and builders of wood-frame houses are unlikely to consider exterior insulation, especially when retrofitting. The detail work around doors and windows is difficult, and the labor costs—whether measured in time or money—are prohibitive. Who wants to change their lovely clapboard to stucco, anyway?

Few companies wanted to be pinned down on the cost of exterior insulation jobs because they vary greatly and are ultimately set by contractors. But about $4 a square foot for a solid straight wall should pay for installation of even the most complicated system. Simpler systems may cost as little as $2.50 a square foot. Walls with windows or doors will probably cost more.

These prices are not likely to be competitive with those of vinyl, aluminum siding, or shingling, but they are comparable with those of new brick or stucco. And many industry experts claim a life expectancy of 25 years or more.

Are longevity, lower energy costs, and tremendous insulating value all decided pluses for exterior insulation? Yes, but there's one more advantage. Seventy-two percent of the architects in one survey expected an increase in their use of these systems over the next five years—but not necessarily for its practical value.

"It's got a pure, sculptural look that can go over everything except the roof," says White—*by Mark Bittman.*

POLYSTYRENE INSULATION BOARD

REINFORCING MESH

ADHESIVE

EXTERIOR FINISH

Insulation board (photo, top) is fastened to house wall with spot patches of adhesive. Reinforcing mesh is added (photo, middle) and covered with next adhesive layer. Edges of mesh overlap by 2½ inches. Final step, adding a finish, varies with color and texture desired. Each layer, as shown in drawing, must be smooth to obtain best results.

SOME MANUFACTURERS OF EXTERIOR INSULATION PRODUCTS
Conproco Corp., Box 368, Hookset, NH 03106; Cota Industries, Inc., 5512 14th St. S.E., Des Moines, IA 50320; Dow Chemical, Midland, MI 48640; Dryvit System, Inc., Box 1014, W. Warwick, RI 02893; Exterior Insulation Manufacturers Assn., 1000 Vermont Ave. N.W., Washington, DC 20005; H. B. Fuller Co., 315 S. Hicks Rd., Palatine, IL 60067; Insul. Crete Co., Inc., 4311 Triangle St., Mc Farland, WI 53558; ISPO USA, Inc., Box 382, Mansfield, MA 02048; Kern-Tac, Inc., 4421 Orchard St. S., Tacoma, WA 98466; SENCON, Inc., 21 Elm St. W., Chicago, IL 60610; STO Energy Conservation, Inc., 2189F Flintstone Dr., Tucker, GA 30084; Synergy Methods, Inc., 1367 Elmwood Ave., Cranston, RI 02910; Therm-Clad, Inc., Box 40096, Tucson, AZ 85717; Thoro Systems Products, 7800 38th St. N.W., Miami, FL 33166; W. R. Bonsal Co., 8201 Arrowridge Blvd., Charlotte, NC 28210.

eight heating-system add-ons

You know the importance of annual maintenance and fine-tuning to keeping your heating system performing at its best. If you heat with gas or oil, you've probably had the burner's firing rate reduced—or at least have investigated the possibility. What else can you do to reduce heating costs?

Add-on devices may be the answer. Over the years I have installed and evaluated many of these, but judging their effectiveness can be tricky. Heating systems, houses, and life-styles are not all alike, and a device that produces significant savings in my home may be of little benefit in yours. However, because of the way they work, some add-on devices should improve the performance of nearly any heating system for which they are intended. They are the ones I have included here.

Another feature these items have in common: their installation is within the skills of most do-it-yourselfers. And the latest models seem to be easier to install than previous versions I've used. DIY installation could save you upwards of $200, but check your local building codes; there are some areas where professional installation is required.

I have listed the items in the order of priority I would assign to them *if they are needed*. You wouldn't, of course, install a booster fan if there is adequate airflow through all ducts, or a humidifier if you live in a tight, damp house.

Some devices must be installed when the heating system is off. Be sure the power is disconnected before inspecting, installing, or testing equipment with electrical hookups.

Setback thermostats. These are available for hydronic (hot-water) and forced-air systems (including heat pumps). By reducing the house temperature at night or when you're away—automatically—they can reduce heating bills substantially. I recommend the multiple-setback kind, which allows you to reduce the temperature more than once during a 24-hour period.

I also recommend the "anticipator" type such as the Intellistat 2 (made by Euro-Med. b.v., Box 1092, 3260 AB, Oud-Beijerland, the Netherlands). This type monitors the number and duration of furnace running cycles, compares that information with the setback differential, then calculates the starting time required to bring the temperature up at the preset time —and, on a heat pump, it does all this without kicking in the resistance heat. The Intellistat 2 has other advanced features (see caption) and is simple to program.

Read the instructions and operator's manual carefully at the outset, and consult the wiring diagram for your heating system. Before you remove your old thermostat, make a diagram of each terminal designation and the color of wire connected to it. Connect the wires to the corresponding terminals on the new stat.

Fresh-air intakes. If your house has a low air-infiltration rate and you heat with fossil fuel, a fresh-air intake may improve your heating system's performance. An air intake can be as simple as a duct from outside that delivers combustion air for the burner, or as sophisticated as a whole-house heat exchanger.

The Skuttle air intake (Skuttle Mfg. Co., Rte. 1, Marietta, OH 45750) is somewhere between these in sophistication. It ducts outside air into the return-air duct of a warm-air furnace. Its barometric damper allows air to flow in whenever a negative pressure exists in the house. In a tight house, negative pressure can occur when the furnace or other combustion appliance is on or when bathroom or kitchen vents are running.

To install the Skuttle you cut a hole in the return-air duct and mount the unit in the opening. Then cut an opening in the outside wall, and pass the connecting duct through, terminating it with a screened cap.

The best way I've found to adjust the Skuttle is to open the doors and windows in the house and turn on the furnace blower. This equalizes the pressure inside and out. Next, adjust the weighted arm on the barometric damper until the damper is just closed. Now when a negative pressure exists, you'll find the damper will open to let in air.

Humidifiers. Properly humidified air reduces the rate of evaporation from your skin and thus makes you feel warmer at lower thermostat settings. There are humidifiers for use with heat pumps as well as fossil-fuel forced-air systems.

A humidifier can be installed under a duct, on the warm-air plenum, or as a "bypass" version between the return and supply plenums. Several units, such as the Aqua-Mist (3980 N. Liberty St., Winston-Salem, NC 27105) shown, are specially suited for DIY installations because they have plug-in transformers and operate on low voltage. Once the humidifier and controls are mounted, you tap into a nearby cold waterline (see caption).

Dampers. When some rooms are too hot and others too cold in a forced-air

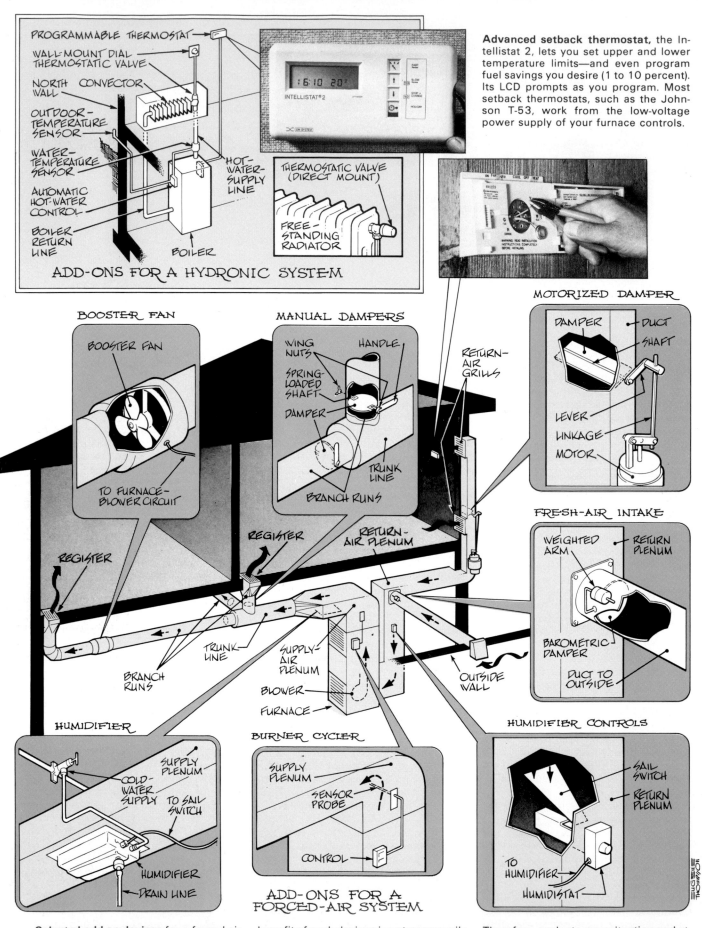

Advanced setback thermostat, the Intellistat 2, lets you set upper and lower temperature limits—and even program fuel savings you desire (1 to 10 percent). Its LCD prompts as you program. Most setback thermostats, such as the Johnson T-53, work from the low-voltage power supply of your furnace controls.

ADD-ONS FOR A HYDRONIC SYSTEM

ADD-ONS FOR A FORCED-AIR SYSTEM

Selected add-on devices for a forced-air heating system are shown in the diagram above; some for a hydronic (hot-water) system are in the diagram at top left. The benefit of such devices is not necessarily additive (if you install two devices that would each have saved 10 percent, total saving likely will not be 20 percent). Therefore, evaluate your situation and attack obvious weaknesses first. Then live with those changes before making others.

system, you may be able to solve both problems by installing dampers in the supply ducts. In use, you turn the damper to reduce airflow to the overheated rooms; and that increases the airflow to harder-to-heat areas. You can also use dampers to shut off heat to rooms when they're not in use. Manual dampers are available to fit standard round ducts and cost about $5 to $18 each. Sheet-metal shops will fabricate rectangular dampers; in my area they charge roughly $15 to $65, depending on size.

To install a damper you separate the branch duct from the main trunk line at the first joint. If the joint is stuck, apply a detergent-and-water solution and allow it to soak for five minutes. Place the damper within the duct as close as possible to the trunk line, and drill two holes for the damper shaft. Use a grounded or cordless drill. Install the damper, then put the handle on the outside, placing it in the same plane as the damper for accurate adjustment.

Motorized dampers, controlled by a switch or a thermostat, are often used in inaccessible areas, where heat is to be zoned, or where excess heat is available, as in a room with a wood stove. You install them just as you would the manuals. In addition, you install a plug-in, low-voltage transformer to provide the power for the motor.

Thermostatic radiator valves. These are to a hot-water system what damp-ers are to the hot-air system—only better because they provide temperature control for individual radiators. They work on hot-water and two-pipe steam systems.

With the heating system shut down and pressure off, you remove the old valve and install the new one. Use standard plumber's tape on all threaded fittings. Some thermostatic valves have a remote sensing tube; others have a sensor on the control knob. If a remote tube is used, be sure to locate it away from windows.

Booster fans. When a long supply duct in a forced-air system delivers too little air to distant rooms, a booster fan may solve the problem for much less than it would cost to enlarge the duct. A booster fan comes within a section of duct, which you install in place of an existing section. Some plug into an outlet and run constantly, but that can create drafts when the furnace isn't running. Most are connected to the furnace-blower circuit or to a sail switch and come on only with the blower. Follow the manufacturer's instructions carefully to make the electrical connections.

Automatic hot-water controls. For hydronic systems, these devices are called outdoor-reset controls, boiler-temperature programmers, or computers. Normally the burner maintains the boiler water at a fixed temperature. With these controls, when the outside temperature rises, the boiler-water temperature is al-lowed to fall. They are particularly useful in moderate climates and in climates with frequent temperature swings in winter months.

Mechanical installation is easy: The indoor sensor clamps to the supply pipe as close to the boiler as possible and is wrapped with insulation. The outdoor sensor is located on a north wall. Both are wired to the control unit, which is wired into the low-voltage control circuit of the burner. Some models also require a 115-V input from the power line.

Burner cyclers. The simplest of these are timing devices called "duty cyclers." They turn off the burner at preset times during the burning cycle.

Another type, the Heat Miser, made by Economic Energy Products (Grass Valley, CA 95945), is temperature actuated. It is calibrated to the furnace duct temperature and cycles the burner just enough to maintain the necessary temperature.

In theory at least, cyclers allow the air, which continues to circulate across the hot heat exchanger, to deliver heat to the house while the burner is off. Actual savings vary, but generally, older furnaces with massive heat exchangers benefit most. You wire cyclers into the low-voltage control circuit of the burner and install any remote sensors according to the manufacturer's instructions—*by Evan Powell. Drawings by Eugene Thompson.*

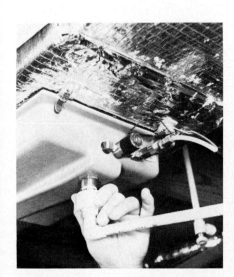

Humidifiers can be installed on supply duct or plenum. Many newer models, such as Aqua-Mist, are self-flushing and require floor drain for runoff.

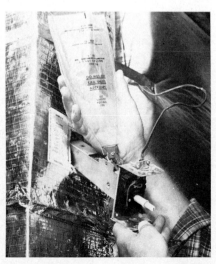

Humidistat and sail switch install in the return plenum. When humidistat calls for moisture and sail switch is tripped by airflow, humidifier is energized.

Self-piercing valve included with most humidifiers makes it simple to connect waterline. (For iron pipes you drill a 1/4-inch hole and use a saddle valve.)

grandfather clock

Mind power. That's what it takes to build large, complex projects. Joinery in this project is no different than in a smaller one—but there are so many more joints! It takes a great deal of concentration to see how they all come together.

Preparation

I found a number of clock-kit suppliers who sell everything from the basic clockworks to a prefabricated case. I finally chose to buy basic clockworks from The Heritage Clock Company, Heritage Park, Lexington, NC 27292. The works come with Westminster chimes, a moving moon dial, and an 8-inch dial face.

Size of the face is important. Knowing the diameter lets you revise the working drawings to fit your own choice of clockworks. The size and radius of the dial face determine size and shape of the dial face frame, the door, the scroll board, and the size of the clock housing—and, in fact, the size of the complete hood assembly and proportions of the entire clock. As drawn, my clock is slightly taller than a typical door (about 6 feet, 8 inches). It's shorter than the classic 7-foot grandfather clock, but it looks good in a typical American home with 8-foot ceilings.

Ornate hood features elegant gooseneck molding, hand-turned spindles and finials.

After working up the drawings, I found that this project requires about 30 board-feet of lumber. I bought 30 percent more than that to allow for bad wood and mistakes. You can make a clock out of almost any wood, but most clock cases are built from either cherry, walnut, or mahogany. I chose cherry.

Once I'd solved all the big design problems, I mounted the actual clockworks to a piece of plywood and hung it in my shop to check out the critical dimensions. Be sure to pack the works away again before you begin the project. The sawdust you kick up while making the clock case could ruin the clockworks.

I decided to divide the project up into three basic components: hood, waist, and base. Cutting a huge undertaking into smaller tasks helps bring things into focus.

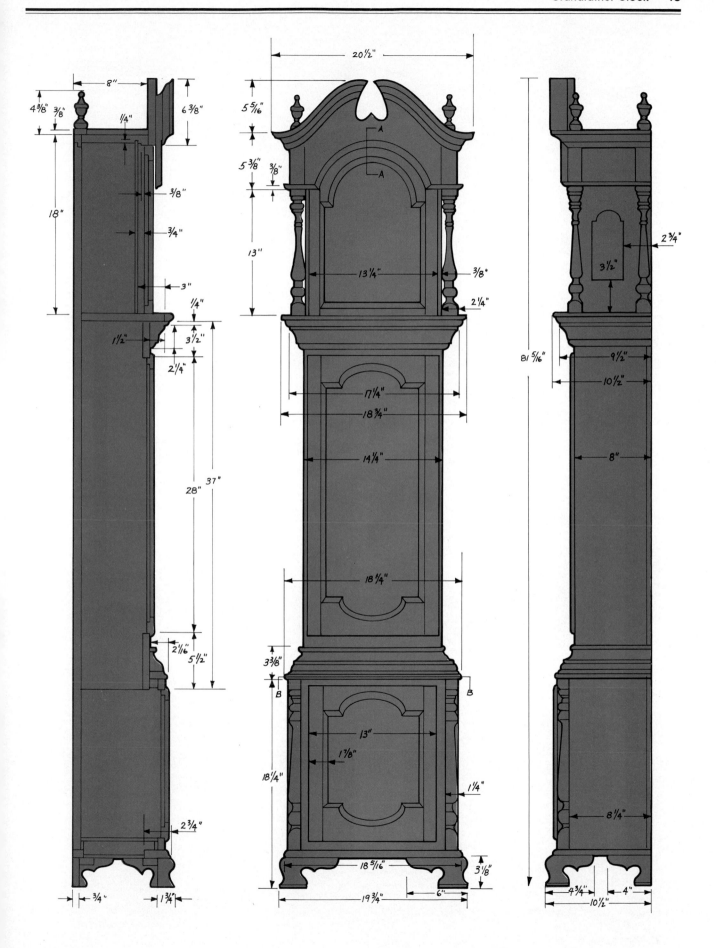

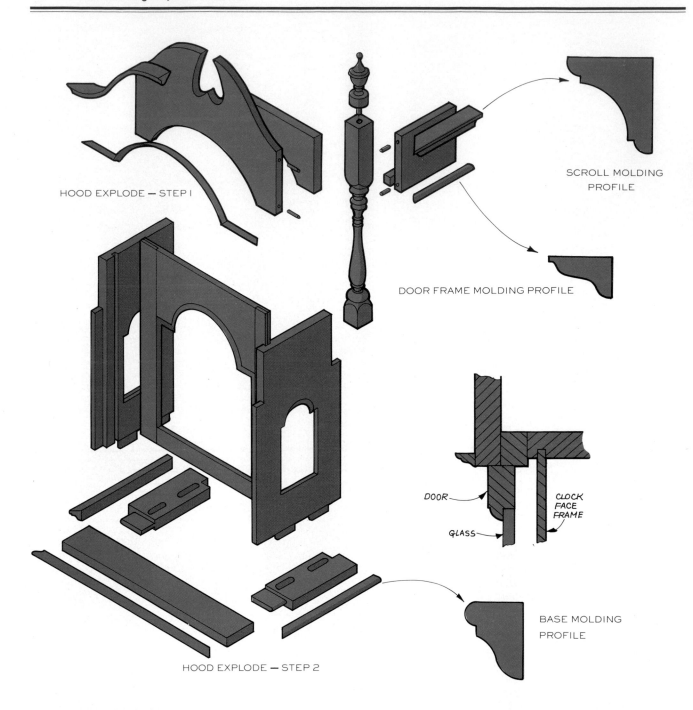

HOOD EXPLODE — STEP I

SCROLL MOLDING
PROFILE

DOOR FRAME MOLDING PROFILE

DOOR

CLOCK
FACE
FRAME

GLASS

BASE MOLDING
PROFILE

HOOD EXPLODE — STEP 2

Start with the hood

Make the sides and the dial face frame. Cut the joinery and and dry-assemble the frame to check the fit of the joints. Set in the grooves between the two sides to measure the width for the scroll board and the size of the hood base.

Cut the spindle stock and the scroll board, and dowel these *dry* to the sides. Don't glue anything up yet. Don't turn or shape any parts. Just concentrate on getting the joinery right. The finials are turned from the same size stock as the spindles, so cut them to size.

With the scroll board, the sides, and the base fitted together, figure the dimensions of the lower hood moldings. You can get many of these dimensions from the working drawings, I know, but there will be little variances in the sizes of the parts as you work. It's best to measure some dimensions as you go.

When you've fit the basic hood parts together, begin to shape the pieces. Cut the sound ports in the hood sides with a piercing cut on your jigsaw. Use a hand-held router to put a bead on the edge of these ports, and carve the inside corners to make them look as if they were mitered.

When you do the lathe work, proceed from the ends of a spindle toward the middle. Cut the large diameters first, then the smaller diameters. That way, there will be be less chatter and whip. Mark and turn a piece of scrap first so that you can work out any problems with the turning before you cut good stock.

Save the sanding until after you've turned all four spindles. Then, if you make a mistake on the last one, you can go back and alter the other three easily. Don't drill the ends of the spindles for joinery of the spindle to the finials yet, either. That would make it difficult to get them back on the lathe for a final sanding and finishing.

Once you're finished with the lathe, set up to make the

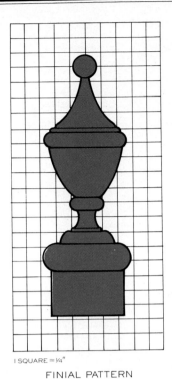

I SQUARE = ¼"

FINIAL PATTERN

I SQUARE = ¼"

SCROLL BOARD PATTERN

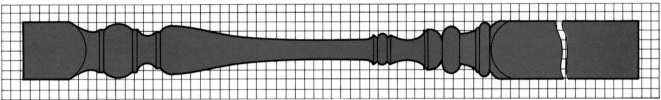

I SQUARE = ¼"

HOOD COLUMN PATTERN

moldings. Start from the bottom of the hood and work up —from the simple to the most difficult. As you make the moldings, avoid curly, figured stock. This wood looks nice, but anything less than the straightest of straight-grained woods tends to split apart when you run it through a molder or shaper. I first cut an edge on reasonably large blanks, then cut the molding off the blank. This is much safer than trying to mill thin pieces of stock.

You'll find the door frame molding is particularly delicate. Cut the contour of the door frame in a wide board, then use a shaper with rub collars and a starter pin to mold the edge. (The board should be long enough to make all the molding you need—both straight and curved.) After shaping, resaw the board to the proper thickness and belt-sand the backside. Then cut the molding off the blank with a bandsaw, and sand the top edge smooth.

When you get to the scroll board molding, start with the straight sides. Make the large cove with a cove cut on your table saw, passing the wood over the blade at an angle (figure 1). Don't cut too much stock at once; cut just ⅛ inch deeper with each pass until the cove reaches the proper depth. Once you've done that, mill a bead on the top and bottom edges with a shaper.

To make the gooseneck molding on the front of the scroll board, cut the S-shape in several pieces of ¼-inch-thick stock, and glue these up like stair steps. Carve out the cove with a hand gouge, doing your best to match the cove on the straight pieces. Mill the bead on the top and bottom of these curved moldings in the same way you do it on the straight moldings.

Finish the spindles and finials, protecting the surfaces to be glued with masking tape. Drill the last of the joinery, and finish-sand all the other hood parts with the exception of the moldings. Assemble the hood on your workbench so that you can make the final measurements for the moldings.

Cut all the moldings to length and miter them. Use a long, tall miter gauge extension to cut the miters on the arched door frame molding (figure 2). This same miter gauge extension with a nail strategically placed helps to cut the miters in the gooseneck molding. True up the miters on a disc sander to get a good fit, then glue them to the hood assembly.

Hang the door on the knife hinge so that it swings open to the right; traditionally that's the way all case clock doors swing. The knife hinges, the pull, and the bullet catch that you need for the door are available from Paxton Hardware, Upper Falls, MD 21156.

Making the waist

After the complexity of the hood, building the waist is a welcome rest. This is basically a long box with a glass door and a few moldings on the top and bottom.

Cut the sides and front rails to size. Assemble them, then get started on the moldings. Again, choose straight-grained wood for these parts. Cut the coves on the table saw similar to the way you made the scroll board molding. The important difference is that the cove profile for the waist is not a quarter-circle, but a quarter-*ellipse*. To cut

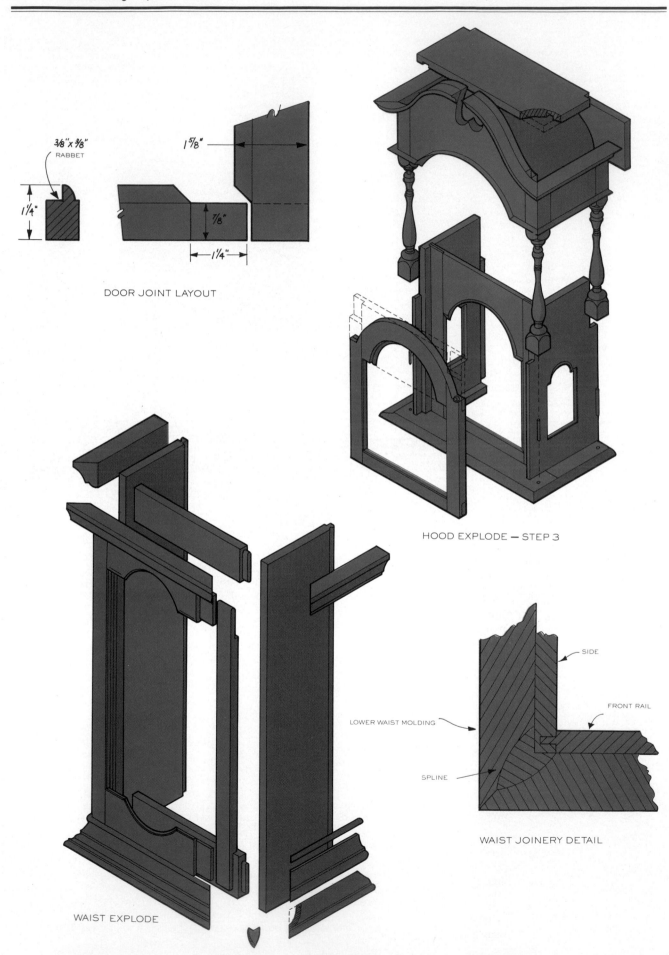

3/8" x 3/8"
RABBET

1 5/8"

1 1/4"

7/8"

1 1/4"

DOOR JOINT LAYOUT

HOOD EXPLODE — STEP 3

SIDE

FRONT RAIL

LOWER WAIST MOLDING

SPLINE

WAIST JOINERY DETAIL

WAIST EXPLODE

this shape, tilt the saw 5 degrees for the upper molding, and 13 degrees for the lower molding.

Position the fence for this operation so that the blade pulls the stock *into* the fence, rather than away from it. You may also want to use a second guide fence on the other side of the cut to keep the stock from dropping down into the blade as the cove gets deeper. Use pushblocks throughout the whole cove-cutting operation for safety's sake. Be extra careful, since you have to remove the saw guard for this operation.

Remove the millmarks in the cove with a scraper and hand sanding. Be careful to preserve the hard edges where the cove starts and stops; this helps define the lines of the piece. Don't bother sanding the molding completely smooth at this point. Before you get around to finishing the entire clock, the wood grain on all the separate pieces will have raised slightly due to temperature and humidity.

The lower waist molding is a three-piece affair of which the cove is only the middle part. Cut the other two parts on a shaper or molder, and glue up the three pieces. Then miter both the top and bottom molding to fit the assembled waist. None of these miter joints have to support any weight, so they needn't be clamped. Just press them together in your hands for a few minutes to make sure there is a good bond, then let the glue cure.

Hold off on making the door for right now. The waist and base doors are similar in construction, so it's best to make these at the same time.

Making the base

Cut the sides of the base and the parts for the base front. Join the front parts with mortises and tenons. You could also join them with dowels, but this is already such a classy project, so why use anything but classic construction?

Underneath the lower rail is what looks like a bit of ogee molding. In reality, it's a frame that supports the whole clock, distributing the weight onto the feet. This frame allows you to make a hidden compartment by installing a false bottom in the base. Make this molded frame with blind splines to reinforce the corners.

From the hood to the base, all the doors on this clock use simple lap joints at the corners. Both the rails and the stiles incorporate thumbnail molding, mitered at the corners. This molding looks as if it was applied separately, but it is sawn and shaped as an integral part of each door frame part. The vertical line of the clock is continued from top to bottom by the doors, making the door rails all the same length.

On the waist and base doors, the bottom rail is wider than the top rail. This gives the door a balanced look. The base door stiles are 1/4 inch wider than the waist door stiles to add a little visual bulk to the base. Width of the vertical front frame stiles is dictated by the finished dimensions of the split turnings on either side of the base and by the final dimensions of the door opening.

You can save some time by doing a "production run" to make the parts of the doors. Cut all the joinery and the elliptical contours, then sand the sawn edges. Cut the thumbnail molding on a shaper, and use a bandsaw to make the miters.

The bracket feet take some time to make but really aren't that difficult. Cove-cut the stock on the table saw, contour the top edge, then do the scrollwork on a bandsaw. Miter the adjoining edges, and cut grooves for splines. Glue up the feet, and assemble them to the underside of the base frame.

Turn each quarter column from a single blank, then split each blank on your bandsaw. To make a straight line

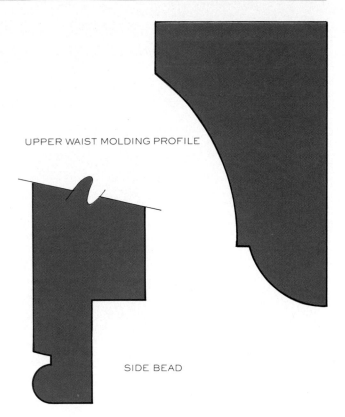

UPPER WAIST MOLDING PROFILE

SIDE BEAD

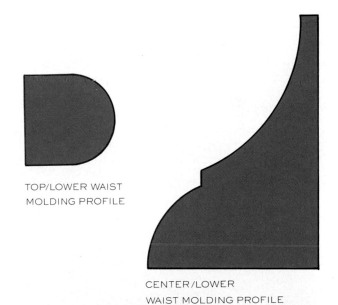

TOP/LOWER WAIST
MOLDING PROFILE

CENTER/LOWER
WAIST MOLDING PROFILE

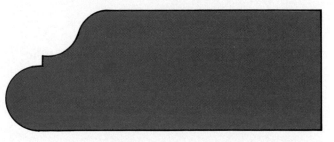

BASE/LOWER WAIST MOLDING PROFILE

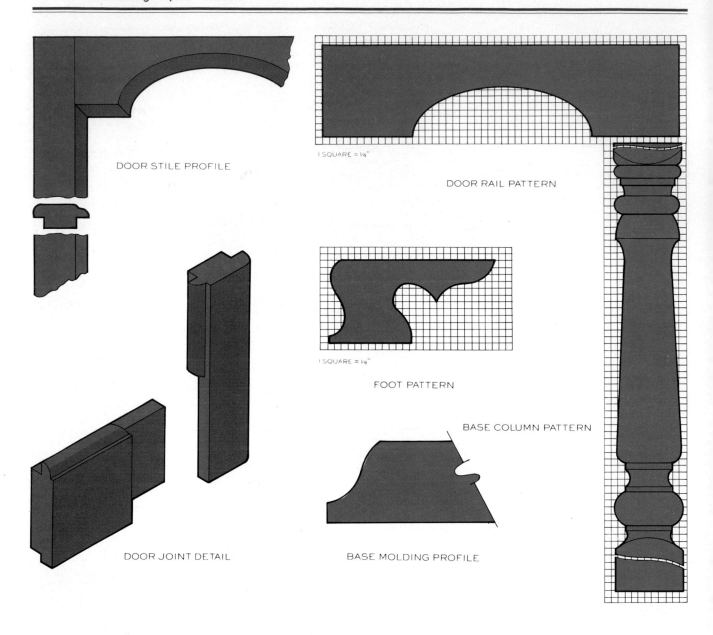

DOOR STILE PROFILE

DOOR RAIL PATTERN

I SQUARE = ¼"

FOOT PATTERN

I SQUARE = ¼"

DOOR JOINT DETAIL

BASE COLUMN PATTERN

BASE MOLDING PROFILE

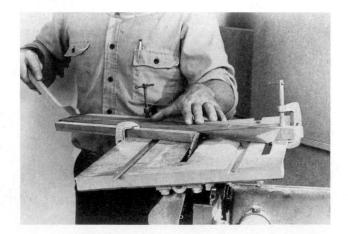

Fig. 1. Cut the coves in the moldings on your table saw. A fence and guide block keep stock positioned correctly. Use push blocks for added safety.

Fig. 2. Oversize miter gauge extension helps in cutting the arched and S-shaped moldings.

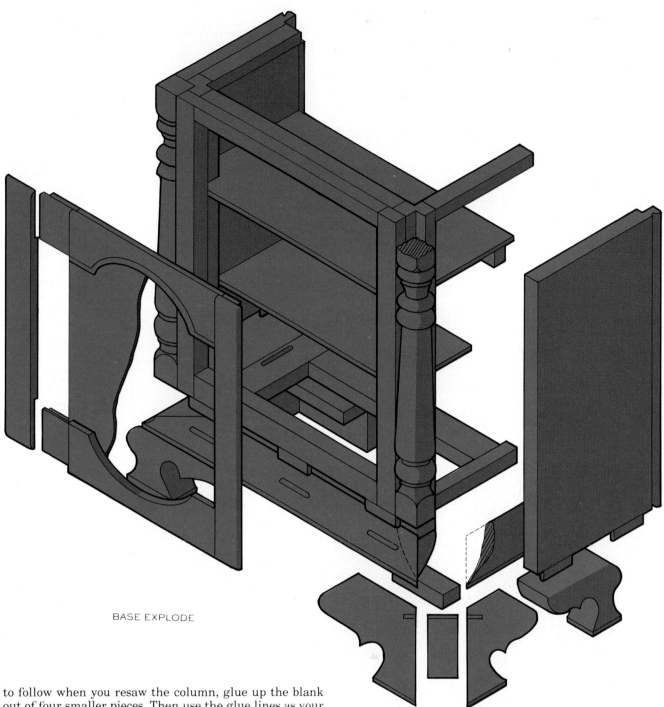

BASE EXPLODE

to follow when you resaw the column, glue up the blank out of four smaller pieces. Then use the glue lines as your cutlines. Remove the saw marks on a jointer, and make sure the backs of the split columns are perfectly flat. Assemble the parts of the base, and hang the doors on both the waist and the base.

Finally, cut the very last piece—the back. This part is made from ¾-inch hardwood plywood, veneered on the front side to match the rest of the wood in your clock case.

Final assembly

Put the entire case together and check the fit of all the joints. When you're satisfied that everything fits properly, join the three components—hood, waist, and base—with wood screws. *Do not* glue these parts together, and do not glue the back to the clock case. You'll need to remove the back and partially disassemble the clock to install the works and to clean them from time to time.

Finish-sand all parts, taking care to keep the corners of the moldings and the other parts sharp and clean. Start

with No. 80 sandpaper, and work your way down to No. 150. Apply a good oil finish and rub it in with No. 220. As you work, the fine sawdust will mix with the oil and fill in the wood grain or any other imperfections in the wood.

Finish the inside of the clock as well as the outside. Use the same number of coats so that the case won't warp. Then apply three good coats of paste wax with No. 0000 steel wool and buff them out.

Once you've installed the works according to the manufacturer's directions, wind up the clock and stand back to view your handiwork. If you're like me, you'll find yourself spending a little time each day admiring it—*by Jim McCann.*

This project first appeared in **HANDS ON!** *magazine. Our thanks to Shopsmith, Inc., for allowing us to publish it here.*

revolutionary lowboy

"This Low-boy is said to have been made by one of our Stimson uncles who fought in the American Revolution." So reads a scrawled inscription inside the center drawer, just behind the carved shell.

While Uncle Stimpson's soldierly deeds have since been forgotten, this piece of furniture remains as a monument to his cabinetmaking skills as well as an elegant example of colonial craftsmanship.

Shaping the cabriole legs

The legs not only support the case, but are an integral part of the framework. Because cabriole or S-shaped legs are inherently weak at the knees and the ankles, select straight-grained lumber to make these parts.

To ensure accurate joints, cut the joinery in the legs *before* you shape them. Use a hand-held router to make the mortises. To make the dovetail slots, first drill stopped holes in the stock. Then widen the holes with a hand chisel to make the dovetail shape. There are six single-dovetail joints in this project. To avoid much of the usual hand fitting, make yourself a dovetail template according to the specifications in the drawings. Use this template to mark both slots and the mating dovetails.

When you've finished the leg joinery, mark the cabriole shape on the two *outside* faces of the leg stock. Mount the stock on a lathe and turn just the foot. Be careful not to turn up past the top of the "pad." Then cut the cabriole shape in the first outside face with a bandsaw. Tape the

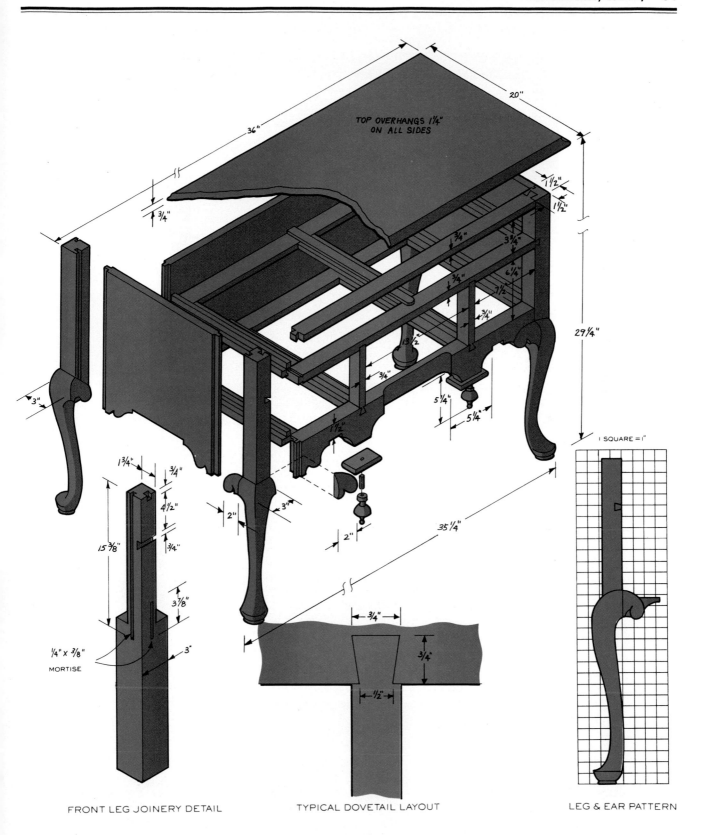

TOP OVERHANGS 1¼"
ON ALL SIDES

FRONT LEG JOINERY DETAIL

TYPICAL DOVETAIL LAYOUT

LEG & EAR PATTERN

waste back to the board, and turn the stock 90 degrees so that the second outside face is up (figure 1). Cut the shape again. When you remove the tape and the waste, you'll have a cabriole leg with a pad foot. Then blend the leg and foot together by carefully rounding the stock at the ankle with a rasp.

Making the web frames

The upper and lower drawers are hung on two web frames. You can make the stiles and back rails of these frames from cheap utility wood or leftover scraps, since these parts don't show. The front rails, however, do show; make them from the same wood as the rest of the project. The

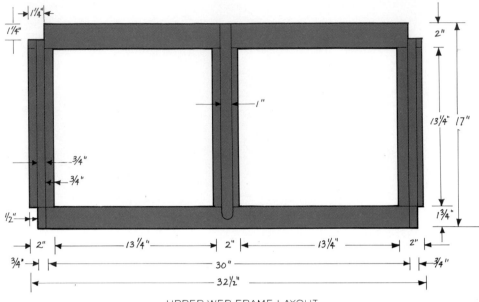

UPPER WEB FRAME LAYOUT

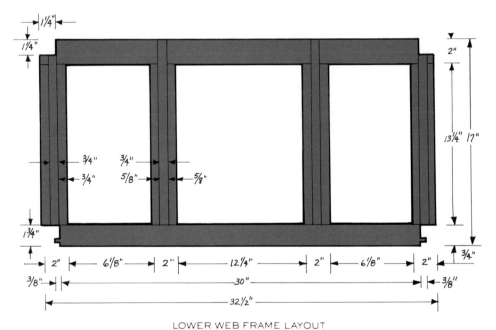

LOWER WEB FRAME LAYOUT

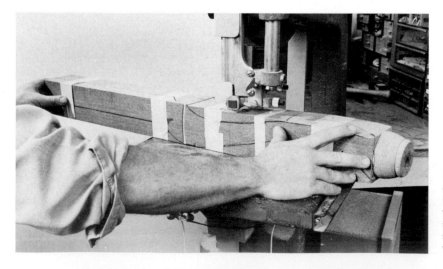

Fig. 1. Cut the cabriole shape on a bandsaw in two passes. Cut one face and tape the waste back to the leg. Turn the stock 90 degrees and make a second cut, then remove the waste.

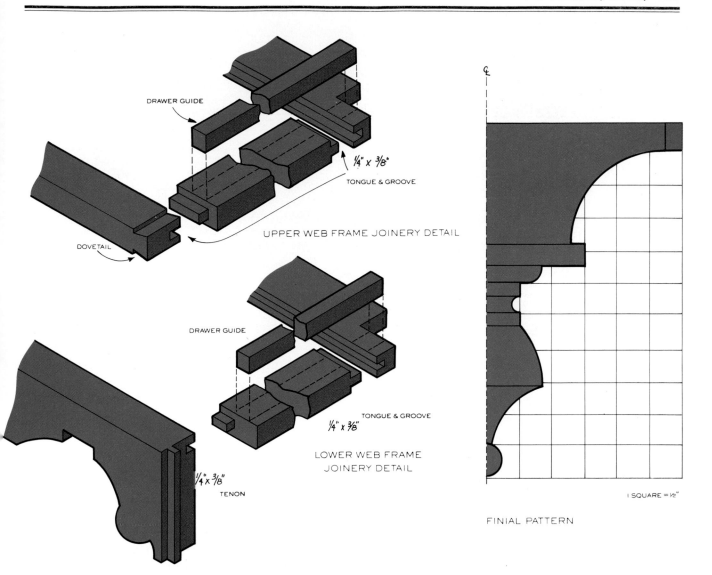

DRAWER GUIDE

DOVETAIL

¼" x ⅜"

TONGUE & GROOVE

UPPER WEB FRAME JOINERY DETAIL

DRAWER GUIDE

¼" x ⅜"

TONGUE & GROOVE

LOWER WEB FRAME
JOINERY DETAIL

¼" x ⅜"

TENON

₵

I SQUARE = ½"

FINIAL PATTERN

upper web frame incorporates a drawer guide. Use a hardwood such as beech or rock maple for this part, which will see more wear and tear than the rest of the parts combined.

Cut the grooves in the rails with a dado cutter mounted to your table saw. The tenons on the ends of the stiles and the lower front rail can be cut with this same setup. Use a simple tenoning jig that straddles your rip fence to keep the boards vertical to the work table. Dado the underside of the upper front rail and cut dovetail slots in the lower front rail for the lower drawer dividers. Using a bandsaw or saber saw, make the decorative shapes in the lower front rail, then assemble the web frames with glue.

Assembling the case

Cut dadoes to support the web frames in the side and back panels. Also, rabbet the edges of these panels to make tenons. Dry-assemble the legs, web frames, and panels to check the fit of the joints. *Do not* glue the assembly together at this time.

While the case is temporarily assembled, cut the top rail, cleats, and lower drawer dividers. Rout slotted holes in the top rail and cleats, as shown in the drawings. Later, you'll use these holes to attach the top. Using your template, bandsaw the dovetails in the top rail and drawer

dividers, and fit these parts to the assembly. The cleats simply butt up against the panels and require little fitting.

When you're satisfied that all the parts of the case fit properly, disassemble them. Finish-sand all outside surfaces, then reassemble the case with glue. Before the glue sets up, check that the assembly is square.

While the glue dries on the case, join stock edge to edge to make the top. The annual rings on this top board should all face the same direction. When the top is mounted to the lowboy, the rings should curve *away* from the case. That way, the tendency for the top to warp can be controlled with a few well-placed screws.

When you have determined the "up" side of the top, rout an ogee along the edge. Then attach the top to the case with roundhead wood screws and washers, passing the screws up through the slots in the cleats and into the underside of the top. *Do not* glue the top to the case. Let it float, so that it can expand and contract with changes in the weather.

Next, shape the ears for the legs and glue them in place. When the glue dries, reinforce these parts by passing wood screws through the lower front rail or panels into the back side of the ears. Blend ears to the legs with carving chisels and rasps. Finally, turn the finials and dowel them to the underside of lower front rail.

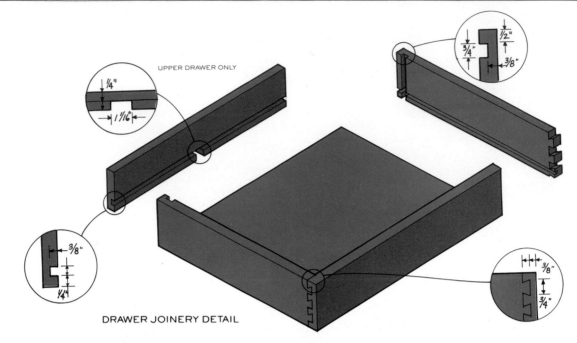

UPPER DRAWER ONLY

DRAWER JOINERY DETAIL

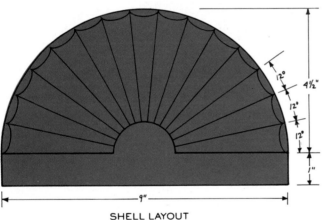

SHELL LAYOUT

Fitting the drawers

Drawer construction is classically simple. The drawer fronts attach to the sides with half-blind dovetails; the backs attach to the sides with a dado; and the bottoms rest in grooves near the bottom edge of the fronts, backs, and sides. The dovetails can be made easily with your router and a dovetail template. There are, however, a few special considerations.

These are flush drawers. They are stopped when the sides butt up against the back panels, so length of the sides is critical. You may want to cut the sides slightly long and sand them down to the proper length when you fit the drawers.

The drawers are guided by strips of wood on the web frames that rub against the drawer sides. The top drawer has an extra guide in the center. Notch the back of the top drawer to fit this guide, as shown in the drawings.

Sides, backs, and bottoms of drawers are rarely seen and are usually made from cheap woods. But if you plan to use your lowboy as a serving table, you may want to make the drawer bottoms from aromatic cedar to keep table linens smelling sweet.

The front of the lower middle drawer is twice the width of the other drawer fronts, so that you have room to carve the recessed shell. A popular motif in eighteenth century furniture, shell carvings are not difficult to carve; they just require a little care and patience. Start by marking out the shell on the drawer front. With a veiner chisel, trace the rays, digging down between each ray to a depth of ½ to ⅝ inch (figure 2). Then use a straight chisel to round rays.

Finishing the lowboy

A hand-rubbed varnish finish lets you avoid painstaking rubbing between coats on the lowboy's intricate surfaces. If you've selected an open-grain hardwood such as walnut or oak, first fill the pores with wood filler. Coat the entire project, inside and out, with sanding sealer. When the sealer dries, lightly sand all exposed surfaces. Apply a thick coat of varnish and allow it to set up for 10 to 15 minutes until tacky. Before varnish dries completely, wipe it off with a rag soaked in tung oil. The varnish that remains behind will dry glass-smooth. Polish it with No. 0000 steel wool and paste wax.

Chippendale drawer pulls complete the lowboy. If you can't find the exact style shown here, you should be able to come pretty close. Here are two sources: The Wise Company, 6503 St. Claude Avenue, P.O. Box 118, Arabi, LA 70032; Horton Brasses, Nooks Hill Road, P.O. Box 95F, Cromwell, CT 06416—*by Nick Engler.*

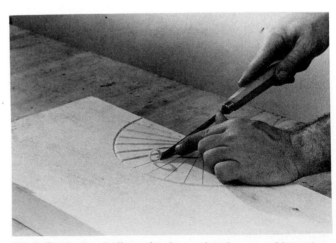

Fig. 2. Begin the shell carving by tracing the rays with a veiner or "parting tool."

queen anne
drop-leaf table

Courtesy of Sotheby's, Inc., © 1985.

If you've ever needed more table than you have room to keep, this classic drop-leaf table could be the answer. When both leaves are down, the table takes up little space and still seats two people. With one leaf up, there's room for up to six diners. Put both leaves up, and ten can eat comfortably. And if you don't mind bumping knees and rubbing elbows, there's space for twelve!

Turning the legs

Begin this project by making the legs. To ensure accurate joints, cut the joinery in the upper end of each leg *before* you turn it. Use a hand-held router to make the slot mortises. Once you've cut the mortises, turn each leg twice. Cut the long taper with the lower end of the leg mounted

off center (figure 1), then remount the stock on center to turn the foot. The off-center taper gives the legs their distinctive shape.

Off-center turning isn't difficult, but it does require some special cautions and considerations.

First, remove as much stock as possible from the two *outside* faces of the leg stock with a bandsaw or saber saw (figure 2). Cut one face as shown in the drawings, tape the waste back to the leg stock, then cut the second face. Removing excess stock in this manner will help minimize leg vibration as you turn it.

When you mount the stock on the lathe, make sure that both the drive center and the tailstock center penetrate the wood at least 1/8 inch. If you glued up stock to make

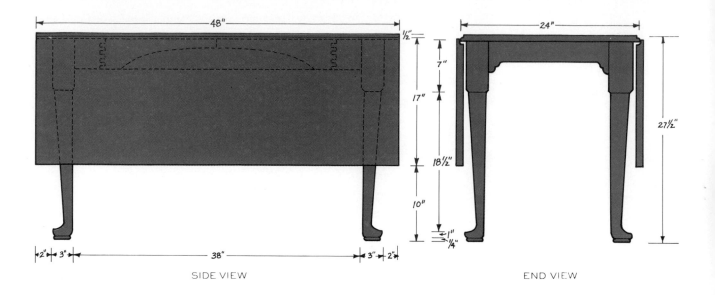

SIDE VIEW   END VIEW

the required thickness for the leg, let the glue cure for at least 24 hours before turning the stock. Turn at the slowest possible speed, no faster than 700 RPM. Turn the taper down to the ankle, but be careful not to cut stock from the ankle or the foot.

When you remount the stock on center to turn the foot, again, make sure the centers are properly engaged, and turn at the slowest possible speed. Turn the foot, but *not* the ankle or the taper (figure 3). Dismount the stock from the lathe and use a Surform rasp to shape the ankle, blending the taper and the foot together.

Joining the legs to the apron

Cut the tenons in the ends of the aprons, using a dado cutter on your table saw or a straight bit in your router. These tenons should fit the mortises snugly, but not too tight; otherwise there won't be any room for glue.

Cut the decorative pattern in the lower edge of the short aprons with a bandsaw, scroll saw, or saber saw. The long aprons need no decoration. They do, however, require several dadoes on the inside faces where the stiffeners join the aprons. Make these dadoes with a dado cutter or router. Dry-assemble the legs, aprons, and stiffeners to check the fit. Hold these pieces together temporarily with bar clamps or band clamps, but *do not* glue them up at this time.

The leaves are held in the horizontal or "open" position by fold-out brackets—two to each leaf. These brackets hinge on stationary pivot blocks and fold back in against the long aprons when the leaves are down. Because the hinge formed by the bracket and pivot block must support a good deal of weight, it's best to make both pieces from an extremely hard wood. Rock maple or beech is best. This wood may not match the hardwood you've chosen for the project, but these parts will be hidden by the leaves most of the time.

To make a wooden hinge, cut fingers in the adjoining ends of a pivot block and a bracket on your bandsaw. Round the corners of the bracket fingers with a disc sander, so that the corners won't interfere with the hinge action. Clamp the pivot block and bracket together, interlocking the fingers, and drill a long hole down through the middle of each finger, starting from the top. Be careful not to drill completely through the bottom finger; stop the hole

just before you break through. This stopped hole will keep the pivot pin from dropping out the bottom of the hinge.

Hinge the pivot blocks and brackets together with metal pins, then temporarily clamp the pivot blocks in place on the side aprons. Check the hinge action; the brackets should swing freely through 90 degrees without binding. If they do bind, you may have to sand more stock from the corners of the fingers.

When you're satisfied that all the joints fit and that the hinges work properly, disassemble the parts. Reassemble them with glue and clamps. Check the assembly for squareness before the glue sets up. When the glue has cured, remove the clamps and reinforce the joints between the side aprons, stiffeners, and pivot blocks with wood screws. You may also want to pin the tenons in the mortises with short dowels.

Attaching the top

Glue stock edge to edge to make up the required widths for the table top and the two leaves. The conventional wisdom for gluing up wide stock is to alternate the direction of the annual rings. If the boards cup, each board will cup in the opposite direction from its neighbors, and the cups will cancel each other out.

That is probably the best method for gluing up the two leaves, which are not reinforced or braced. The table top *is* braced. It's fastened to the aprons by cleats. Many professional woodworkers have found that when you can brace a wide board, it's better to glue the stock with the annual rings all curving *away* from the brace. Then you can easily prevent the cup with the placement of a few well-placed screws.

One more way you can prevent cupping is to make the table top and leaves from costlier *quarter-sawn* lumber, if there's a custom sawmill nearby where you can get it. In quarter-sawn wood, the annual rings are perpendicular to the width and there's very little tendency to cup.

When you've glued up the wide stock and cut it to size, make the drop-leaf joint in the top and the leaves with a hand-held router. Then turn the boards face down on a wide, flat surface and arrange them so that the joints mesh. Position the hinges temporarily and mark the boards where you need to install them.

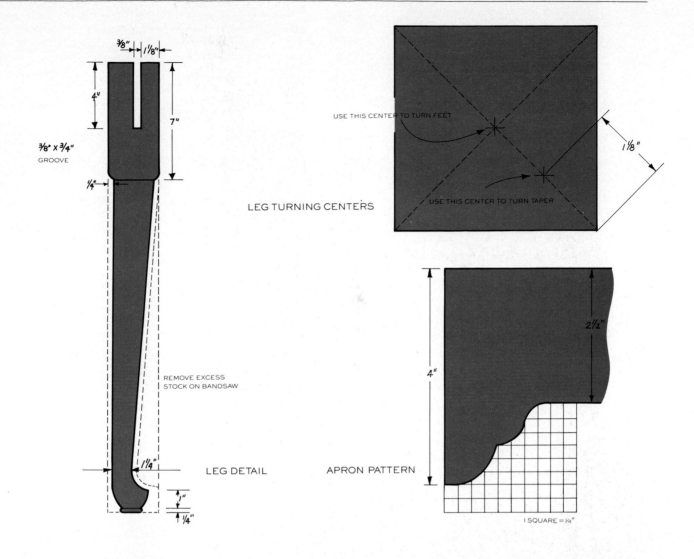

3/8" x 3/4"
GROOVE

3/8"   1 1/8"

4"

7"

1/4"

REMOVE EXCESS
STOCK ON BANDSAW

1 1/4"

LEG DETAIL

1"
1/4"

USE THIS CENTER TO TURN FEET

USE THIS CENTER TO TURN TAPER

LEG TURNING CENTERS

1 1/8"

APRON PATTERN

2 1/2"

4"

1 SQUARE = 1/4"

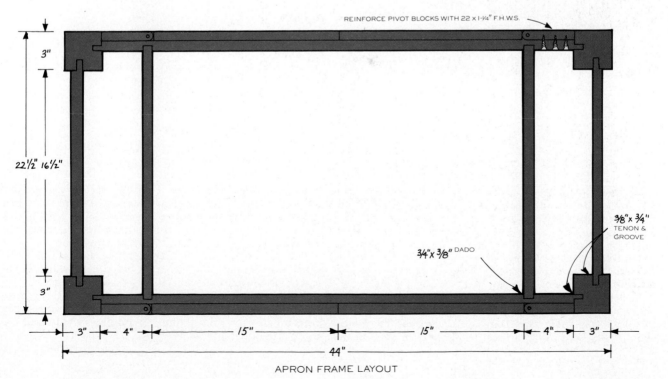

REINFORCE PIVOT BLOCKS WITH 22 x 1-1/4" F.H.W.S.

3"

22 1/2"   16 1/2"

3"

3/8" x 3/4"
TENON &
GROOVE

3/4" x 3/8" DADO

3"   4"   15"   15"   4"   3"

44"

APRON FRAME LAYOUT

Fig. 1. Turn the taper with the lower end of the leg stock mounted slightly off center.

Fig. 2. Remove as much excess stock as possible from the legs before you turn them. Cut this waste from the two outside faces of the legs, using a bandsaw or saber saw to make the compound cut.

Fig. 3. To turn the pad foot, remount the stock on center.

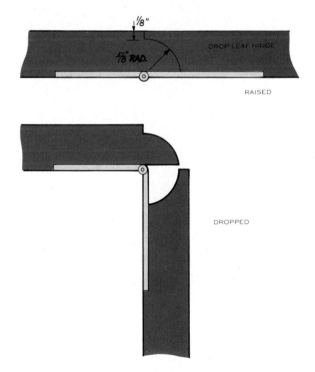

DROP-LEAF JOINERY DETAIL

Unlike most hinges—which are positioned so that the pin straddles the joint between two boards—the hinge pin in drop-leaf hinges should rest at the center of the arc of the drop-leaf joint. Calculate the proper position for your hinges in relation to the joint, and attach them to the table top and leaves accordingly. Depending on how you've cut the joint, you may have to chisel shallow grooves for the hinge pins.

Attach cleats to the inside faces of the aprons and stiffeners with glue and wood screws. Drill holes in the cleats to attach the table top from the underside. The holes should be slightly larger than the shanks of the screws you'll use to attach the top. That way the top can expand and contract with changes in temperature and humidity.

Center the top on the aprons, and attach it with round-head screws and washers. *Do not* glue the top in place. The top must be free to "breath" with the weather.

Finish is up to you. Be careful, however, to apply the same number of coats to *all* sides of the table parts, whether they show or not. This is especially important for the table top and leaves. If a board has fewer coats of finish on one side than the other, each side of the board will absorb moisture from the air at a different rate and the board will warp—*by Nick Engler.*

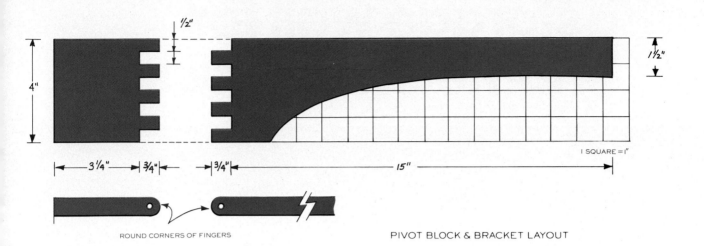

½"

4"

1½"

3¼"   ¾"   ¾"   15"

1 SQUARE = 1"

ROUND CORNERS OF FINGERS

PIVOT BLOCK & BRACKET LAYOUT

DROP-LEAF TABLE PARTIAL EXPLODE

storage wall for home electronics

Installing separate components for hi-fi, video, and computer systems can clutter your home with hardware and interconnection cables. One solution is this modular storage center, custom designed by well-known furniture designer Geza Zambory. The freestanding wall modules offer lots of storage space. They'll also open into a bar, a media center, and a home-office computer desk.

The four-module system shown re-quires a little more than 10 feet of wall space. But if your room space (or budget) is limited, you can build any of the modules; they're designed in two widths and can be arranged in any sequence.

Accessory compartments are 19 in-ches deep—adequate for virtually all electronic equipment. Optional clear-or smoked-acrylic doors help keep dust out. Access to wiring is via de-tachable front brass strips.

Computer buffs will appreciate the clamshell door opening for a mi-crocomputer that creates a shaded overhead light and a sturdy desk sur-face. Beneath the computer a printer stand on casters rolls out to either side. If you decide to use the desk for conventional typing or writing, the castered stand can hold shelving or vertical files.

TV-door panels slide from view and leave room to pull the drawer for-

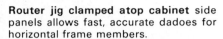
Router jig clamped atop cabinet side panels allows fast, accurate dadoes for horizontal frame members.

Lights for the bar and computer station can be operated by automatic switches in door frames. Lights for display compartments may be tied to a single wall switch. Television and VCR are from Sears, Roebuck and Co.; audio components are from Harvey Electronics, White Plains, N.Y.; IBM computer equipment is from Sears Business Systems Centers' White Plains branch.

ward. This ensures adequate ventilation around the TV set, and a lazy Susan for the receiver lets you adjust the viewing angle.

More detailed construction plans with step-by-step photos and layout diagrams for the most economical cuts in ¾-inch plywood panels are available. (Send $10, payable to G. Zambory, Box J, Shenorock, NY 10587. New York State residents add 58 cents sales tax.) The modules shown were made from cabinet-grade panels with one-sided oak-veneer face. Interiors are surfaced with plastic laminate here, but you may prefer two-sided plywood for staining or painting. And you can substitute strips of wood for the brass. Module frames are glued and screwed.

As for tools, you'll need either a table saw or a circular saw and router, plus a power drill and clamps. In case you can't find suitable hardware locally, you'll find mail-order sources in the plans packet—*by Neil Soderstrom. Drawing by Carl De Groote. Construction by Reinhardt Dickwisch.*

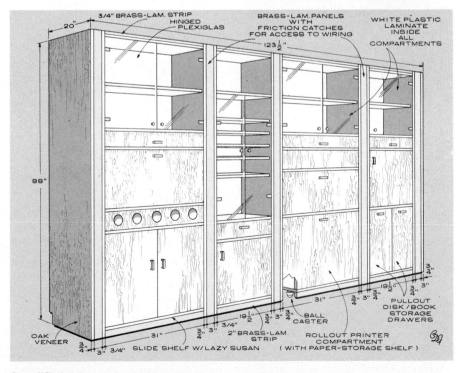

Simplified right-angle marking and cuts throughout make this project less complex than most. Casters installed on the computer-printer stand (bottom of second module from right) let the stand roll out to either side of the station.

double-duty room

Like a lot of homes, mine isn't so big that I can devote a whole room to activities that occur just a few times a year. And it certainly isn't so big that I can waste two rooms that way. If I had a dining room, I'd use it less than once a month. A guest room? Maybe half that often.

Still, there are times when we do need such rooms. My solution? Combine them both. Now, what used to be a little-used guest room is a dining room—with built-in buffets and cabinets for china, tablecloths, silver, and so on—that also contains a disappear-

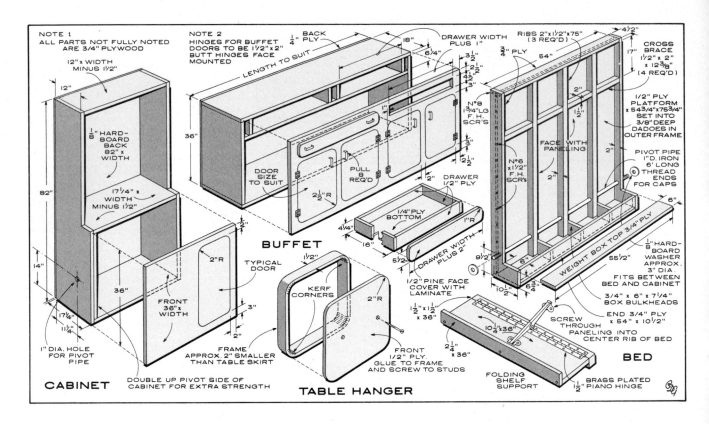

Cabinets (A) flanking fold-up bed are made with cabinet-grade ³/₄-inch particleboard. This material is heavier, stronger, and smoother than underlayment grades. Glue and screw cabinets using white or yellow glue and 1³/₄-inch screws. Fasten back to cabinet with glue and 1-inch screws. All screw-heads are countersunk and capped with polyester auto-body filler, belt-sanded smooth and flush. Apply laminate, then cut out doors (see photo caption). Cover door backs with laminate, too, to prevent warping. Add shelves as desired using standard pin or spade-type supports in ¹/₄-inch holes. Fasten cabinets in place by driving screws through bottom into floor. Buffet (B) is built much the same as cabinets. Drawers are simple butt-joined plywood with bottoms glued and nailed to frame. They ride on Knape and Vogt ball-bearing slides. Mount drawers—without pine faces—on sliding hardware. Then close them and temporarily tack pine faces in position using hot-metal glue, carefully aligning them before the glue cools. Hold them in place by hand until the glue sets. Bolt-through drawer pulls—when

added—will hold drawer faces firmly in place. The plywood platform for bed (C) is made of two identical pieces 27³/₈ inches wide. The bed's outer frame captures the platform in a dado. After frame and platform are assembled, glue and screw the three ribs to the platform, running the center rib directly over the seam in the platform. Next add cross-brace parts and counterweight box bulkheads. Both the bed frame and the counterweight box are covered with laminate and mounted on a pivot made from pipe. Paneling is glued and nailed to bottom of bed, and folding leg is screwed in place over the paneling. To make table hanger (D), cut frame to size, and kerf at corners to facilitate bending. Cut out plywood front, and glue frame to back of front. Let glue dry, then apply laminate to edges of the hanger. To do this, use a torch or heat gun to warm laminate, and prebend it around curves in frame. Then cement in place as usual. Use flathead screws through front and into wall studs to secure the hanger to wall. Apply laminate to its front, and trim the excess laminate with a router.

In the dining-room mode circular table in the center of the room provides seating space for up to eight. Bed is folded against the wall between the two cabinets in the background, its underside covered with prefinished oak paneling. Table hangs out of the way, and bed folds down (below), turning room into cozy sleeping space.

Door openings (above left) for buffet and cabinets are cut after laminate is applied, using a super-fine blade such as a Trojan X-FS to prevent chipping. To cut the openings accurately, draw their outlines on laminate, and drill starting hole for jigsaw behind where one hinge will mount. Tilt saw shoe 5 degrees to bevel door edges for clearance. First, saw only hinge edge of door, then face-mount hinges and finish cut. Door will be perfectly hung with kerf-wide clearances all around. Laminate for both the buffet top and the left-hand cabinet top (above) is applied in one piece to eliminate need for tricky joint. Carefully cut and dry-fit the piece as shown here before cementing in place. Use slip sheets to ensure proper positioning. The counterweight box beneath pivot pipe (left) makes the pivoting bed easier to raise and lower. Box is filled with rocks "buttered" in place with concrete so they don't rattle.

ing bed. Most of the time we leave it set up as a dining room, using the table year-round for sewing, crafts projects, or updating household accounts.

But if we have overnight guests, the table top goes up on the wall, and the bed pops down from between two cabinets. Pillows and blankets come out of the closet, and we have a comfortable and cozy place for friends and relatives to sleep.

All this fits neatly into a 12-by-12-foot room, with space left over to store a sewing machine, ironing board, crafts, and games, plus eight folding chairs to go with the dining table.

Best of all, the room was inexpensive and easy to convert. Although the drawings and photos on these pages may make the project look complicated at first, nothing could be simpler. With the exception of cutting a dado in the bed frame, everything else is basic butt-joint, glue-and-screw construction. Even the cabinet doors hang themselves automatically and fit perfectly. If you can cut particleboard accurately, you can build a room like this.

Despite the simplicity, everything looks good. The reason? All those basic butt joints and screw heads are

covered with a plastic laminate. If you have never worked with these laminates, I suggest you give them a try. They are by far the fastest, easiest way to put a professional finish on a project. With a little practice, you can cover a piece like one of these cabinets in an hour or two. A first-class paint job could take four or five days and might not look as good or last as long as laminate does.

So if you have a room in your home that's not earning its keep, consider giving it a double life—*by A.J. Hand. Drawing by Carl De Groote.*

two computer carrels

Once you bring the computer home, where do you put it? Two do-it-yourselfers have worked out different approaches to the problem. Each has custom features that make it unique, and each can be further tailored to your needs. They can be built largely of low-cost plywood—or even scrap lumber.

veneered stand

I custom-designed the veneered stand for my Apple computer with one disk drive and an Epson printer. But you can adapt the stand to any small computer-printer combination. Because the desk top simply rests on the two drawer sections, the entire stand can be moved easily by one person.

A unique feature is the open-sided design of the support units (see diagram). The back half of each has been left open for easy access and increased storage capabilities. The open section on the right unit provides storage for manuals and books; the half-side on the left-hand unit permits easy loading of bulk printer paper. A paper slot in the desk top feeds the paper into the printer.

I deliberately made the left-hand support unit slightly larger than the right. The left-hand drawer is the proper size for hanging files. The right-hand one stores diskettes snugly, with no room for added clutter. You can, of course, make each drawer stand the same size.

Though the cost of the desk shown is well below that of commercially made versions, you can cut costs even further. You could substitute birch-

Though custom-tailored to meet the author's needs, this computer stand is basically a simple slab resting on two boxes. But oak veneers make it a substantial-looking piece of furniture.

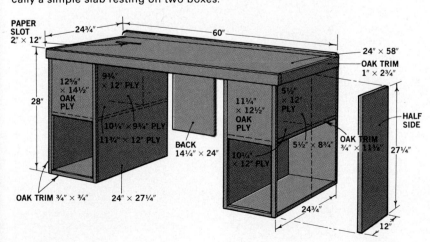

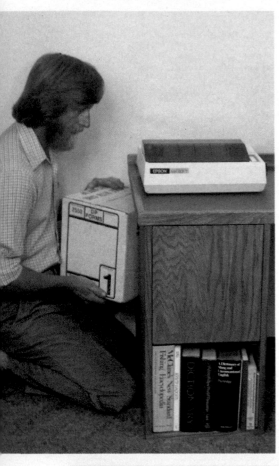

veneer plywood (either A/A or A/B shop grades) for the oak veneer that I used for the stand sides and drawer faces. And you could use cheaper wood than solid-oak strips for your edging.

A table saw makes it easy to cut the plywood to size, but you can do the job with a hand-held circular saw. If you don't own a router, borrow or rent one —you need it and a special bit to trim the plastic laminate for the desk top.

Begin construction by cutting the desk top from ¾-inch shop-grade plywood. Measure and cut the paper slot with a saber saw.

Glue and clamp hardwood trim flush to the front of the desk before applying the plastic laminate. Cut

Open rear compartment in the veneered-oak stand allows for easy storage of large boxes of computer fan-fold paper.

Disk drives and monitor stack neatly above the computer on the drop shelf of this laminated-trestle carrel. Monitor stand shown came with computer; a similar stand could be built.

this oversize, then brush contact cement onto both the desk top and backside of the laminate. Tip the laminate in place so its front edge butts against the trim piece. Then, using the familiar slip-sheet or removable-sticks technique, press the coated surfaces firmly together.

With the router, trim the laminate's remaining three sides flush with the desk top, then touch up the edges with a file. Align the side-trim pieces with the front oak strip, and glue them in place. Place the bottom of the rear trim section flush with the desk edge; the trim then forms a raised lip that keeps things from falling off the back.

Now make the plywood frame for the two support stands, install the shelves, then make drawer sides and backs. Plan the face cuts for the drawers carefully to make most-effective use of grain patterns on the plywood-face veneer. Finally, install the sliding-drawer hardware.

I built the veneered stand shown in one day but spent several hours finishing it. The time was worth it; with the computer sitting on its own desk, we can eat at the dining-room table again—*by Don Geary. Drawing by Edward Lipinski.*

laminated trestle

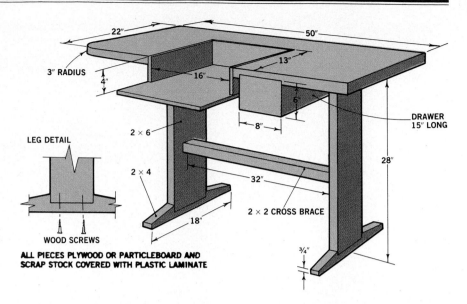

LEG DETAIL

WOOD SCREWS

ALL PIECES PLYWOOD OR PARTICLEBOARD AND SCRAP STOCK COVERED WITH PLASTIC LAMINATE

I wanted to design a computer desk that would function as an efficient work station yet would suit both my budget and the decor of my home office.

The trestle desk I produced is compact, sturdy, and attractive. To lower the computer keyboard to proper typing height, I inserted a pocketlike enclosure with a dropped shelf into the desk top. The "pocket" has an open back, so all cables and power cords are hidden from view.

Because I covered all surfaces with plastic laminate, I was able to build the entire desk from scrap materials. Obviously, you can skip the laminate and finish the desk with paint, varnish, or stain.

I also built a free-standing printer stand with a paper shelf and storage drawer. The stand is a simple box covered with matching plastic laminate. A slot in the top allows the paper to feed from inside. If desired, the stand may be built as part of the desk instead of as a separate unit.

I began by figuring out my workspace needs and then juggling those dimensions to fit into the space available. Layout on graph paper was important in determining scale.

I found that trestle-type legs are the easiest to construct and are very stable. Two-by-six stock joined into a "T" make the legs (see drawing), and the crosspiece of the "T" is securely attached to the upright piece with several large countersunk screws. Glue adds strength to the joint. The brace that connects both legs can be made of any scrap; I used a piece of 2 × 3.

The desk top can be made of ¾-inch particleboard or plywood. Be sure that it is flat, without warpage. To minimize the chance of later warping, I strengthened the desk top on the underside by securely attaching a piece of ½-inch angle iron. This runs the length of the top and acts as a "spine."

To give the desk a more solid look, you can add a plywood strip around the entire top and sand it flush with the edge. Create the desk's corner curves by tracing around a gallon paint can before cutting.

To form the computer pocket, first lay out the dimensions of your com-

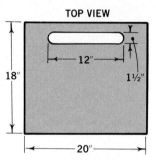

TOP VIEW

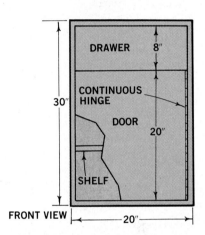

FRONT VIEW

puter, adding about an inch margin in all directions. Cut out this piece carefully and save it to use as the drop shelf for the computer. Next, cut out the pocket sides, but don't assemble the unit until you've laminated the faces on all the pieces. Next, assemble the drawers. I made just one, but a larger desk could hold more. Each drawer hangs via dado grooves that engage metal strips fixed to the underside of the desk top.

Attaching the plastic laminate was easy—and it was my first experience with the material. All the mounting screws and nails should be countersunk so they can be covered with laminate. For a professional-looking job, you must use a router with a laminate bit.

But the most important point to remember is that the surface you look at the *most* should be laminated *last*. For example, laminate the edges of the desk top before you to the top, so you won't be constantly staring at the seams.

One final note: Be sure you computer is adequately ventilated. You may need to cut air holes in the pocket sides for cross ventilation—*by Bryan Shumaker. Drawings by Edward Lipinski.*

Sturdy trestle legs and a unique drop shelf distinguish this home-built computer desk. A separate stand stores supplies while hiding printer paper. Slot feeds paper to printer.

Unit is an attractive bookcase-secretary when against the wall, with three shelves above the cabinet and two below behind doors with decorative brass grillework. Left end swings around so unit is perpendicular to wall, creating 4-foot-wide room divider to allow privacy in corner of room. Heavy-duty plastic casters attached to bottom make easy swinging. Panel in back of unit swings down to become a dressing table (below). It is held in horizontal position by brass letdown bracket on right side, and is kept in vertical position by magnetic catch. It is attached with continuous brass hinge.

swinging-bookcase room divider

If you'd like to add space to your home and can't, you can still make the most of the space you have. One way is to turn a corner of your living room into an extra bedroom with this wide bookcase that swings out to become a room divider. It has a secretary cabinet with a door that folds down to become a writing surface, revealing a letter cabinet and drawer with Corian front panels.

When the unit is swung around so that it's perpendicular to the wall, the rear panel folds down to level position and becomes a dressing table, and a makeup mirror swings down for the convenience of lady guests. A lamp panel also revolves to front or back to light either area.

The bookcase/divider is made of ladder frame sides using 1-by-2-inch stock, with 1-by-12-inch shelves at the top and 1-by-15-inch shelves at the bottom. A special piece of wood 15 inches wide by 46½ inches long by 1 inch thick was cut for use as the secretary desk top; it is held in place with a 46-inch brass continuous hinge. Decorative die-cut ⅛-inch hardboard covers the area behind the top three shelves. The doors of the front bottom of the unit are made of frames of 1-by-4-inch stock with decorative brass grillework attached inside. The letter cabinet and drawer with ¼-inch Corian front panels are inside the secretary enclosure—*by John W. Sill. Drawings by Carl De Groote.*

Optional letter cabinet is made of ¼-inch plywood except for top which is of ½-inch plywood to take No. 10 1¼-inch screws which hold unit to shelf above. Cabinet door and drawer front panel are ¼-inch Corian. The door and drawer panel are attached with epoxy to hinges so that no connectors are visible from front.

Lamp rests on fitted platform on panel in cabinet back. The panel pivots conveniently to illuminate either front (top) or rear dressing table (bottom). Pivot is ⅛-inch dowel at top and bottom of panel shown in the drawing. The lamp cord is fed through hole in right corner of cabinet base. *Important:* Be certain to give the lamp cord ample play.

Swing down make-up mirror is attached by hinges to shelf bottom and held up by cabinet catch. It is made of ¼-inch plywood base and frame with revolving make-up mirror attached in center hole. Miniature light sockets are attached with ¼-inch screws in each corner, and lights are wired in series with switch in cord.

1 **Accurate marking and drilling** are important when preparing for doweling. Mark ends of sidebars exactly in center and ½-inch from each side for two dowels. Make a deep hole with awl in mark to guide drill bit.

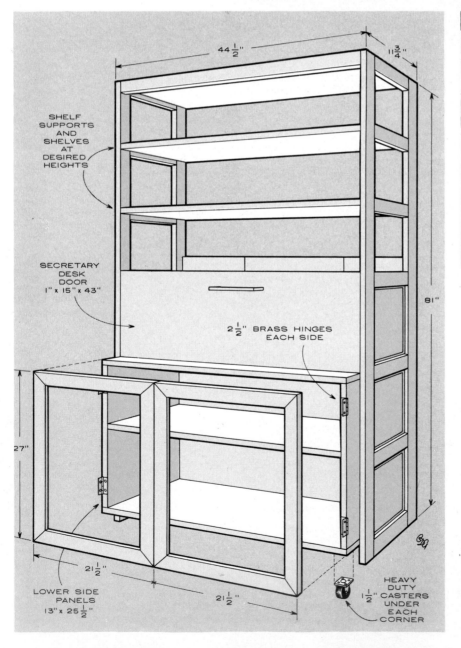

SHELF SUPPORTS AND SHELVES AT DESIRED HEIGHTS

44 ½"

11 ¾"

81"

SECRETARY DESK DOOR 1" x 15" x 43"

2 ½" BRASS HINGES EACH SIDE

27"

21 ½"

21 ½"

LOWER SIDE PANELS 13" x 25 ½"

HEAVY DUTY 1 ½" CASTERS UNDER EACH CORNER

3 **Lay all pieces** of each side in place with dowels in holes to check fit. Some holes might need slightly more drilling to adjust fit. Glue pieces of each side together making sure they are square and on a flat surface. Use several bar clamps across front and back.

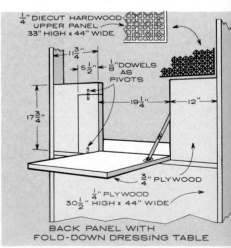

¼" DIECUT HARDWOOD UPPER PANEL 33" HIGH x 44" WIDE

11 ¾"

5 ½"

⅛" DOWELS AS PIVOTS

19 ¼"

12"

17 ¾"

¾" PLYWOOD

¼" PLYWOOD 30 ½" HIGH x 44" WIDE

BACK PANEL WITH FOLD-DOWN DRESSING TABLE

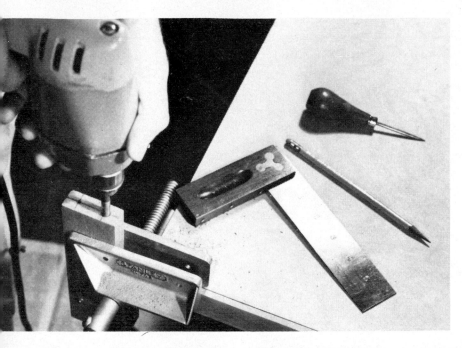

2 **Drill straight down,** pressing firmly into hole to ream out cleanly with revolving bit. Hole should be about 1 inch deep to allow an ample pocket for glue beneath dowel.

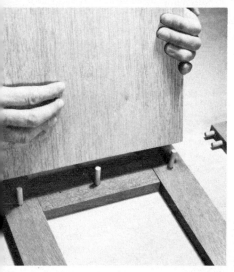

4 **Shelves are secured** to sides with three dowels in each end. Each dowel hole is drilled ½ inch into side pieces and about 1 inch into shelf ends. After checking for fit and squareness, glue pieces together using several web clamps to hold unit together. Corner miter clamps are useful here, too.

5 **Letter cabinet** is made of ¼-inch plywood, except for top piece which is ½-inch plywood, according to measurements in drawing. Top piece is thicker to take No. 10 1¼-inch screws which hold cabinet to shelf above it. Letter dividers have indentation cuts in front and slide into ¼-inch grooves cut with router in top and bottom horizontal pieces.

6 **Drawer is also made of** ¼-inch plywood, using butt joints with brads and glue. Then Corian front piece, with handle in place, is cemented to drawer front with epoxy, held with clamps.

two-faced bed/wardrobe divider

Bedrooms don't come any more compact than this. Built as a divider partition in an island location, as shown here, the unit provides not only the bed alcove and clothes closets, but a handsome display wall on the back plus end walls for mounting light switches and outlets. Or you could butt the unit against an existing wall for a peninsula divider—or build it flat against a wall if you don't have space to divide.

Whatever location you choose, you'll have added a bedroom that's readily available for overnight guests or for regular use by family members. Because there can be no bedside tables here, the sleeping alcove features

Four accordion doors present neutral 11-foot wall until center pair is parted (opposite page) to expose bed frame. Doors fold to each side so bed can be pivoted down; note opened sliding panel for storage (right of fan). Doors fold farther open for access to clothes (below). Switches for light and fan are on right partition. Enameled wall above headboard is ideal for fragile art that shouldn't be exposed to sun. Back face of waferboard (above) is left natural as background for display.

built-in amenities such as the little "pockets" at each side for storing those things you'll want to keep handy during the night—medicines, tissues, eyeglasses, and wristwatch. The light fixture on the alcove ceiling is ideal for reading in bed, and switches for both it and the fan's speed control are mounted on an alcove wall where you can reach them without rising.

Frame-panel construction uses inexpensive ¾-inch-thick waferboard over a frame of 2 × 2s and 2 × 4s. In my loft location, shown here, the height to be filled (from the floor to an overhead structural beam) was greater than the standard 8-foot length of structural panels, so I stood the panels atop dressed 2 × 4s set on edge to serve as baseboards.

The "public" faces of the structure were left natural. The wood-chip mosaic of a quality waferboard is most attractive when finished with clear shellac or a low-luster polyurethane varnish. Joints and corners are capped with molding strips painted a contrasting color before application. The bedroom faces of the unit were enameled. A prime coat plus a semigloss topcoat brushed on waferboard gives a strikingly textured surface

suggesting rough-troweled plaster. With its many depressions waferboard isn't easy material to finish, but

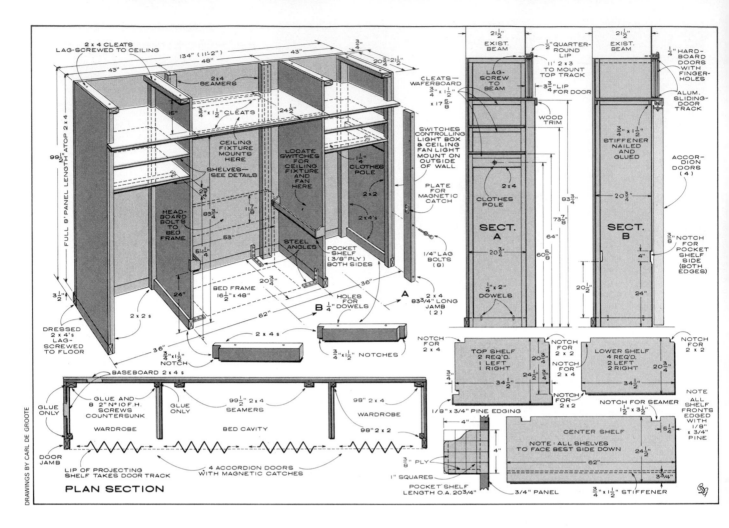

DRAWINGS BY CARL DE GROOTE

PLAN SECTION

the results are worth the effort. And there's little surface preparation involved except on faces you'll leave natural. On these some sanding is required to minimize wax-burn spots that occur during manufacturing. In assembling the closet units, I selected the least-blemished faces for the public side because I'd be painting the faces on the bedroom side. Here are other construction tips (in addition to clamping photos):

● Start construction by ripping the panels to width: four pieces at 20¾ inches and two at 43 inches. If you're

using a portable circular saw, face the good side down.

● Before any subassembly, cut the recesses for the pocket-shelf ends on the edges of the two inner partitions. The four 2 × 2s and four 2 × 4s used for vertical framing are all more than 8 feet long, so they must be cut from stock 10-footers.

● When gluing panels to framing, sand surface areas to remove all traces of manufacturing wax before applying glue. After the vertical members are attached, cut four pieces of 2 × 4 20¾ inches long. Rabbet notches ¾ inch deep and 1½ inches wide on both ends of the end baseboards and one end of each partition baseboard. Two ¼-inch dowels are used to attach these to their panel edges.

● You can cut shelf cleats from waferboard scraps, attaching them with glue and 1¼-inch finishing nails. Cut the shelves from ¾-inch plywood, notching as shown above.

Photos (6) and (7) show the final assembly steps for the bed cabinet. The two wardrobe assemblies are spaced slightly more than 4 feet apart on an 11-foot-2-inch 2 × 4 baseboard anchored to the floor with steel angles. Cabinet assembly is completed by

bridging these units with a full 4-by-8-foot panel of waferboard (6), gluing and screwing it into the vertical 2 × 4 seamers already attached to the wardrobe panels.

The pivoting-bed headboard frame is anchored to the floor within the alcove (7) before you set the pivoting bedspring frame atop it. Then you link the two with heavy springs such as the one shown in the lower-left corner of the photo. You add only as many as needed to balance the weight of your mattress for easy lifting.

Doors to close the upper storage compartments are simple panels of ¼-inch hardboard sliding on aluminum tracks. The full-width accordion door is actually four folding panels hung from a continuous aluminum track screwed to the bottom of the protruding shelf. (The track will come in four pieces when you buy the doors.) The doors come with magnetic catches on each stile; magnets of adjacent doors catch one another. At the outer ends you must provide a jamb on which you can mount a metal plate for these doors to close against. I simply bolted a vertical 2 × 4 on edge, as shown in the dimensional sketch—*Al Lees. Cabinetry by Rosario Capotosto. Drawings by Carl De Groote.*

The following manufacturers were selected by POPULAR SCIENCE for participation in this project. Retail prices are listed where appropriate, as a guide only; for further data, contact the source.

Source	Item
Louisiana-Pacific Corp. 111 S.W. Fifth Ave. Portland OR 97204	Waferwood, five panels (¾ in. × 4 ft. × 8 ft.)
Murphy Door Bed Co. 40 E. 34th St. New York NY 10016	Coil Spring frame, model CRH-54 ($448)
Reynolds Metals Co. Box 27003-A Richmond VA 23261	DIY Aluminum double track, model 3621, for ¼-in. doors (two 6-ft. sets)
Robbins & Myers, Inc. 2500 Frisco Ave. Memphis TN 38114	Hunter Comfort Breeze 52-in. ceiling fan, model 22531 ($235), plus light-adapter kit
Wood Specialty Products 24300 60th Ave. W. Mountlake Terrace WA 98043	Spacesaver 350 Winwood Floating Doors

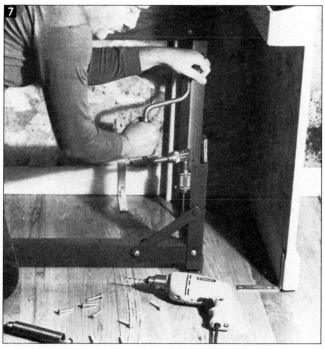

Clamping tricks speed assembly. Scrap block clamped at end (1) allows for cleat. The 1 × 2 blocks are clamped across face of 2 × 4 to hold it flush with panel edge while glue sets. Self-centering doweling jig is ideal for panel drilling (2). Check fit before applying glue (3); poor alignment could split out waferboard. Clamped crosspiece (right in photo) lets you use short pipe clamps (4). Clamp the end units while boring the pilot holes into the back panel (5). See text for comments on photos 6 and 7.

queen anne secretary

During his long life, Vincent Lookermans—son of the wealthiest man in the colony of New York—filled his home with some of the finest furniture ever made in the colonies. An inventory taken upon his death lists "1 old Walnut Desk" he had stored "In the Back Room." The assessor valued the desk as $4.10. Today, it has been reassessed at almost $18,000!

The secretary is made in two pieces; the bottom part is a drop-front desk, and the top is a bookcase. You needn't attempt this project all at once to enjoy it. The drop-front desk will look just fine by itself while you take a breather and get ready to make the bookcase.

Drop-front desk—start with the feet

The desk rests on a frame base which forms four "bracket" feet. The front corners of this base are mitered, while the back corners are assembled with rabbet joints, as shown in the drawings. The sides and front are rabbeted at the top to hold the desk case. Cut all joinery first, and fit the pieces together. Then you can cut the decorative shapes that will form the feet.

Glue the base together and check it with a framing square. *This is important!* If the base isn't square, the rest of the project will be out of kilter. When the glue is dry, reinforce the joints with glue blocks and wood screws.

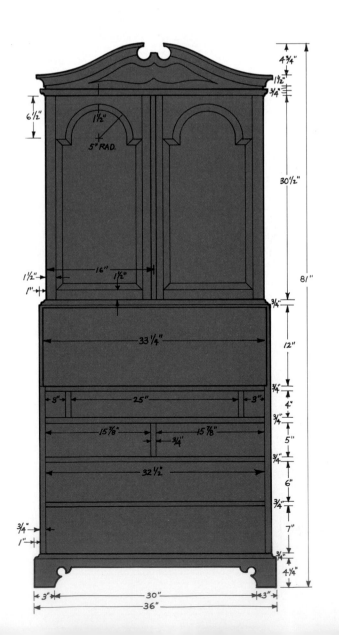

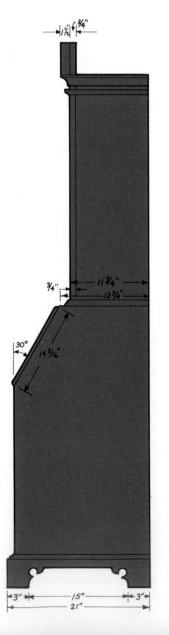

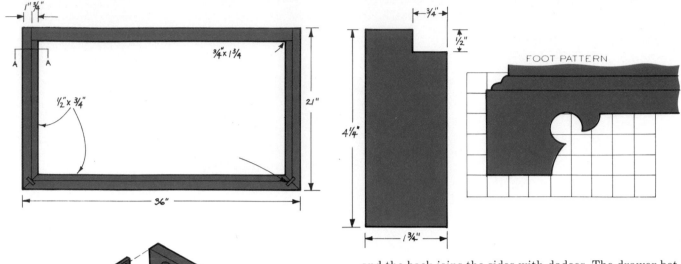

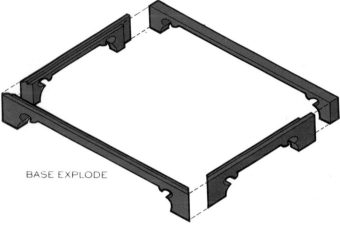

BASE EXPLODE

Building the case

The desk case consists of two sides, a top, a back, and five shelves. Except for the top, which is solid wood, all of these parts are made from cabinet-grade plywood, and the front edges are veneered to hide the plies. Tradional solid-wood construction would necessitate special joinery to allow for expansion and contraction of as much as ¼ inch across every 12 inches of width. Plywood, on the other hand, is relatively stable. Using it to make most of the large parts simplifies construction.

Cut the dadoes and rabbets in the case parts with a router or dado cutter mounted on your table saw. If you use a router, clamp a board to the parts to serve as a guide. Hold the router firmly against this guide as you work. Don't take big bites. Make the dado in several passes, cutting just ⅛ inch deeper with each pass to avoid "hogging" the bit and burning the cutting edges.

Dry-assemble the parts to check the fit of the joints. Set the assembled case on the base to see that it rests solidly inside the lip formed by the rabbets. When you're satisfied, disassemble the parts, then reassemble them again with glue. *Do not* glue the top to the case at this time. Leave it loose so that you can easily install the pigeonholes.

Cover the exposed edges of the plywood with veneer tape. Completely cover the visible plies with glue, then apply the tape to the edge. Hold it in place with masking tape while the glue dries. After the glue sets up, trim the tape flush with a razor blade or a sharp utility knife.

Fitting the drawers

The case holds seven flush drawers. While the sizes of these drawers differ, their construction is the same. The front is assembled to the sides with half-blind dovetails,

and the back joins the sides with dadoes. The drawer bottoms rest in grooves in the drawer fronts, backs, and sides.

Make the dovetails with a router and a dovetail template. If you don't have a template, you can substitute "lock joints"—locking tongues and dadoes, as used on the pigeonhole drawers—for the half-blind dovetails. Cut the grooves and dadoes with a dado cutter mounted on your table saw. Notch the backs of the five largest drawers, as shown in the drawings. The backs of the two smaller drawers are not notched.

Each of the drawer fronts has a small "cock bead" around the edges. The easiest way to cut this bead is with a homemade beading tool (figure 1). Break off a short length of an old hacksaw blade and grind it as shown in the drawings. Mount the blade in a handle, and use it as you would a scraper. Draw it in one direction across the surface of the drawer front until the bead is fully formed. Use very light pressure, especially when cutting a bead across the grain.

Assemble the drawers, and fit them in the case. Mark the position of the drawer guides on the shelves, remove the drawers, and tack the drawer guides in place temporarily. Again, check the fit of the drawers and see if they slide smoothly across the guides. When you're satisfied the guides are properly positioned and the drawers work well, glue the drawer guides in place on the shelves.

Fitting the drop-lid

Like the top, the drop-lid is made from a solid piece of wood. Shape the top and side edges with a cabinet lip cutter, so that the lid will overlap the top and sides of the case. Leave the bottom edge square.

Pull out the two small drawers from the case and lay the lid across them. (These drawers double as supports for the drop-lid.) Butt the lower edge of the lid against the edge of the top shelf. Place the hinges where your want them and mark their position on the desk parts. Rout out mortises for the hinges, attach the lid to the desk, and check the fit when the lid is closed. If there's a gap at the top when the lid is closed, sand a little stock off the desk sides near the bottom edge of the lid. When the lid closes properly, sand a little more stock away and apply new veneer to the edge. If there's a gap at the bottom, cut the mortises a little longer and move the hinges back slightly on the top shelf.

Making the pigeonholes

The pigeonholes shown in the drawings are the kind and size that were installed in the desk when it was built around 1740. The standard sizes of letters and envelopes,

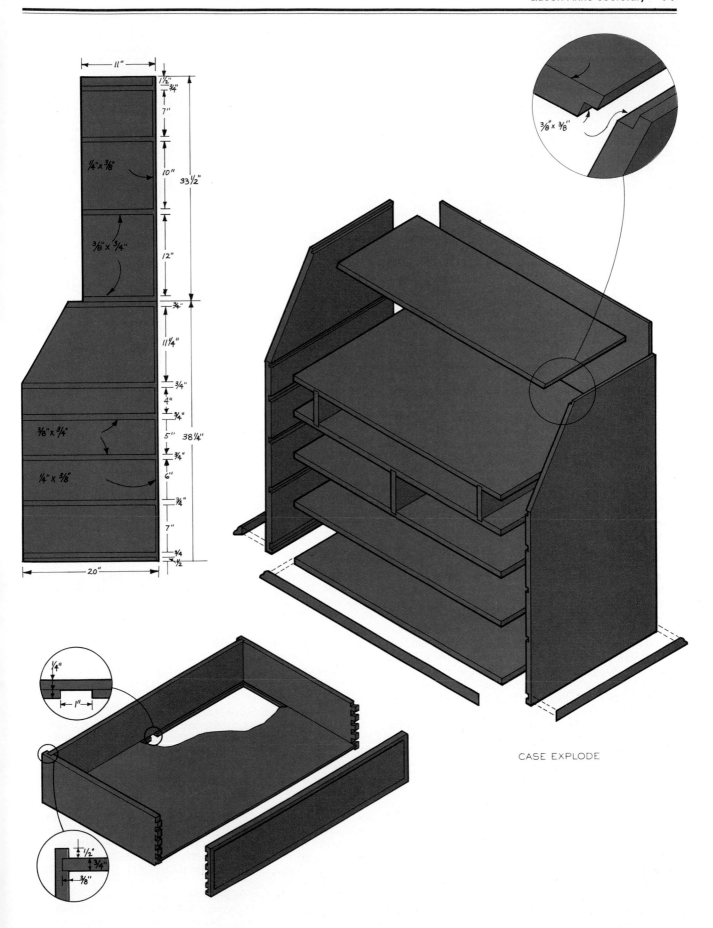

3/8" x 3/8"

11"

1½"
¾"
7"

¼" x ⅜"   10"   33½"

⅜" x ¾"   12"

¾"

11¼"

¾"
4"
¾"
⅜" x ¾"   5"   38¼"
¾"
¼" x ⅜"   6"
¾"
7"
¾
½

20"

¼"
1"

½"
¾"
⅜"

CASE EXPLODE

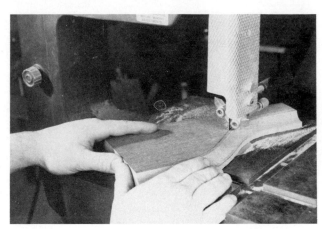

Fig. 1. Make a beading tool from an old hacksaw blade to cut the cock beads around the edges of the drawers.

Fig. 2. To make gooseneck molding, first shape the edge of a curved board, then cut the molding free of the waste. Never shape a thin, curved board; it may come apart in your hands.

however, has changed considerably since the early eighteenth century. You may want to design your own pigeonholes according to modern envelope sizes.

Whatever the design of your pigeonholes, they should contain four elements to remain representative of the period: open compartments, small stamp drawers, slender column-front drawers, and at least one compartment with a locking door. Here's how to build each of these elements:

Open compartments. Pigeonholes are an arrangement of small shelves and dividers. The open compartments are places where the craftsman chose not to put a drawer or a door. Fit these shelves and dividers together with simple dadoes and rabbets, as shown in the drawings. Make the long shelves from 1/2-inch-thick stock, and the large dividers from 3/8-inch stock. Smaller shelves and dividers can be made from 1/4-inch stock. Scallop the front of the shelves and/or dividers surrounding open compartments to make it easier to retrieve papers stored in them. After you have installed the shelves and the dividers, glue the desk top in place.

Stamp drawers. The fronts, backs, and sides of these small drawers are put together with lock joints. To make a lock joint, first cut a dado in the drawer sides on your table saw. Using the same setup, cut a groove in the end of the drawer front or back, forming two tongues. A tenoning jig helps keep the drawer part vertical to the worktable. Complete the joint by cutting the inside tongues to the proper lengths. To speed up construction, cut all the drawer parts to size, then cut all the dadoes, then all the tongues, and so on. Notice that the front of the stamp drawers are scalloped to match the scallops in the shelves. Make these scallops on a bandsaw before you assemble the drawers.

Column-front drawers. The drawers are actually hidden compartments. If made correctly, the columns look like decorative, non-functional parts of the desk. Cut the flutes in the drawer fronts with a small bead cutter mounted in a molder or shaper. Assemble the fronts, backs, and sides with lock joints in the same manner as the stamp drawers. Glue short lengths of molding to the top and bottom edges of the drawer fronts to serve as finger pulls.

Locking compartment. This is just a compartment with a flush door and a lock. To make the door, cut a scrap of 3/8-inch-thick stock to fit the front of the compartment.

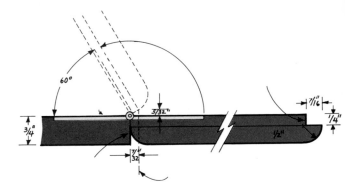

Mortise one side for small brass hinges, and drill the other side for a cam lock. Small cam locks are available from several sources, one of which is The Wise Company, 6503 St. Claude Avenue, P.O. Box 118, Arabi, LA 70032.

Bookcase—making the shelves

Like the desk case, most of the bookcase is made from plywood to simplify construction. Join the shelves to the sides with dadoes, and cover the exposed edges with veneer tape.

The top is a false-front "bonnet," made of solid wood. Cut the top and the applied panel out on a bandsaw. Round the edges of the applied panel with a bead cutter mounted in your shaper or router. Glue the panel to the top, then glue and screw the top to the bookcase.

Both the top and bottom of the bookcase are decorated with molding. The top gets two moldings—a straight molding that sets the top apart from the doors, and a "gooseneck" molding that follows the contours of the bonnet top. The straight molding is fairly simple. Cut the molding with a shaper or router and apply it to the bottom edge of the top. While you're making this molding, make enough to put molding around the bottom, but *do not* apply it to the bookcase yet.

The gooseneck molding is somewhat more involved. It's built up in two parts—a bead and a cove—and the front pieces each have two curved edges, top and bottom. First cut the *bottom* curve in a wide board on your bandsaw.

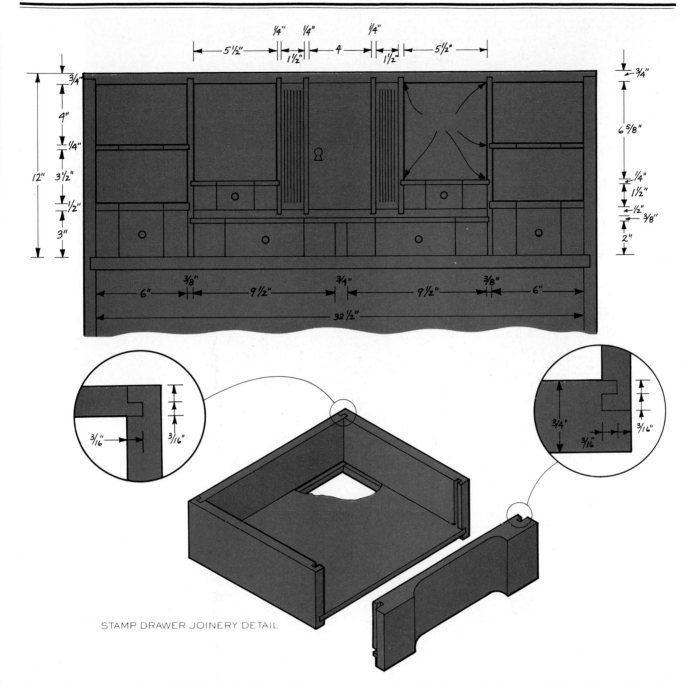

STAMP DRAWER JOINERY DETAIL

Shape the curved edge of this board with a shaper or router, then cut the *top* curve to separate the molding from the waste stock. (figure 2). *Do not* try to cut the curved moldings to width before you shape them. The shaper will only tear the thin strips.

Apply the gooseneck molding to the bookcase. Then sit the bookcase on the desk and attach the two assemblies with wood screws. Attach the bottom molding to the top of the desk, but *not* to the bookcase. Butt this molding up to the bookcase, but leave it unattached. That way, if you ever have to move this project, you can easily disassemble the components.

Making the doors

The bookcase is enclosed by two arched paneled doors. The frames of these doors are joined with through-mortises and tenons. Cut out the arches in the upper rails with your bandsaw, then cut tenons on the ends of both the upper and lower rails. To make the through-mortises, first drill

a series of holes through the width of the stiles, then square the edges of the mortises with a chisel.

Assemble the frames with glue, and peg the mortises with short dowels. When the glue has cured, cut a decorative bead around the interior of the door frames on the *outside* surfaces, and a rabbet on the *inside* surface. Use a router to make both the bead and the rabbet. Square off the corners with a hand chisel, removing the stock that the router can't reach.

Cut arched panels to fit the frames. You have several choices on how to make these panels, depending on how you would like your finished project to appear:

Raised panels. The original secretary sports two raised wooden panels. Raise the three straight sides of each panel on a table saw, with the blade tilted at a slight angle. Then carefully carve the arched side to match the straight sides.

Glass panels. Most specialty glass shops with be able to cut arched panes for you. And if you want to go to the expense, some shops will be able to bevel the glass.

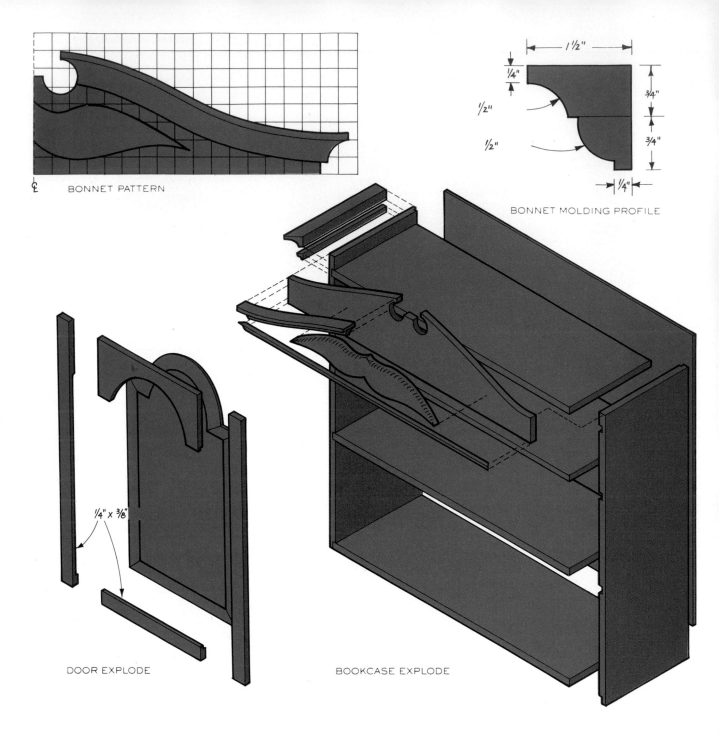

BONNET PATTERN

BONNET MOLDING PROFILE

DOOR EXPLODE

BOOKCASE EXPLODE

1/4" x 3/8"

Flat panels. The easiest panels to make are flat wood panels. Cut these from 1/4-inch-thick stock or veneered plywood with a saber saw or bandsaw.

Hold the panels in the door frames with small metal or plastic "dogs". These tiny tabs are available at most hardware stores, in among the screen door fittings. *Do not* glue wooden panels in place; let them float in the frames so that they can expand and contract with changes in the weather.

Mortise the door frames and the bookcase for hinges, then hang the doors. The doors should clear the top and bottom molding by approximately 1/16 inch when they open, so that they don't bind.

Finishing the project

Hardware on this secretary is pretty fancy as Queen Anne furniture goes, indicating that it may not be original. Queen Anne drawer pulls traditionally had simple "bat

wing" escutcheons and brass bails, with keyhole escutcheons shaped to match the pulls.

You can order period hardware—both plain and fancy—from several sources, including the Wise Company that was mentioned earlier. Here are two more sources: Horton Brasses, Nooks Hill Road, P.O. Box 95F, Cromwell, CT 06416; Wolchonok & Son, 155 East 52nd Street, New York, NY 10022.

The original finish was probably a hand-rubbed oil finish. There are several good products on today's market that duplicate the look of hand-rubbed oil, such as Minwax oil finishes and Watco Danish oil. Whatever finish you use, be careful to apply just as many coats to the inside of the secretary as you do to the outside. This extra precaution helps prevent warping and keeps all components of the project square—*by Nick Engler. Color photo courtesy of Sotheby's, Inc.,* © *1985.*

make your own tambour doors

They're sliders, but unlike conventional bypass doors, tambours disappear into the cabinet to expose the entire contents. Construction isn't complicated, but you must take care if the doors are to function efficiently. Two vital factors: The case must be square, and—because the doors are guided by grooves or tracks in opposite panels—the guides must match.

You can buy the slats or make them. Suitable ready-mades include

Now you see it, now you don't. Tambour doors are especially appropriate for masking equipment that should be heard and not seen. A pair of sliding doors on this cabinet would only let you open half at a time, and hinged panels need swing space. You get a variety of textures (below) by using molding or strips of hardboard.

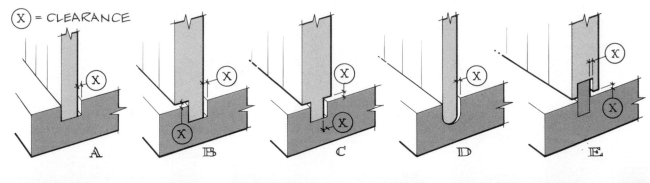

Ⓧ = CLEARANCE

A   B   C   D   E

Take your pick of track techniques: First photo and sketch show full-width slats riding in groove; second photo shows

¾-inch-thick slats rabbeted to form tongue for narrower groove (sketches B and C). Track can also be round-bottom

groove (sketch D) or splinelike projection of ⅛-inch-thick plywood (third photo, sketch E).

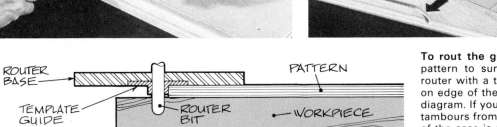

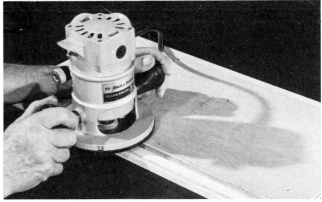

ROUTER BASE
TEMPLATE GUIDE
ROUTER BIT
PATTERN
WORKPIECE

To rout the grooves, tack an accurate pattern to surface (left photo). Fit the router with a template guide that bears on edge of the pattern, as shown in the diagram. If you want to be able to insert tambours from the rear (before the back of the case is attached), make a pattern with run-out (arrow).

the moldings sketched on the next page. The problem lies in finding moldings to match the lumber you use for the case (unless you plan to paint the project). It's hard to find moldings in fancy hardwood such as teak.

Making flat slats is easy—rip as many as you need from wide boards, then pass them between a fence and drum sander (see sketch).

To create molded slats, you'll need a shaper or drill-press accessories.

Don't attempt to shape slats after they've been cut. Instead, shape the edge of a wide board, then rip off the edge to the thickness you need. Shape the newly sawed edge, and repeat the process until you've cut all the strips you need. When one board becomes too narrow for safety, start another.

Slat thicknesses and widths are variable—thin and narrow for delicacy, wider and thicker for a substantial appearance. As a guide, figure

that slat width can range from ¼ to 1 inch; slat thickness from 3/16 to ¾ inch.

Thin slats can ride directly in the grooves. For slats thicker than ¼ inch, each end should be rabbeted on one or both faces to form tongues; you won't want grooves much more than ¼ inch wide. If you're cutting slats from a wide board, shape the tongue before doing the ripping; if you're using ready-mades, secure the slats to a flat surface with several battens and do the forming with a portable router.

To cut the grooves, fit your router with a template guide and tack a pattern panel to the face of the board. Work with a ¼-inch bit, and make the groove about ¼ inch deep. The radius of the corner curves will depend on the width of the slats. As slats make the turn, they run tangent to the curve, so the narrower the slats, the smaller the radius can be. A radius of 1½ to 2 inches is fine for slats up to about ¾ inch wide.

Tambour doors are usually assembled by coating the backs of slats with glue before laying a sheet of light canvas across them. It may be simpler, however, to work with one of the many self-adhesive materials available. I've tried such unorthodox backings as self-adhesive felt, plastic-coated or flocked wallpapers, and shelf liners—even duct tape. They can be applied in strips or as overall backings. Keep all slats square as you apply the backing. Use a carpenter's square as a jig.

To insert the finished doors in their grooves, run out the guide grooves at the rear of the case. If the width of the opening is more than the length of the door, cut the top groove enough deeper than the bottom one to let you push the panel up and tilt back the bottom so it falls into the bottom groove (see sketch). With these two methods, you can finish the doors before putting them in place—*by R.J. DeCristoforo. Drawings by Eugene Thompson.*

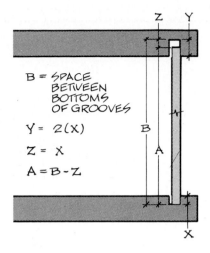

$B = $ SPACE BETWEEN BOTTOMS OF GROOVES

$Y = 2(X)$

$Z = X$

$A = B - Z$

You can design your cabinet with an extra-deep top groove so door panels can be inserted after case assembly.

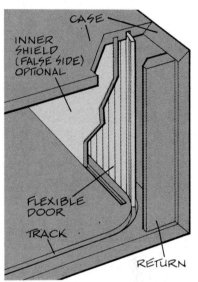

"Returns" are masking blocks glued inside cabinet corners to conceal door mechanics. As shown in the cutaway photo, a bevel on the leading edge helps clearance. If stored items might clog the track, add a shield (drawing).

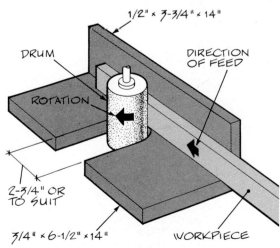

1/2" × 3-3/4" × 14"

DRUM

DIRECTION OF FEED

ROTATION

2-3/4" OR TO SUIT

3/4" × 6-1/2" × 14"

WORKPIECE

Jig for use with drum sander in a drill press helps you smooth door slats and bring them to uniform thickness.

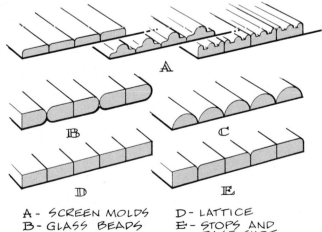

A
B
C
D
E

A - SCREEN MOLDS
B - GLASS BEADS
C - HALF ROUNDS
D - LATTICE
E - STOPS AND BASE SHOE

Ready-made moldings can give a variety of patterns to tambour doors. They're all attached to backing in same way.

organize your garage with waferboard

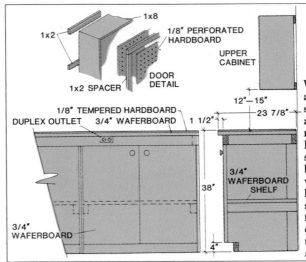

1x8
1x2
1/8" PERFORATED HARDBOARD
UPPER CABINET
DOOR DETAIL
1x2 SPACER
1/8" TEMPERED HARDBOARD
DUPLEX OUTLET   3/4" WAFERBOARD
1 1/2"
12"—15"
23 7/8"
38"
3/4" WAFERBOARD SHELF
4"
3/4" WAFERBOARD

DRAWINGS BY GERHARD RICHTER

Workbench and tool-storage area at right provide space for a radial-arm saw and vise as well as plenty of room for laying out projects. Drawings (left) show construction details of workbench made largely from waferboard and of overhead cabinets built from standard lumber and perforated hardboard. This cabinet design permits tools to be hung on both insides and outsides of doors.

Insulating your garage can provide a warm place to work in the winter while holding down heating costs. If you've already undertaken or are contemplating insulating your garage, why not expand the project so that it includes the work and storage areas you'll need?

You can build a workbench, cabinets, and shelves in your garage with the same inexpensive waferboard panels used to sheathe the interior walls after glass-fiber or other insulation has been installed. These plans show how you can use waferboard as the primary building material to transform your garage into more than just a shelter for your car.

The projects call for ¾-inch-thick sheets of waferboard to build the storage and work areas. Thinner panels, ¼ or ⁷⁄₁₆ inch, are normally specified for interior sheathing work such as covering insulated walls. White glue and four-penny nails are used in the simple butt-joint construction employed throughout.

The upper cabinets are fastened to the wall above the workbench by driving screws into the wall studs through 1 × 2 strips at top and bottom.

The shelves and cabinets shown were finished with primer followed by a coat of semi gloss acrylic latex paint. The exposed waferboard surfaces of the workbench and sheathed garage walls can, if you like, be finished with shellac, varnish, or urethane for a

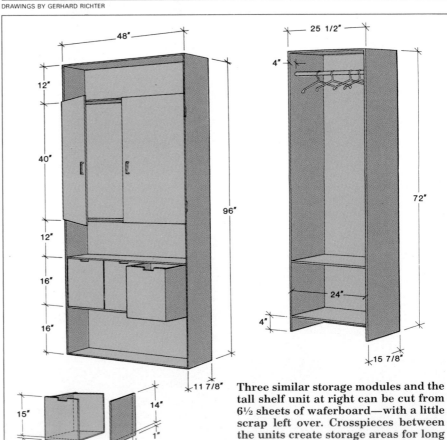

48"
12"
40"
12"
16"
16"
96"
11 7/8"
25 1/2"
4"
72"
24"
4"
15 7/8"
15"
1"
1"
16"
14"
10"   1"
1"

Three similar storage modules and the tall shelf unit at right can be cut from 6½ sheets of waferboard—with a little scrap left over. Crosspieces between the units create storage areas for long objects such as skis. In the drawing above, a 1⅛-in. softwood dowel serves to make a clothes rack.

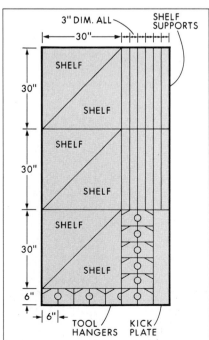

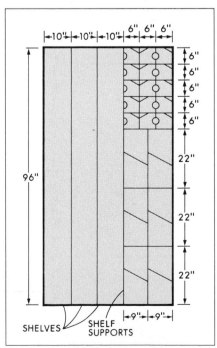

natural effect as well as protection. You can also apply an undercoat of stain to highlight the waferboard's chaotic grain patterns, which some people find pleasing.

Designers at Louisiana-Pacific Corp. (111 S.W. Fifth Ave., Portland, OR 97204), manufacturers of waferboard under the Waferwood brand name, have proved ingenious at designing simple stud-wall storage projects and figuring out how many pieces can be cut from a panel of the factory-sanded material. They worked out the accompanying cutting diagrams, which show how you can cut out the semicircular notches in 13 pairs of tool-hanger brackets by using a 1½-inch spade bit in a power drill. The remaining six unpaired notches are cut with a saber saw. This virtually no-scrap layout even provides a kick plate for the bottommost angled corner shelf—*by Stuart F. Brown. Drawings by Gerhard Richter.*

Corner of garage wall with exposed studs was transformed into a space-saving storage area with shelves (photo above), supports, and garden-tool-storage brackets cut from only two sheets of waferboard (see diagrams).

nine do-it-yourself safety devices for power tools

My hands first appeared in a photograph more than 30 years ago, showing how to use a power tool. Since then, they've been in thousands of pictures, and they're still the same hands—older but whole. I've never fallen off a ladder, tripped over debris, suffered an electrical shock, or had to rush to an ophthalmologist to have a foreign substance removed from my eye, either.

Why? It's not entirely luck. I like to attribute my unscathed anatomy to my healthy mistrust of tools. For one thing, I don't rely on the safety features of power tools or the guards that come with them. I design a special fixture when I feel that one is needed.

There is often a double benefit in doing this; a safety jig can also help me to work more accurately.

The point is, there is no such thing as a "safe" tool, even though some might rate pretty high on a scale of safety.

The danger to the woodworker, paradoxically, often becomes greater as he gets more experienced. I'm talking about overconfidence. I have a friend (I know he won't mind my telling the story) who has worked for years making truly heirloom-quality furniture. One day, needing a very short piece of molding, he decided to skip the good practice of shaping a large piece and then cutting off what

he needed. He figured that, this once, he could shape a small piece. I won't go into detail, but he no longer has all ten fingers. Sadly, this kind of accident—whether in industry or in the home shop—is far too frequent.

The router is probably one of the least hazardous of the power wood cutters, but using it overconfidently can result in lacerated fingers. As a friend with a bandaged hand said to me: "Don't ever trust a router bit." I say: "Don't ever trust any tool."

Safety Jigs

All of the jigs shown are used in my shop. At times, I'll admit, setting

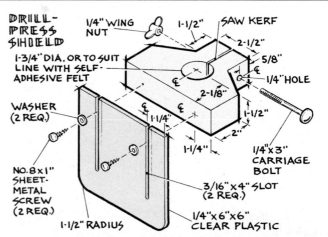

When using a drill press for routing, keep your hands away from the moving parts with this adjustable clear-plastic safety shield, which is designed for a collar that moves with the quill. The mounting bracket is made of hardwood, bored to accommodate the collar and then kerfed at the back.

ADJUSTABLE PUSHER

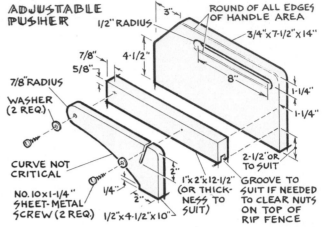

ROUND OF ALL EDGES OF HANDLE AREA

3"
1/2" RADIUS
4-1/2"
7/8"
5/8"
7/8" RADIUS
WASHER (2 REQ.)
CURVE NOT CRITICAL
NO. 10 x 1-1/4" SHEET-METAL SCREW (2 REQ.)
1/4"
2"
1/2" x 4-1/2" x 10"
2"
3/4" x 7-1/2" x 14"
8"
1-1/4"
1-1/4"
2-1/2" OR TO SUIT
1" x 2" x 12-1/2" (OR THICKNESS TO SUIT)
GROOVE TO SUIT IF NEEDED TO CLEAR NUTS ON TOP OF RIP FENCE

Strip cutting on a table saw is safer with this pusher, which is made to ride the rip fence. It's adjustable for various wood thicknesses; you tighten the screws of the hook so it stays put as you work. You may still be able to use the saw's guard or anti-kickback fingers, depending on the workpiece.

VERTICAL TABLE

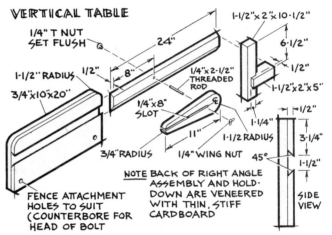

1/4" T NUT SET FLUSH
1-1/2" RADIUS
1/2"
8"
24"
3/4" x 10" x 20"
1/4" x 2-1/2" THREADED ROD
1/4" x 8" SLOT
11"
3/4" RADIUS
1/4" WING NUT
1-1/2" RADIUS
1-1/4"
1-1/2" x 2" x 10-1/2"
6-1/2"
1/2"
1-1/2" x 2" x 5"
FENCE ATTACHMENT HOLES TO SUIT (COUNTERBORE FOR HEAD OF BOLT
NOTE BACK OF RIGHT ANGLE ASSEMBLY AND HOLD-DOWN ARE VENEERED WITH THIN, STIFF CARDBOARD
1/2"
3-1/4"
45°
1-1/2"
SIDE VIEW

Tenoning jobs are dangerous when only the rip fence is used for support. With a jig, the work is held securely and accurately; hands never come close to the saw blade. This jig is a vertical table with its own miter gauge and hold-down. Blade-to-work distances are set by the rip fence.

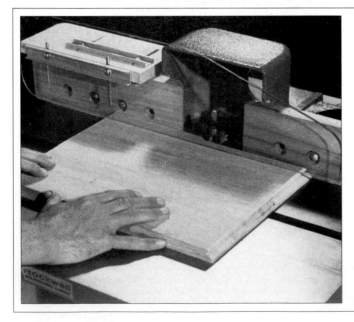

SHAPER-FENCE SHIELD

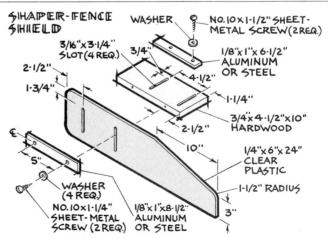

WASHER
NO. 10 x 1-1/2" SHEET-METAL SCREW (2 REQ.)
3/16" x 3-1/4" SLOT (4 REQ.)
3/4"
1/8" x 1" x 6-1/2" ALUMINUM OR STEEL
2-1/2"
1-3/4"
4-1/2"
1-1/4"
2-1/2"
3/4" x 4-1/2" x 10" HARDWOOD
10"
1/4" x 6" x 24" CLEAR PLASTIC
1-1/2" RADIUS
5"
WASHER (4 REQ.)
NO. 10 x 1-1/4" SHEET-METAL SCREW (2 REQ.)
1/8" x 1" x 8-1/2" ALUMINUM OR STEEL
3"

A thick workpiece? Despite that, you can situate this adjustable shaper safety shield as close as necessary to the cutter. It can be used regardless of the cutter's rotation. When feeding from right to left, invert the bracket, and mount it on the opposite fence; turn the shield end-for-end.

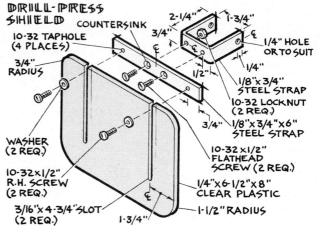

DRILL-PRESS SHIELD

COUNTERSINK

10-32 TAPHOLE (4 PLACES)

2-1/4" 1-3/4"

3/4"

1/4" HOLE OR TO SUIT

3/4" RADIUS

1/4"

1/8"x 3/4" STEEL STRAP

10-32 LOCKNUT (2 REQ.)

1/8"x3/4"x6" STEEL STRAP

1/2"

3/4"

WASHER (2 REQ.)

10-32x1/2" R.H. SCREW (2 REQ.)

10-32 x 1/2" FLATHEAD SCREW (2 REQ.)

1/4"x 6-1/2"x 8" CLEAR PLASTIC

3/16"x 4-3/4" SLOT (2 REQ.)

1-3/4"

1-1/2" RADIUS

For routing on a drill press: This type of shield is designed for a machine that does not have a collar that moves with the quill. The shield's mounting bracket is secured with the same bolt that tightens the casting for the depth-stop rod. Adjust shield after locking cutting tool in position.

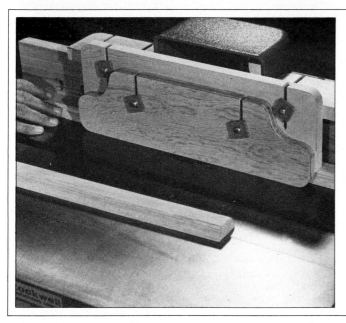

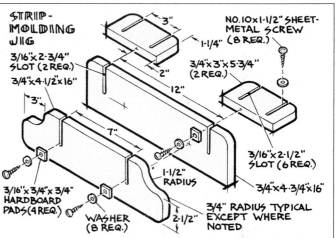

STRIP-MOLDING JIG

3"

NO.10x1-1/2" SHEET-METAL SCREW (8 REQ.)

3/16"x 2-3/4" SLOT (2 REQ.)

1-1/4"

3/4"x4-1/2"x16"

2"

3/4"x3"x5-3/4" (2 REQ.)

12"

3"

7"

3/16"x 2-1/2" SLOT (6 REQ.)

1-1/2" RADIUS

3/4"x4-3/4"x16"

3/16"x 3/4"x 3/4" HARDBOARD PADS (4 REQ.)

WASHER (8 REQ.)

2-1/2"

3/4" RADIUS TYPICAL EXCEPT WHERE NOTED

Strip-molding jig increases safety without sacrificing accuracy and convenience. Feed pre-cut workpieces in one end, and pull them out the other. The jig is adjustable to accommodate various stock sizes. The inner part acts as a hold-down; the outer section holds work against the fence.

them up seems a nuisance—but then I consider the possible alternatives. Some of the jigs are work holders and movers, others are simple shields that keep your hands away from cutting edges. Some, like the strip-molding jig for a shaper, allow you to work faster and more accurately, and at the same time provide additional safety. If you have the same tool pictured or one that is similar, especially in size, you can duplicate the projects by following the drawings. Otherwise, you might have to modify the design to suit your equipment—*by R.J. DeCristoforo. Drawings by Gerhard Richter.*

General power-tool precautions

Before you turn on any tool, learn what it does and how it does it. Do a dry run whenever you encounter a procedure that is strange to you. Do the complete procedure with the power off so you can preview work movement and hand placement.

The most efficient way to use a table-saw blade is with a high projection because this buries fewer teeth in the stock. The safest way, however, is to have a minimum projection or, at most, one no higher than the length of the tooth (that is, so you don't see more than the gullet depth above the stock). This rule must be broken when using a hollow-ground blade because a higher-than-usual projection is necessary to prevent burning.

Use the guards that are supplied with the tool. With some tools there are cuts that can't be made with the guards in position. Be extremely careful, or determine whether you might be better off using another tool or technique for such a cut.

Don't work after you've had a drink or when you're tired. Don't socialize while working. (All my friends and neighbors know better than to startle me by just walking into my shop. When they hear the sound of a tool, they wait until it stops before entering.)

Have a shop uniform: hard shoes with steel toes; a tight-fitting shirt or one with half sleeves; no rings, wrist watches, ties, or unbound long hair. Safety goggles are always a must. A dust mask makes sense even when doing jobs other than sanding: Many sawing, shaping, and routing operations can produce particles best kept out of your lungs. Headphone-type hearing protectors can be as important as any safety device. Good ear protectors will screen out high frequencies but still allow normal conversation and won't eliminate the noises you should hear.

Most important is awareness that safety is a state of mind. It's a small price to pay for staying whole.

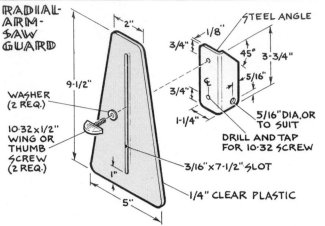

RADIAL-ARM-SAW GUARD

2"
9-1/2"
WASHER (2 REQ.)
10·32 x 1/2" WING OR THUMB SCREW (2 REQ.)
1"
5"
1/8"
3/4"
STEEL ANGLE
45°
3-3/4"
5/16"
3/4"
1-1/4"
5/16" DIA. OR TO SUIT
DRILL AND TAP FOR 10·32 SCREW
3/16" x 7-1/2" SLOT
1/4" CLEAR PLASTIC

Adding a plastic shield to a radial-arm saw covers the blade from the front without blocking vision. Adjustable shield mounts on a piece of angle iron that slips into split casting at the front end of the tool's guard. It's secured to the saw with the same bolt used to lock the anti-kickback unit.

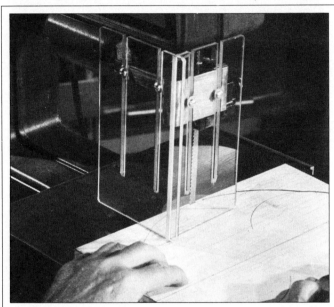

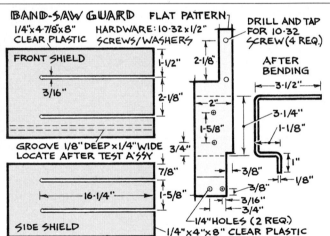

BAND-SAW GUARD   FLAT PATTERN

1/4" x 4-7/8" x 8" CLEAR PLASTIC
HARDWARE: 10·32 x 1/2" SCREWS/WASHERS
DRILL AND TAP FOR 10·32 SCREW (4 REQ.)

FRONT SHIELD
1-1/2"
3/16"
2-1/8"
2-1/8"
2"
1-5/8"
AFTER BENDING
3-1/2"
3-1/4"
1-1/8"
1"
1/8"

GROOVE 1/8" DEEP x 1/4" WIDE LOCATE AFTER TEST A'SSY
3/4"
7/8"
3/8"
3/8"
3/8"
3/16"
3/4"
16-1/4"
1-5/8"
1/4" HOLES (2 REQ.)
SIDE SHIELD
1/4" x 4" x 8" CLEAR PLASTIC

Guard for a band saw consists of vertically adjustable, independent shields. The blade guides are shown higher than they need to be. The guides can be placed as close to the work as necessary. Mounting bracket is secured with the same screws that hold the regular blade guard.

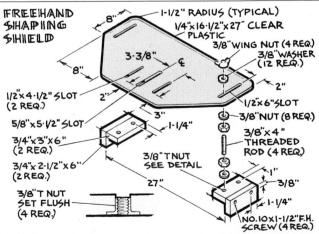

FREEHAND SHAPING SHIELD

8"
8"
3-3/8"
2"
3"
1-1/2" RADIUS (TYPICAL)
1/4" x 16-1/2" x 27" CLEAR PLASTIC
3/8" WING NUT (4 REQ.)
3/8" WASHER (12 REQ.)
2"
1/2" x 6" SLOT
3/8" NUT (8 REQ.)
3/8" x 4" THREADED ROD (4 REQ.)
1"
3/8"
1-1/4"
NO. 10 x 1-1/2" F.H. SCREW (4 REQ.)
1/2" x 4-1/2" SLOT (2 REQ.)
5/8" x 5-1/2" SLOT
3/4" x 3" x 6" (2 REQ.)
1-1/4"
3/4" x 2-1/2" x 6" (2 REQ.)
3/8" T NUT SEE DETAIL
27"
3/8" T NUT SET FLUSH (4 REQ.)

A large, clear-plastic shield provides extra protection when doing freehand shaping against collars. The whole unit is adjustable so it can cover a large part of the workpiece. Shorter slots provide access to the spindle and fulcrum pins. Adjust shield so it will be as close to work as possible.

flip-top bench for compact tools

A workbench is a key component in most workshops. It's where tools are brought as they're needed. But when I began designing a custom bench for a collection of the new breed of bench-top power tools, I decided to make it a complete woodworking station. It's larger than conventional units to meet two needs: space required for all the tools and surface area required for fabrication and assembly work.

Cutouts in the bench top accommodate most of the tools: an 8-inch table saw (Black & Decker), a 10-inch band saw (Skil), a 1/2-inch drill press (Shopcraft), a belt sander-grinder (Rockwell), and a bench grinder and disc sander (Black & Decker). I chose these as a representative sample of what's available in this new class of power tools. In addition, I included a lathe (Shopcraft) and two Record woodworking vises.

Shelves beneath provide storage space for additional tools. You set these on the bench top when you need them and attach them with screws through T nuts. I provided T-nut mounts for various small tools and

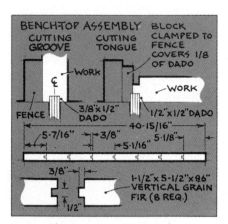

1 **Bench top can be made of** 2 × 6 vertical-grain fir formed on a table saw for tongue-and-groove assembly. Seven of the eight pieces must be rip-cut to remove 1/16 inch from the groove edge to ensure square mating edges. That, plus the 3/8-inch overlap at the joints, means the width of the bench top will be 40 15/16 inches. Cuts are made as diagramed: You pass the stock vertically over the saw blade to form the groove and use two passes with the work flat to form the tongue. Shape the groove about 1/32 inch deeper to be sure that edges will butt and allow room for glue. Don't make the fit too tight; an easy slip-fit is correct.

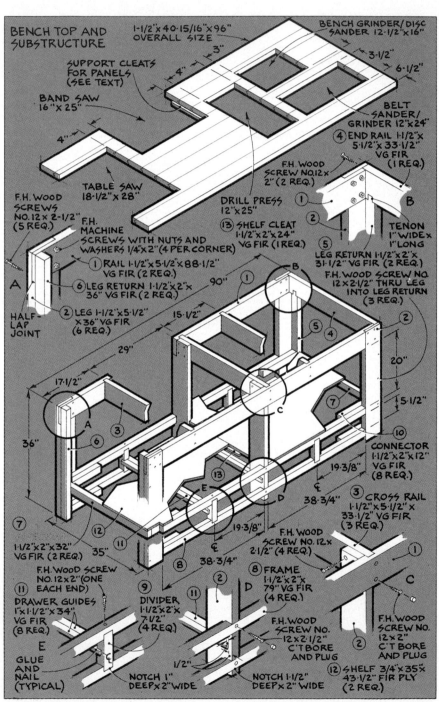

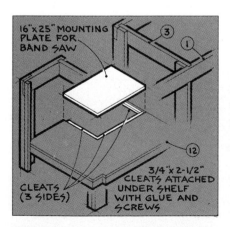

2 **Substructure is assembled next.** Details show how joints are made. End laps are easy to form on radial arm saw but can be done with handsaw. (Form shoulder first, then cut out waste.) Center leg is notched for rail and lower frame pieces. Assemble these parts, then add end rail and leg returns.

Make subassemblies of frames, dividers, and connectors, and add them to substructure. Attach connectors (allowing for stretchers) to frames and legs with glue and No. 12-by-2 1/2-inch flathead wood screws. Make drawer guides, and attach with glue and single 4d finishing nail at each end. Cut shelves to size, then

lay out and form notches. Lefthand shelf has panel cutout that will be mounting plate for band saw (lower-left detail). Cleats around opening support panel. Attach shelves with 4d box nails spaced about 10 inches apart. Don't forget to include shelf cleat, which supports both shelves at center joint.

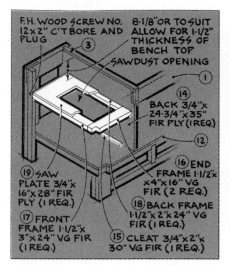

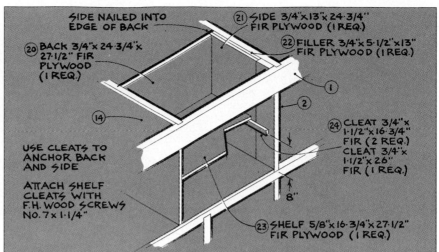

3 **Make table-saw compartment:** Form the back and attach it by nailing into cross rail (3) and bottom cleat. Make frame as subassembly using glue and corrugated nails at joints. Put it in place with screws through back piece and through leg returns. Cut opening for sawdust in saw plate; attach plate with glue and 5d box nails. Saw table must be flush with bench top.

4 **Enclosed cabinet:** Cut side and filler, and nail into cross rail (3). Nail side into bottom cleat (13 in drawing 2). Anchor back by nailing into edge through side piece; add a cleat behind at bottom. Install cleats and shelf.

5 **Shape grooved frame pieces** for sliding doors as diagramed. Note that top and bottom grooves are deep enough so that doors can be lifted clear of bottom groove for removal. Enclose front of bench with small (left) and large (right) panel, leaving space for sliding doors: Cut panels to size and form rabbets as shown. Attach panels to substructure with glue and 1-inch nails. Shape trim, and attach it around panels with glue and ³/₄-inch brads. Install frame for doors with glue and 1-inch brads driven into grooves.

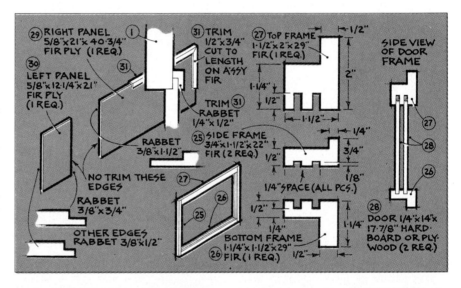

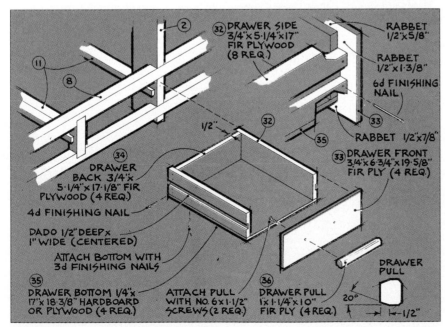

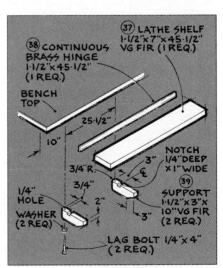

6 **Drawer joinery is basic,** but if you use glue in all joints, drawers will be sturdy. Author attached bottoms *under* sides to maximize depth. Materials listed are for four drawers; there's room for four more behind.

7 **Lathe shelf is attached** to edge of bench with 1½-inch continuous hinge. Shelf supports, which pivot on lag screws, swing out of the way under bench-top overlap when shelf is down. Lag screws anchor the supports when the shelf is up. (Remove sharp lathe centers when tool is not in use.)

even for some larger tools. Drawers below provide more storage.

Building the workbench is not a weekend project. But once the top is made and the substructure assembled, it is functional and, further, can be used for subsequent steps in its own manufacture.

The easiest way to make the bench top is to buy two 25-by-96-inch maple counter tops and glue them together. Then you remove a 9-inch strip, preferably with a cutoff saw, to arrive at the required 41-inch width.

A cheaper method is to assemble eight 96-inch-long vertical-grain-fir 2 × 6s, as shown in drawing 1. Hint: Assemble four of the pieces, then the remaining four, and, finally, the two halves. This will minimize the possi-

Table-saw top is flush with bench top so you can have full length and width for support. There is space around the saw for easy attachment of rip fence and guard. A box placed on the shelf below the saw will catch sawdust.

Ten-inch band saw is bolted to piece that is cut out of lower left-hand shelf, where it is stored when not in use. To use the saw, you lift out the bench-top cutout and put in the mounted saw.

Bench-top cutout is secured with two ¼-by-2-inch flathead machine screws that thread into T nuts installed in support cleats. Same screws anchor band-saw plate when the tool is in use.

Belt sander-grinder is bolted to the underside of its pivoting panel, near hinges: Pull it up for use, then lower for storage. Be sure to use the rubber feet that are supplied with some tools.

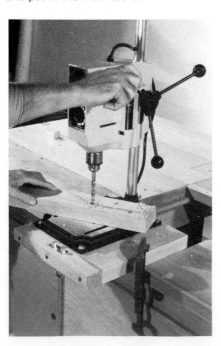

Plate for drill press is two pieces (above) so you can stand close to tool in use (left) and still have space to lower it. Panel with drill uses Soss hinges; the other panel uses continuous hinge. Tool plates can be anchored with a C-clamp. Handles for flip-ups are U-bolts (recessed in grooves).

Flip-up panels must lie flat on bench top when tool is stored. Recessed, heavy-duty Soss hinges (upper left) make this possible. They come with a template so you can locate holes accurately. Author installed two quick-release Record woodworking vises with adjustable dogs on edges of bench.

Seven-by-38-inch lathe becomes functional when hinged lathe shelf is swung up level with bench top. Shelf is supported by brackets that tighten under it for use, then swing under 3-inch benchtop overlap when shelf is down.

Disc sander-grinder pivots out over the lathe shelf when the lathe is down. If there's water in the trough, be sure to empty it before lowering the grinder.

Shelves store extra tools. (Install T nuts in underside of bench top—even in pivoting panels—to mount them for use; countersink holes and plug with flathead screws.) Sides and back of bench are open for access. To move bench you lower casters (Sears Craftsman); when they're up, workbench rests on floor.

bility of the assembly bowing under clamp pressure.

Next, construct the substructure. Cut the rails, cross rails, end rail, and legs to length. Drawing 2 shows how to assemble these parts.

Next step: Place the top so that it overlaps the substructure by 3 inches on all sides. Anchor it with No. 12-by-2-inch screws driven into the rails and cross rails. Space the screws 12 to 14 inches apart, and drive them through holes counterbored about 3/4 inch deep. Fill the holes with wood plugs.

The bench top in drawing 2 shows the tool cutouts. Different brands of each tool are similar in size, but you'd be wise to examine individual tools to be sure the cutout sizes will be usable. The openings can be formed with a saber saw, but I used a router because of the resulting smooth edges. To make the cuts, I tack-nailed guides to the bench top and followed them with a router equipped with a template guide. It's best to make repeat passes, deepening the groove about 1/4 inch each time. Work with a 1/4-inch router bit. This reduces the size of the cutout panels, so you must compensate by gluing on 1/4-inch-thick strips of wood to fill the gaps.

The piece cut out for the table saw is discarded. The piece that is removed when the band saw is in use rests on cleats. The band saw itself is mounted on an identical piece cut from the lower shelf (drawing 2), where it rests when not in use.

The remaining three cutout panels are hinged so they can pivot, sewing-machine style, to the use position. These openings require cleats, which should extend into the opening 1/2 inch or so and should be opposite the hinge end, except for the two-piece drill-press panel. Here the cleats run the long dimension of the opening.

Finishing

Sand individual pieces before assembling. When the bench is complete or at any stage where you wish to use it, do a final sanding with fine sandpaper. Apply a liberal coat of sanding sealer to all surfaces following package directions. Sand once more when the sealer is thoroughly dry, and, after removing the dust with a tack cloth, apply a second coat. Wipe off the excess, and wait at least 24 hours for the second coat to dry. Then sand again. Remove the dust, and coat the bench liberally with paste wax, rubbing it to a polish—*by R.J. DeCristoforo. Drawings by Gerhard Richter.*

fanciful functional fences

Picket, board, or post-and-rail—these are the usual constructions chosen for a wood fence. But as this spectrum of striking designs shows, a fence can take many forms—all of them functional. The fence's role can vary according to your needs, such as defining an area, framing a view, or perhaps enclosing a site for privacy.

1 Brick-post-serpentine

2 Staggered-box-beam

3 Two-tiered-louver

4 Trellis-shaded-slat

5 Post-and-beam

6 Board-and-batten

7 Lattice-top-board

All but one of the redwood fences in this portfolio provide privacy, in varying degrees. The louvered fence in photo 3 gives the feeling of seclusion while admitting glimpses of the view beyond. The stepped-board fence (7) presents a massive barrier to the outside, but its lattice top lightens the look.

Erecting a privacy fence means making a trade-off between ventilation and seclusion. Erect too ponderous a fence, and you risk creating an airless outdoor room. But a rugged windbreak makes sense for a site where strong prevailing winds make outdoor living uncomfortable. When designing a massive fence, be aware that the more it cuts off the winds, the stronger the fence must be.

The staggered-box-beam fence (2) is the one nonprivacy fence shown. But it illustrates a quality shared by all of these fences: It is overbuilt for its function. Though it evokes a massive sculpture, the fence was erected to frame the view while setting off a specific spot on the site. This

1 Brick-post-serpentine

Fence fastens to brick via steel hangers embedded during construction of posts. This technique would also work with concrete-block posts. To attach the fence to existing masonry, an angle bracket must be lag-screwed to a lead anchor inserted into a mortar joint.

2 Staggered-box-beam

The stepped platforms of these timber towers serve as seats and as plant rests. Like most of the other fences in this article, this one could be constructed of weather-resistant, pressure-treated lumber instead of the garden-grade redwood that was used here.

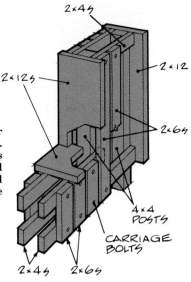

3 Two-tiered-louver

For a neat-looking fence, the louvers should be nailed in place. First nail a triangular block cut from a 2 × 4 next to the post, then set the 1 × 6 louver in place and nail to the block. Nail an angle-cut 2 × 2 against the louver. Another triangular block at the far corner completes the row.

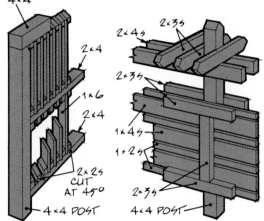

4 Trellis-shaded-slat

Cracks between slats admit air; trellis top provides dappled shade. Left untreated, redwood weathers to a driftwood gray. To stabilize color at buckskin tan, builder applied two coats of clear water repellent, brushing first coat onto all surfaces before assembly.

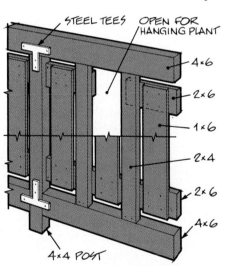

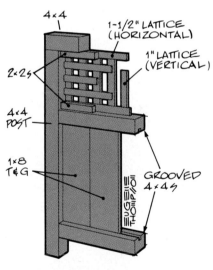

5 Post-and-beam

Floating battens nailed to a 2 × 6 give fence a solid look. The 2 × 6s are face-nailed to center posts and toenailed to end posts. Heavy hardware enhances rugged look while adding support. Hanging plant provides whimsical note to otherwise-serious structure.

6 Board-and-batten

Timbers atop this fence extend out to define a carport on the other side. The timbers can double as supports for hanging plants. To provide a mid-fence cutout for a hanging plant without losing privacy, the circular frame was boxed and the inside painted white.

7 Lattice-top-board

Grooves in 4 × 4 rails accept 1 × 8 slats, making a super-solid privacy fence. Design is only practical with moisture-resistant redwood and pressure-treated lumber; other woods would rot. Lattice top lightens somber look of fence while admitting light and air.

crenelated fence is actually architecture—the hefty pillars have a striking visual impact and buttress the design of the house.

The undulating appearance of the brick-pillared fence (1) was also planned by an architect. The serpentine-looking slats play against the stolid sturdiness of the brick pillars. The sap-streaked slats were carefully alternated to produce the look; the tree poking through the fence enhances the playful illusion of these creative elements.

Another example of an architect's fancy, the floating battens of the post-and-beam fence (5) make it look even more massive on the exterior. Because this fence's function is to shield a site elbowed by a busy street, the fortress illusion sends a signal to passing autos.

The portfolio presented here gives just a sampling of the fanciful designs possible when fences are viewed as architecture as well as enclosure—*by Susan Renner-Smith.* *Drawings by Eugene Thompson.*

high-rise planter deck

Rising above rolling New Jersey woodland is a garden on a redwood deck. The high garden provides a protected planting area for herbs, vegetables, and annual flowers —a welcome respite from marauding groundhogs, deer, and rabbits. I designed the deck as an architectonic complement to a colonial-style tract house. The bold angled walls, formed by the 3-foot-high planters, create two "rooms" for alfresco dining and sunbathing. Each room has a "window" defined by a section of open railing. The deck, 9 feet above the sloping site, is reached by a redwood stairway from the driveway and by a door from the utility room.

I use the colonnaded covered space under the deck to protect summering house plants and for a shady seating area; 8-inch-diameter Wolmanized utility poles create the shady loggia. The poles rest on pins sunk into 2-by-2-foot concrete footings that extend below the frost line. Double beams bolted together are notched into the

Nine-foot-high columns support planter deck and provide a shady loggia underneath (facing page). Deck has two activity areas: one for dining, another for sunbathing (top photo). The 2 × 8 redwood ledger plate, bolted to house, has joist hangers nailed to it, which support 2 × 8 redwood joists (above, left). Columns rest on concrete footings, which extend below frost line (above, middle). Tops of columns were cut off level to support planters (right).

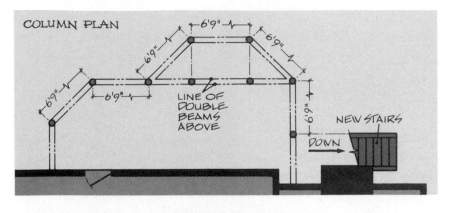

COLUMN PLAN

6'9" 6'9" 6'9"

6'9"

6'9" 6'9"

LINE OF DOUBLE BEAMS ABOVE

NEW STAIRS

DOWN

6'9"

DECK PLAN

PLANTERS

PLANTERS RAIL

RAIL

GAS BARBECUE

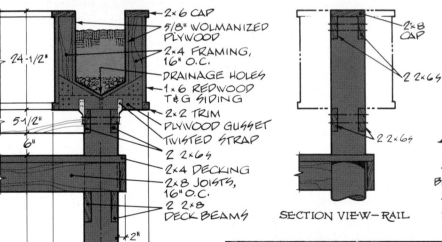

2×6 CAP

5/8" WOLMANIZED PLYWOOD

2×4 FRAMING, 16" O.C.

24-1/2"

DRAINAGE HOLES

1×6 REDWOOD T&G SIDING

2×2 TRIM

PLYWOOD GUSSET

TWISTED STRAP

5-1/2"

2 2×6s

6"

2×4 DECKING

2×8 JOISTS, 16" O.C.

2 2×8 DECK BEAMS

2"

12" 12"

8" DIA. UTILITY POLE

9'2"

1/2" DIA. SILL ANCHOR BOLT

8"

3'6"

12"

24" × 24" CONCRETE FOOTING

SECTION VIEW—PLANTER

104

SECTION VIEW—RAIL

2×8 CAP

2 2×6s

2 2×6s

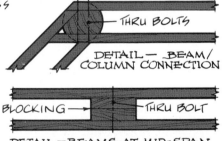

THRU BOLTS

DETAIL—BEAM/ COLUMN CONNECTION

BLOCKING

THRU BOLT

DETAIL—BEAMS AT MID-SPAN

poles to form a continuous column capital. All bolts and nails are hot-dipped galvanized. Wood blocking bolted at the midpoint of the spans provides structural integrity. I specified shallow 2 × 8 redwood beams and joists to keep the underside of the deck as high as possible. The poles continue through the beams to support another set of double 2 × 8 beams, which support the redwood planters. The 16-inch-on-center 2 × 8 joists rest in joist hangers nailed to a ledger plate bolted to the house. The 2 × 4 redwood decking is laid diagonally across the joists at a 45-degree angle. Rather than attaching the decking with the usual flathead galvanized nails, I used 10-penny buttonhead nails suggested by the builder, Allan Sheppard of North Plainfield, New Jersey. These give a unique, finished look.

The planters, framed and sheathed in redwood, are lined with Wolmanized plywood. I coated the inside face of the plywood with Karnak Asphaltic DL emulsion No. 330 to protect it from constant moisture. Half-inch holes drilled into the bottom of each planter section permit drainage—*by Amy Delson, Architect, A.I.A. Design by the author. Drawings by Eugene Thompson.*

Planters were built in modules. After precutting components, builder set up a jig and nailed together frame sections, bracing with plywood. These were toe-nailed 16 inches on center to 2 × 8 beams. Frames were sheathed inside with 1/2-inch Wolmanized plywood, on the outside with 1 × 6 redwood siding.

butcher-block patio stool

These butcher-block bar stools will enliven any existing deck or outdoor serving area.

To make a stool, first cut a 12-inch-diameter disc out of ¾-inch pieces of exterior plywood. Lay seven short 2 × 4s (7 to 15 inches long) on edge, separated with ⅜-inch-plywood spacers. Find the center of each of the 2 × 4s. From these points, measure down from the tops of each a distance of 1¾ inches. Bore a ⁷⁄₁₆-inch hole, centered on this mark, through all the pieces, including the spacers. Now assemble the 2 × 4s and spacers with a threaded rod and nuts. On the assembly draw a circle which is bisected by the threaded rod and tangent to the outside surfaces of the two end 2 × 4s. Cut with a band saw.

Use a saber saw at an angle to cut the top edge of the 2 × 4s. Use a rotary sander with a coarse abrasive disc to smooth the corners, then finish with a belt or orbital sander. Assemble the stool and seat as shown—*by Joseph W. Robicheau. Drawings by Carl De Groote.*

Attractive butcher-block-like bar stool can be left unfinished or stained to match a deck or other outdoor furniture.

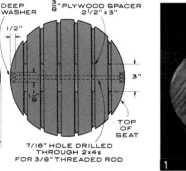

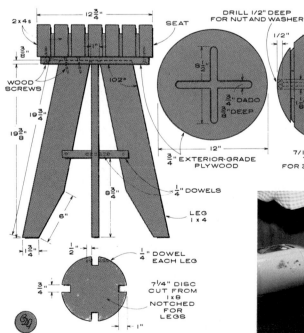

Stool legs fit into the slots on the plywood disc (1). Inside edge of legs must be ½ inch from the center of the disc. Fasten each leg to the plywood disc with two countersunk flathead wood screws (2). Drill ¼-inch hole through the edge of the center reinforcing disc. Apply glue to ¼-by-3-inch dowels, then tap them into place (3) and trim excess with chisel. Secure the stool-top assembly with four countersunk flathead wood screws.

compact patio sports center

Here's the most active storage unit you can build for your backyard or driveway. Our sports center unfolds in a variety of ways to become: a regulation-size table for table tennis, a basketball court complete with regulation-height hoop, or a backboard for tennis, paddleball, racquetball, or handball practice. And when you're through, it all folds back up into a weathertight 2-by-4-by-

Folded up, above, the sports center occupies just 2 by 4 by 8 feet of space in your backyard. But it unfolds to provide a basketball hoop, a full-size Ping-Pong table, and a backboard for handball or tennis practice.

Construction

Assemble the cabinet as shown, using 1½-inch nails driven through the plywood and ¾-inch framing cleats. Clinch the ends and hammer them flush on the inside. Assemble the top, bottom, and sides to the box back with glue, nails, and framing cleats: Vertical cleats are nailed to the ¼-inch back panel, flush with the side edges of the panel. Then nail the 1 × 4s around the inside of the box, flush at the front.

To mount the doors, first hang the outer door by mounting the 3-inch butt hinges as shown, recessing one wing into the right-hand 1 × 4 and the other into the edge of the plywood, using 2-inch screws to sink securely into edge grain. (To avoid splitting the ply, predrill to start the screws.) Mount the top hinge 5 inches down from the top and the bottom hinge 5 inches up from the bottom (with the center hinge 3 inches below the center). Remove the outer door, lay it down finished side up, and place the middle door next to it. Position the hinges as shown, recessing them down

flush with the plywood surface (and puttying over later for a smooth surface, using auto-body putty). The hinge pins will stick out a little, but will not be in the play area. Whenever screw tips stick out the back side, nip them off.

Bend gate hinges as shown to mount the inner door, hang the door, then cut the notches shown to allow the door to swing back for Ping-Pong clearance. Round off the front corner edges of the box to allow further door swing. The box should be anchored with ⅜-inch bolts or lags through a 1 × 4 cleat, and the rear wall anchored to a solid wall or eave to keep it upright when you're opening and closing doors.

To close, fold the inner door in, then fold the middle and outer door together. Mount a sliding barrel bolt to the outer door and the front of the left 1 × 4. Mount one half of a barrel bolt to the middle door at the upper and lower left-hand corners, then mount the other halves of the locks along the right-hand edge of the inner door (when opened out).

8-foot cabinet with enough room inside to conveniently store bats, balls, and racquets as well.

It can be built in sections, beginning with the outer cabinet.

To lock the backboard fully open, first swing the outer and middle doors aside as a unit. Then, open the inner door, fold back the middle door and—while holding the outer and inner doors back—place the edge of the middle door flush with the inner door, and lock flat.

Add the Ping-Pong table

To mount the slide holding the hinges for the center panel, drill and mount the 3/8-inch bolts in the counter top as shown, using the 6-by-36-inch cleat and allowing the bolt ends to stick up. The slide is secured with flat washers and wing nuts.

For a smooth playing surface, the table wing hinges have to be on the bottom of the panels. The gate hinges holding the center legs are mounted to the upper surface, but are inset into the plywood and puttied along the side edge to permit a smooth surface within the playing boundaries.

To fold the table back into the cabinet, loosen the wing nuts on the slide, remove the four end legs by pulling hinge pins, then fold the center leg over onto the top. Lift the center panel, allowing the wings to fold underneath. Now, push in on the assembly to recess the slide, then fold the assembly up inside. Store the end legs in the ball locker. Reverse these steps to unfold.

And now, for basketball

To hang the basketball backboard, start out by gluing and nailing the ceiling reinforcer to the bottom side of the cabinet top (driving nails spaced about 5 inches apart and clinching on the underside), centered with the central cutout of the front edge exactly 9 5/8 inches in from the front of the top 1 × 4. Next, fasten the 6-by-15-inch hinge mount to the bottom of this with its front edge flush with the indent. Mount heavy 8-inch iron angle brackets to the 5-by-by-15-inch bracket mount with four 1/4-inch bolts. Attach the bracket mount to the hinge mount with hinges, as shown. Swing the brackets forward and up until they hit against the bottom of the top 1 × 4. Mark this placement and use a saw and chisel to cut notches so the brackets can fit up flush into the 1 × 4. Now swing the brackets up and close the doors. Mount the backboard holder to the front of the brackets with the bottom edge of the holder down 1 inch below the top of the cabinet. Mount the wings (with hinges on the back) to the sides of the holder so their bottom edges are exactly 1 inch above the bottom of the holder and exactly aligned with the top surface of the box.

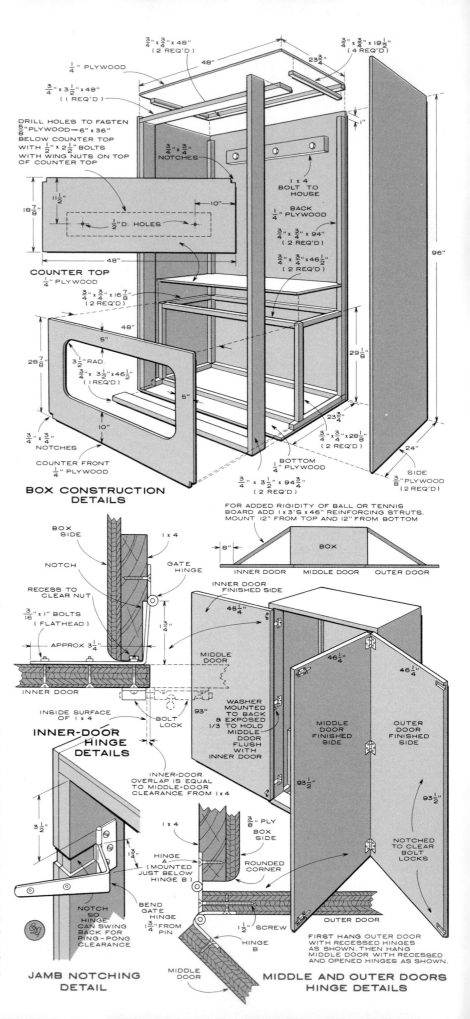

Swing out the overlapping side doors to flank the middle door, and you've got a practice backboard over 11 feet wide and nearly 8 feet high. Other gear stows behind center doors, inside weathertight box.

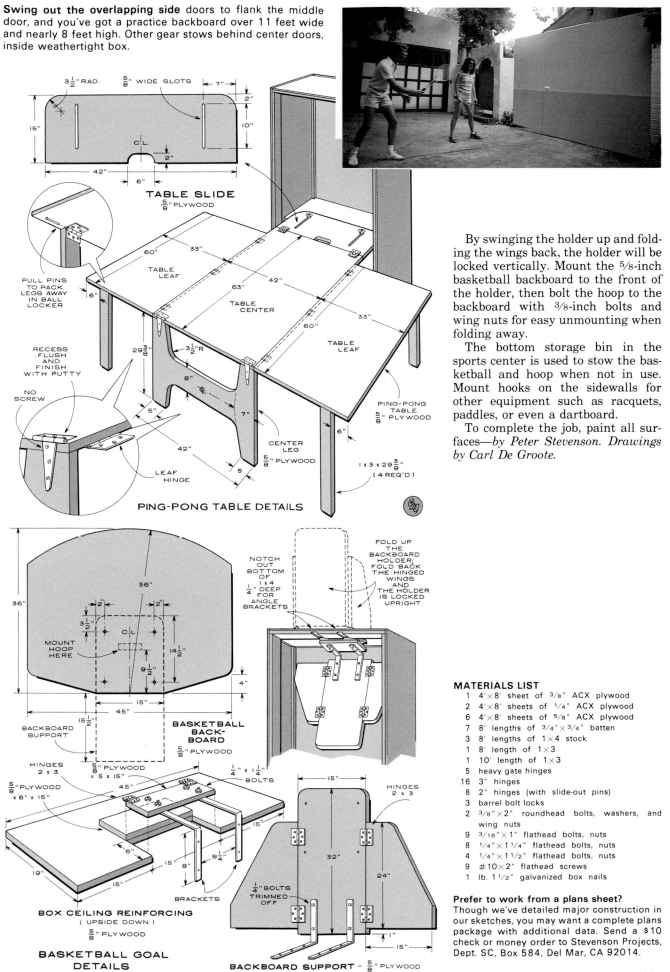

TABLE SLIDE
5/8" PLYWOOD

3 1/2" RAD.   5/8" WIDE SLOTS   7"   2"   15"   10"   C.L.   2"   42"   6"

PULL PINS TO PACK LEGS AWAY IN BALL LOCKER

RECESS FLUSH AND FINISH WITH PUTTY

NO SCREW

TABLE LEAF   60"   33"
TABLE CENTER   63"   42"
TABLE LEAF   60"   33"

29 3/8"   3 1/2"R   8"   7"   5"   42"   5"

CENTER LEG   5/8" PLYWOOD

LEAF HINGE

PING-PONG TABLE   5/8" PLYWOOD

6"

1 x 3 x 29 3/8"   (4 REQ'D)

PING-PONG TABLE DETAILS

By swinging the holder up and folding the wings back, the holder will be locked vertically. Mount the 5/8-inch basketball backboard to the front of the holder, then bolt the hoop to the backboard with 3/8-inch bolts and wing nuts for easy unmounting when folding away.

The bottom storage bin in the sports center is used to stow the basketball and hoop when not in use. Mount hooks on the sidewalls for other equipment such as racquets, paddles, or even a dartboard.

To complete the job, paint all surfaces—*by Peter Stevenson. Drawings by Carl De Groote.*

36"   36"   2"   2"   3 1/2"   C.L.   14 1/2"   9 1/2"   4"   15"   45"   15 1/2"

MOUNT HOOP HERE

BACKBOARD SUPPORT

HINGES 2 x 3

5/8" PLYWOOD x 5 x 15"

BASKETBALL BACK-BOARD
5/8" PLYWOOD

NOTCH OUT BOTTOM OF 1 x 4 1/4" DEEP FOR ANGLE BRACKETS

FOLD UP THE BACKBOARD HOLDER; FOLD BACK THE HINGED WINGS AND THE HOLDER IS LOCKED UPRIGHT

5/8" PLYWOOD x 6" x 15"   45"   1/4" x 1 1/4" BOLTS   15"   15"   6"   15"   8 1/4"   8"   19"   15"

HINGES 2 x 3   32"   24"   1/4" BOLTS TRIMMED OFF   15"   1"   15"

BRACKETS

BOX CEILING REINFORCING
(UPSIDE DOWN)
5/8" PLYWOOD

BASKETBALL GOAL DETAILS

BACKBOARD SUPPORT - 5/8" PLYWOOD

MATERIALS LIST
- 1   4'×8' sheet of 3/8" ACX plywood
- 2   4'×8' sheets of 1/4" ACX plywood
- 6   4'×8' sheets of 5/8" ACX plywood
- 7   8' lengths of 3/4"×3/4" batten
- 3   8' lengths of 1×4 stock
- 1   8' length of 1×3
- 1   10' length of 1×3
- 5   heavy gate hinges
- 16 3" hinges
- 8   2" hinges (with slide-out pins)
- 3   barrel bolt locks
- 2   3/8"×2" roundhead bolts, washers, and wing nuts
- 9   3/16"×1" flathead bolts, nuts
- 8   1/4"×1 1/4" flathead bolts, nuts
- 4   1/4"×1 1/2" flathead bolts, nuts
- 9   #10×2" flathead screws
- 1   lb. 1 1/2" galvanized box nails

Prefer to work from a plans sheet?
Though we've detailed major construction in our sketches, you may want a complete plans package with additional data. Send a $10 check or money order to Stevenson Projects, Dept. SC, Box 584, Del Mar, CA 92014.

all-season skylight gazebo

Build this cozy hideaway in your backyard and you may never want to leave home. Measuring only 16 feet square, the post-and-beam gazebo offers:

● Generous space for a picnic table and LP-gas or charcoal grill.

● A food-preparation counter with sink and running water.

● Storage for cookware, plus a space to tuck away the 12 panels that enclose the gazebo in winter.

The interior's light and airy looks are enhanced by a 30-inch-square skylight that tops off the roof. Solar screening covers three sides to keep the enclosure glare- and bug-free. Because the screening blocks direct sunshine, the interior should stay cooler, as well.

While most post-and-beam structures are relatively easy to build, the gazebo requires some construction skills. Eight 4 × 4 posts, set in concrete footings to the frostline, provide the foundation; these must be accurately positioned.

Assembly then proceeds from floor to roof, roughly in that order. Install support framing for deck, 2×4 top plates, and remainder of 4×4 posts. The floor—2×6 tongue-and-groove decking—ensures that insects can't come from below, either (no air spaces between deck boards are needed in a roofed structure). The roof requires two trusses, as detailed in the construction drawing—*by Richard Stepler. Design by Dave Swartwout. Drawings by Carl De Groote. Photos by Tony Romano.*

Entry to gazebo is via short deck-walk. Normally, siding on left would be removed for warm-weather use.

Storm-window hangers are used to mount the removable siding. We used two hangers per panel.

Handling the panels—Masonite's prestained Woodsman planked siding—is a two-person, twice-a-year task.

You can escape from the elements and the insects inside the solar-screened gazebo. The post-and-beam structure's interior is flooded with light, thanks to skylight and three "open" sides.

Conveniences include food-preparation counter, sink with hot and cold running water, plenty of storage, and propane gas grill.

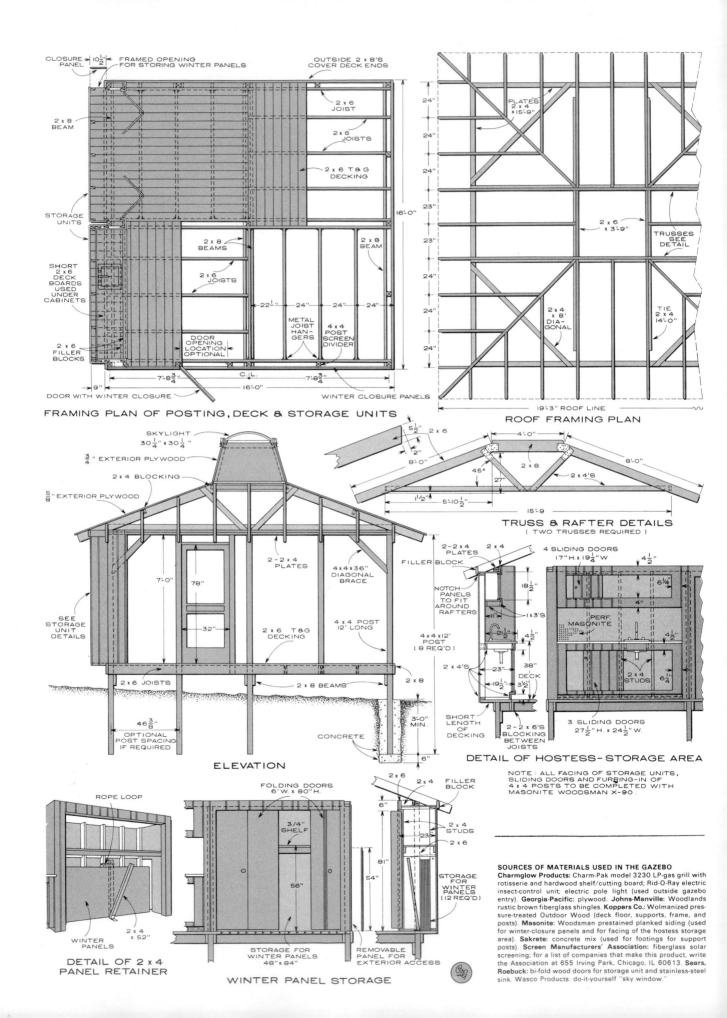

FRAMING PLAN OF POSTING, DECK & STORAGE UNITS

ROOF FRAMING PLAN

TRUSS & RAFTER DETAILS
(TWO TRUSSES REQUIRED)

ELEVATION

DETAIL OF HOSTESS-STORAGE AREA

NOTE: ALL FACING OF STORAGE UNITS, SLIDING DOORS AND FURRING-IN OF 4 x 4 POSTS TO BE COMPLETED WITH MASONITE WOODSMAN X-90.

DETAIL OF 2 x 4 PANEL RETAINER

WINTER PANEL STORAGE

SOURCES OF MATERIALS USED IN THE GAZEBO
Charmglow Products: Charm-Pak model 3230 LP-gas grill with rotisserie and hardwood shelf/cutting board; Rid-O-Ray electric insect-control unit; electric pole light (used outside gazebo entry). **Georgia-Pacific:** plywood. **Johns-Manville:** Woodlands rustic brown fiberglass shingles. **Koppers Co.:** Wolmanized pressure-treated Outdoor Wood (deck floor, supports, frame, and posts). **Masonite:** Woodsman prestained planked siding (used for winter-closure panels and for facing of the hostess storage area). **Sakrete:** concrete mix (used for footings for support posts). **Screen Manufacturers' Association:** fiberglass solar screening; for a list of companies that make this product, write the Association at 655 Irving Park, Chicago, IL 60613. **Sears, Roebuck:** bi-fold wood doors for storage unit and stainless-steel sink. **Wasco Products:** do-it-yourself "sky window."

easy-access woodshed

How many cold winter nights have found you scurrying out to the woodpile to grab fuel for a dying fire, hoping that the logs weren't soggy as you swore with every step that there must be a better way? There is, and it's as close at hand as your deck.

This easy-to-build woodshed occu-pies an end of a deck, offering easy access from your house and close proximity to your fireplace. The wood-shed not only stores firewood within arm's reach, it also keeps it dry through the winter. But the bonuses of this woodshed don't stop there.

Because the woodshed uses the deck's railing as framing members, you save money on material and you save time: One weekend is all you will need to build and stock it.

Firewood is often a nesting place for insects such as carpenter ants and powder-post beetles. Though your fire-wood will be in contact with your deck and adjacent to your house, you can stave off infestation by treating the

deck and the lumber for the shed with preservative. If your deck is raised, you have all the protection you need against termites, which make their homes in mud.

Deck widths and railing heights vary, of course, but here are guidelines and a materials list necessary to build a woodshed 12 feet long, 5½ feet high (at the peak), and 4 feet deep—large enough to hold roughly one-third of a cord of wood.

You'll need about 75 feet of 2 × 4 for posts, beams, and rafters, and a 12-foot length of 2 × 6 for the ridge piece. I recommend fir, which is excellent for framing, or pine. You'll also need four 4-by-8-foot sheets of ⅜-inch exterior-grade plywood and a roll of 15-pound building paper. Any wood destined for outdoor use should be protected from the elements. The two most common methods are painting and staining, although I chose to protect—and dress up—the front posts of my shed with shingles.

Roofing and siding are a matter of choice, though you might want to match the shed's roofing and siding to those on the house. If you shingle the whole woodshed, as I did, plan on five bundles of shakes and use 1½-inch shingle nails. Actually, I used panels of Masonite imitation shakes left over from a roofing project. Asphalt shingles keep costs down, but using them

sacrifices looks. Total cost of the woodshed: about $200, with $125 going to the shingles alone.

Building it

Construction is fast and easy—you don't have to cut many pieces of lumber, and of those cut, many are the same size. Also, much of the framing is already in place because the deck rail forms the back wall and outer end frame of the shed.

The rest of the frame is built from posts made of two 2 × 4s nailed together and 2 × 4 beams and rafters. To finish framing, butt one end post against the house, leaving a slight air gap for circulation, and set the front posts parallel with the existing rail posts. A long mason's level is a reliable, fast way to check the level of the framing. Use 16d nails (all hardware on an outdoor project should be galvanized to prevent rust) to anchor the posts and beams in place.

I figured my rafter angles just by eye and then cut a sample pair to fit. If you prefer to measure the rafters, keep in mind that you'll want rain and snow to slide down the backside of the roof, away from deck and house. A steep-pitched roof in the front and a longer rear slope calls for an off-center roof, which adds measurably to the shed's appearance.

The first set of rafters I cut served

as templates for the other rafters. Although rafters are usually 16 inches on center, I used eight pairs and varied the spacing from 15 to 18 inches on center. I did this to correspond as closely as possible with the overlap of the posts and beams.

When the rafters are cut, use a circular saw to make quick work of notching them. You can knock out the wedge left by the kerfs with a hammer and chisel. Attach rafters at opposite ends of the ridge piece with 10d nails, and lift the ridge into place. Toenail the rest of the rafters, and enclose the shed with plywood boards anchored with 16d nails. I chose to have one side of my woodshed overhang the deck, so I had to notch the plywood (and shingle) to fit over the railing.

Shingles require an underlay of building paper, but I decided to tack down a sheet of polyurethane—another remnant of projects past—which has worked just fine. The imitation shakes I chose, unlike real shingles, don't require a double course. Instead, strips of shingles are nailed along the eave line, and the panels are then laid in courses upward—just like conventional shingles. The shakes go up quickly. As a finishing touch, I decided to add a dash of style to my woodshed by nailing the last row of shingles into a Boston cap—*by Bernard W. Powell.*

Begin by toenailing 2 × 4s in place (left). Nail rafters to both ends of the 2 × 6 ridge pole, and lift the beam into place (above). Nail remaining rafters in place (below left), and enclose with plywood. Tack paper in place before adding roofing and siding (below).

elevated deck with spa

The view across Long Island Sound to the Connecticut coastline can be magnificent—particularly if you're gazing out, glass of wine in hand, from a second-story heated spa high above the north-shore beaches.

That's just the way a Long Island couple wanted to enjoy their waterfront view—and entertain friends. But there were complications: The backyard was steeply sloped and not private. And the small rear windows of the cottage-cum-Tudor-style home didn't afford much of a view.

The solution? A 675-square-foot elevated deck that features:
● A year-round hot tub.
● A raised, glassed-in sun deck.
● An entertainment area with built-in seating.
● A decorative—but structurally necessary—fascia.
● A cooking area with adjacent built-in counter top.
● French doors that lead from den to deck.

The problems were both structural and aesthetic. The deck, 15 feet above the ground, had to support an elevated cedar-stave spa 6 feet in diameter that, when filled with 630 gallons of water and eight people, would weigh 6,500 pounds. Heavy-duty support was needed from the footings, posts, and beams (see construction drawings). For additional support—and for several other reasons—I added a fascia, a horizontal band that acts as a structural diaphragm to brace the deck against racking and twisting tendencies.

Although many deck builders use cross-bracing between posts, that design would have left the deck open—and easily visible from neighboring yards. The fascia ensures privacy while providing the structure with a sense of individuality and offering a visual balance to the house's dominating rear elevation.

The deck runs the full width of the house—another way of integrating the addition with the home's massive rear facade. The deck's length made possible four entrances from the house: the kitchen, the screened porch, the yard, and the den, where elegant French doors were a welcome replacement for a small window.

I began construction by pouring the footings and installing the posts. I used 8 × 8 posts so I could cut seats for the beams and create a sense of equal scale between deck and house. But 6 × 6 posts, as shown in the drawings, would do the job with less bulk. Major beams are composites of three 2 × 12s at 7-foot centers. For additional support under the spa, I installed a grid of 2 × 12 joists laid 12 inches on center.

The fascia consists of ¾-inch exterior plywood nailed post to post. I then framed this in beveled 3 × 4s and 1 × 4 trim.

The observation/sun deck increases the sense of spaciousness and adds a distinctive touch. I set this deck three steps above the main deck: That allows comfortable seating on the tub's 12-inch-wide rim. Next, the ¼-inch tempered glazing was installed and

Footings were set 3 feet below grade: 2½-by-2½-foot footings for under tub, 2-by-2-foot elsewhere, topped with piers (top). Posts were nailed into ¼-inch bent-steel-plate base anchors. The 4 × 8 ledger was fastened to foundation by ¾-inch-diameter bolts. Beams were toe-nailed to ledger, and joists were strapped to foundation's top plate with 16-gauge steel (above). Seats in posts took beams, secured with ¾-inch bolts (above photo, section at far right).

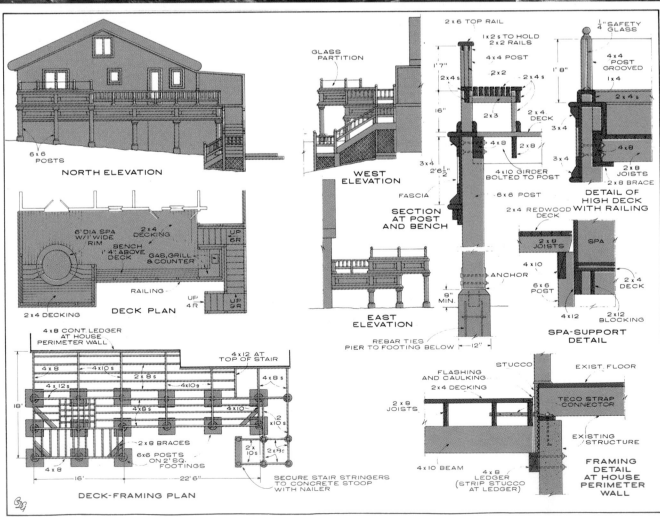

NORTH ELEVATION

6 x 6 POSTS

DECK PLAN

6' DIA SPA W/1' WIDE RIM

2 x 4 DECKING

BENCH 1' 4" ABOVE DECK

GAS, GRILL & COUNTER

RAILING

UP 6R

UP 9R

UP 4R

2 x 4 DECKING

DECK-FRAMING PLAN

4 x 8 CONT. LEDGER AT HOUSE PERIMETER WALL

4 x 8

4 x 10 s

4 x 12 s

2 x 8 s

4 x 10 s

4 x 12 AT TOP OF STAIR

4 x 8 s

4 x 8 s

4 x 8 s

4 x 10

2 x 10 s

18'

2 x 8 BRACES

6 x 6 POSTS ON 2' SQ. FOOTINGS

4 x 8

2 x 10 s

2 x 8

SECURE STAIR STRINGERS TO CONCRETE STOOP WITH NAILER

16'

22' 6"

WEST ELEVATION

GLASS PARTITION

EAST ELEVATION

SECTION AT POST AND BENCH

2 x 6 TOP RAIL

1 x 2 s TO HOLD 2 x 2 RAILS

4 x 4 POST

1' 7"

2 x 4 s

2 x 2

2 x 4 s

16"

2 x 3

2 x 4 DECK

4 x 8

2 x 8

3 x 4

2 x 6 1/2"

4 x 10 GIRDER BOLTED TO POST

FASCIA

6 x 6 POST

ANCHOR

8" MIN.

REBAR TIES PIER TO FOOTING BELOW

12"

DETAIL OF HIGH DECK WITH RAILING

1/4" SAFETY GLASS

4 x 4 POST GROOVED

1 x 4

2 x 4 s

3 x 4

4 x 8

3 x 4

2 x 8 JOISTS

2 x 8 BRACE

SPA-SUPPORT DETAIL

2 x 4 REDWOOD DECK

2 x 8 JOISTS

SPA

4 x 10

6 x 6 POST

2 x 4 DECK

4 x 12

2 x 12 BLOCKING

FRAMING DETAIL AT HOUSE PERIMETER WALL

STUCCO

EXIST. FLOOR

FLASHING AND CAULKING

2 x 4 DECKING

2 x 8 JOISTS

TECO STRAP CONNECTOR

EXISTING STRUCTURE

4 x 10 BEAM

4 x 8 LEDGER (STRIP STUCCO AT LEDGER)

Impressive-size deck has heated spa protected with rollable cedar-slat top and shielded by observation/sun deck with safety-glass enclosure (right). Built-in seating accommodates sun-hungry guests, and there's a convenient enclosed shower (top). Even grill area (left) features pleasant view. Note built-in counter top.

secured in quarter-round molding at the base and post extensions. This wind screen deflects gusts over the heads of tub users and allows a clear view of the beach front and water.

The owners planned on using the spa in all seasons, so all exposed plumbing had to be insulated and weatherized. A thermostat was installed under the deck to control the temperature. The gas heater is kept in the garage.

For the stairs, I used 2 × 12 stringers with 1½-by-1½-inch steel angles to receive treads of three 2 × 4s. Double 2 × 10s support the two landings.

I used simple wood-lattice screens to hide the underside of the stairs and deck. The balusters were 2 × 2s set between 2 × 6 rails. As a decorative touch—and to match the stairs to the windbreak—I capped the newel posts with spherical finials.

Built-in benches provide plenty of seating. The benches, which measure 16 inches high and 20 inches deep, were built from 2 × 4s set ½ inch apart within a frame of flat-laid 2 × 4s. Bench posts are 4 × 4s along the backs, 2 × 4s in front (see section) with beveled 2 × 4s as base plinths. The deck's top rail, which is built of continuous 2 × 6s with 1 × 2 stops and 2 × 2 balusters, stands about 36 inches high.

Finally, because the deck would be used at night, I installed concealed low-voltage lights under the steps and along the underside of the built-in seating. I also installed a single overhead fixture that has two sodium-vapor lamps and three electrical outlets. The deck was finished with Samuel Cabot's Driftwood Gray semi-transparent stain—*by Jack Hillbrand. Photos by Greg Sharko. Drawings by Carl De Groote.*

parquet deck

"These new deck tiles are ideal for the do-it-yourselfer," says Chicago architect Tom Hood. "Each tile is finished, so no cutting or sanding is required."

Hood designed his 16-by-24-foot deck around the 2-foot-square Moore-Tile. The mahogany tiles are approximately 1 inch thick and consist of eight slats stapled to three backer slats. Because South American mahogany is such a dense wood, there is no splintering problem, and the tiles are highly resistant to rot and insect damage.

A striking basket-weave-pattern deck is formed by laying mahogany tiles in alternating directions. The square tiles are especially suited for building rectangular-shaped decks. For contrast the builder used cedar for risers and edge trim. This deck sits on 4-by-4-inch poured-concrete posts, but pressure-treated wood posts can also be used. Sheet-metal framing anchors secure the posts to the pressure-treated beams that support the 2 × 8 joists. These joists must be spaced 12 inches on center instead of the usual 16-inch spacing.

At $10 to $12 a tile, this decking material costs about the same as redwood or pressure-treated lumber. But because of their size, the tiles are faster to install than standard decking. A Moore-Tile deck requires about 25 percent fewer fasteners than an equivalent-size plank deck. And it's easier to align 2-foot-square modules than it is to work with cumbersome 6-foot-long planks.

The square tile has other advantages, according to Hood. He first planned his deck on graph paper, using 2-foot squares as basic building blocks. He found uses for the versatile tiles as stair treads, vertical skirting, and walkways.

"If you lay out your deck in 2-foot increments and use standard-size lumber, you have a minimum of cutting and waste," Hood says. He framed his deck in No. 2 pressure-treated lumber and used cedar rails and posts for trim.

The framework is the most difficult part of any deck. With Moore-Tile you can hire a carpenter to erect the framework (especially if your location is on a sloping site), but you can save money by laying the decking yourself. (Of course, before beginning any deck installation you should also check local building codes.)

Crafting the checkerboard
Building the deck frame to support these tiles is done the same way you'd construct a standard lumber deck—except for joist spacing. The 1/2-inch tile slats require a joist every 12 inches for support instead of the more common 16-inches-on-center spacing. (This means you need about 30 percent more lumber for the joists. But as a bonus you get a sturdier deck.)

If you want the tiles flush with the deck edge, allow 9 3/4 inches instead of 10 1/2 inches between outer joists and the next joist. This adjustment will put the tile edge flush with the outside edge of the joist.

Installing the tiles is much like laying a tile floor except that you start along the outside edges of the deck instead of an inner wall. "Alternating tile direction creates a basket-weave pattern that hides minor errors," Hood says.

Lay the first tile at an outside corner, using a framing square. Then rough-lay the tiles along both edges of the deck. Trim tiles to fit when necessary. You can cut as much as needed when trimming the slats—but if you cut more than 3 inches across the slats, you'll cut off the backer slat. To keep slats in place while cutting, install a new backer slat inside the old one before you cut.

Moore-Tile can be nailed or screwed. "I found No. eight 1 3/4-inch brass flathead screws, bought in bulk at a hardware supplier, the most economical," says Hood. "We used 500 screws that cost around $50." The brass quickly tarnishes and blends in with the wood. Stainless-steel screws

Fastening holes must be predrilled (above). Cedar shims can be wedged under tiles if joist surfaces are irregular. Tiles require a screw per corner, but only two screws per tile are needed to mount for skirting (right). Cedar trim hides exposed edges of tile.

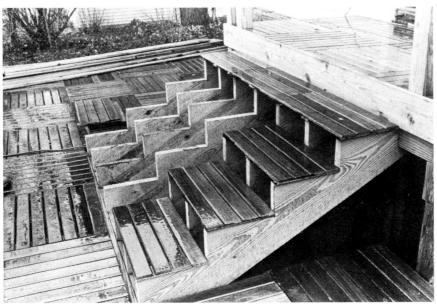

Match tiles for color after cutting to make stair treads. Predrill to prevent splitting. Though cedar was used for risers here, tiles may be used instead.

For walkways in low-traffic areas, such as alongside house (right), tiles can be laid right atop gravel bed contained in frame of pressure-treated wood (above). For heavy-traffic areas, excavate shallow trench to hold frame.

are a bit more expensive but will not tarnish with age like the brass.

Screw holes must be predrilled through the dense hardwood tile. Using two electric drills speeds the job. Keep a countersinking bit (Screwmate is a good one) in one for drilling the pilot holes, and a screwdriver bit in the other for quick installation of the four screws per tile.

Hood gave the deck tiles two coats of Thompson's Water Sealer, using a long-nap paint roller. One coat was applied before the tiles were laid, and the final coat was applied after the deck was completed.

What about maintenance? "If a deck is located under shade or sap trees, it's a good idea to remove leaves before winter to avoid discoloration," Hood says. "This happens on any type of decking but can be easily avoided."

Beyond decking

The versatile tiles are suited for more than decking. Cut in half, they make stair treads. Stringer spacing is the same 12-inches-on-center as that of the joists. Tiles can also be laid vertically to make a deck skirting.

Moore-Tile is also suited for creating walkways and even small patios. Because the mahogany tiles are rot resistant, they can be laid over a gravel bed or directly onto a plastic sheet if the walkway is not a high-traffic area.

For a walkway built on grade, use pressure-treated 2 × 4s—laid parallel and 24 inches apart—as a walkway frame. Hold the frame in place with wood stakes driven into the ground on the inside.

Nail 2-foot lengths of 2 × 4 across the frame at 4-foot intervals to hold the side rails parallel. Then place plastic between the 2 × 4s to hold back weeds. Fill with gravel, smoothing it to about 1 inch from the top of the 2 × 4s. Finally, insert the tiles, and backfill against the form if necessary.

The deck tiles have a variety of other uses, according to the importer (William G. Moore & Son Inc. of Delaware, 482 Manor Rd., Box 1278, Staten Island, NY 10314). The tiles can transform an urban "tar beach" into a handsome roof deck simply by applying flashing adhesive to the backer slats and pressing in place. The tiles can be screwed directly into a run-down existing deck once loose and broken slats are nailed in place. Finally, the tiles can be glued atop an existing concrete or flagstone patio. Or they can be fitted into a perimeter frame attached to the patio—*by Gene and Katie Hamilton.*

cocky catamaran

Spray flies off the hull like a jet from a fire hose (top) as the 4.9 meter scoots along at 15 knots. Advanced-design features include antidive planes (visible in photo above, just below hull-joining strut) and a drilled-out boom. For construction plans, send a $10 check or money order to Stevenson Projects, Box 584, Del Mar, CA 92014.

Water shoots off the lee bow as the sailboat speeds across the bay. It tacks, producing a classic rooster-tail wake—the signature of a high-speed catamaran. Yet this exciting performer is not a costly, advanced-design production boat but our latest home-built craft: the 4.9-meter catamaran. As it speeds along at up to 15 knots, it may not outpace the $4,000 craft that inspired its design—but it can make an impressive attempt. Best of all, this 16-footer costs less than $600 to build.

Like the Mini-Cat we built in 1980, our 4.9-meter has deep, high-aspect hulls—longer than they are wide by a ratio of 20:1. These skinny, symmetrical hulls are shaped to tack smoothly without a dagger board. The 110-square-foot mainsail also has a high aspect ratio for most-efficient sailing in brisk winds. Like the Mini-Cat, the 4.9-meter has an airfoil-shape wing mast (see diagram at end of chapter) that automatically pivots to face the wind. Internal halyards cut drag further.

But this catamaran differs from the Mini-Cat in more ways than length. The jib has an easy-handling club-foot rig. When tacking, you just steer while the 45-square-foot jib swings over on its own mini-boom, keeping a good shape that you can adjust later.

You can also adjust the pivoting wing mast's angle of attack: Simply tighten a turnbuckle. And you can tune the mainsail to the best airfoil shape for prevailing winds by adjusting the lines linking the sail's bottom batten to the boom. This perforated boom is both lighter and sportier-looking than conventional booms.

The 4.9-meter even boasts some features that you won't find on most production boats. The kickup rudders have lines running up inside the tiller for easier and safer lock-down at speed. (On more-conventional craft, you must raise the tiller for a moment to lock the rudders down—a risky maneuver at high speeds.)

A unique set of antidive planes attached to the inner face of each hull at the bow (see diagram) helps protect against pitchpoling. The airfoil-shape planes ride out of the water during normal sailing, but when the skinny hulls pierce a wave, the planes act like hydrofoils to pull the boat up, keeping the craft from pitching forward.

Another custom touch: Instead of mounting the main-

sheet pulley flush with the deck, as is standard, we inserted a spring between it and the deck. This keeps it from falling over when tacking and thus fouling the lines.

To transport the 4.9-meter, we modified our rugged wooden boat trailer. Details are included in our plans (see caption on opening page for ordering data). Once at the water, two people can carry the unrigged boat down the beach. Rigged, with rudders added, two people can still lift it into the water. And by unfastening the trampoline and loosening ten nuts, the whole boat can be disassembled for easy storage.

We were able to build the 16-foot cat using materials found at lumberyards and hardware stores—no marine-supply stocks are needed. The solid-lumber deck and bottom make hull construction easy. The hulls are the same sort of simple box section we used on the Mini-Cat. We mounted two stringers on the hull's outside to double as splash rails. For storage, we made hatches out of 4-inch rubber drain plugs with plastic drain caps for tops.

As usual, we made sails from tough, polyethylene tarp that's wide enough to require no sewing. The battens are pieces of plastic pipe inserted into pockets made from webbing used for lawn furniture.

The trampoline is also made from three layers of the tarp, with grommets as drain holes. All four edges of this deck are rolled around a 1 × 2 that's sandwiched between frame members.

A final clever touch: The folding lift handle for the mast is a standard kickup door stop—*by Susanne and Peter Stevenson. Drawing by Eugene Thompson.*

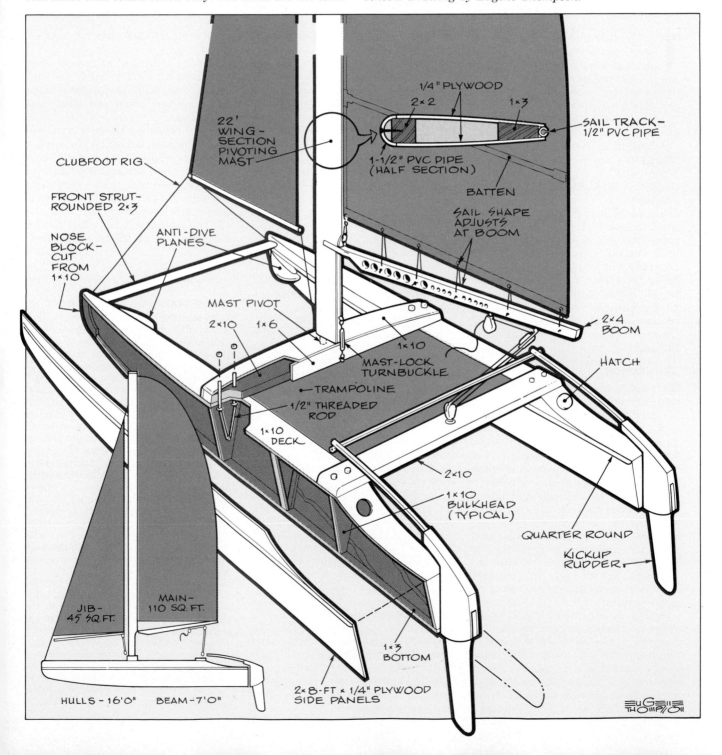

wood-epoxy construction

The handsome wooden boat you see here is more than five years old and has always been stored outside. Every other year we sand it lightly and roll on two coats of ultraviolet-shield marine varnish. That's all it takes to keep the boat sound and glowing.

A low-maintenance wooden boat? Indeed it is, and we built it ourselves. We've built others, too—from dories to five-ton sailboats—and so can you. The technique we use is the key to the low upkeep, for it encapsulates all the wood in epoxy. That seals out moisture—the source of most problems with wooden boats. The technique is also excellent for other projects, especially those that must live in a wet world. We've built oars, furniture, wind-generator vanes, stair banisters, fuel and water tanks, flowerpots, and the little hot tub you see on a succeeding page.

Why wood?

It's readily available, for one thing, and easy to work with common tools. It's good-looking, lightweight, strong, and stiff—when it's dry. When saturated with moisture, however, wood becomes heavy, and its strength may be reduced by half. The trick is to dry the wood and then seal it. But paint, varnish, and even fiberglass in polyester resins are not true moisture barriers. In time, enough moisture may penetrate them to cause weakening of the fibers and perhaps even dry rot. (Dry rot is a misnomer because the dry-rot fungi can only live in wood that is close to saturation point: 20-percent moisture).

Epoxy, on the other hand, is an excellent moisture barrier. As with the familiar epoxy adhesive you buy at the hardware store, you combine the epoxy resin and a hardener, and the mixture cures through polymerization. The liquid mix, with a viscosity slightly thicker than varnish,

changes to an impermeable solid when cured.

The epoxy is used both as an adhesive to bond mating parts and as a sealing finish for the entire structure. It forms tenacious bonds and is generally as flexible as the wood itself, so the structure can deflect without cracking the epoxy surface. The epoxy darkens the wood, but the wood retains its natural appearance; it can be sanded and varnished or painted. Because no moisture can get under the paint, cracking and lifting problems do not occur.

Boatbuilders call this technique cold-molding—as opposed to hot-molding, which uses large ovens to cure the structure. It has been developed and refined over the last decade by Gougeon Brothers, Inc., a boat-building firm in Bay City, Michigan. Initially, the company used the technique to build high-strength-to-weight-ratio ice boats for racing. Now it's used for everything from canoes and kayaks to today's state-of-the-art ocean racers.

Gougeon Brothers also formulates the epoxy and has developed a complete line of collateral products (called the WEST System). Included are fillers and fairing compounds with such names as microfibers (short cotton fibers that are added to the resin for bonding critical joints), coloidal silica (a fine powder used to control viscosity of the resin), and microballoons (hollow phenolic spheres used to make a low-density fairing), as well as fiberglass cloth, graphite powder, and a good deal more.

Our boat is an 8-foot-long Norwegian pram. With judicious use of light components, we built it to weigh less than 50 pounds—a comfortable weight for cartopping. The hull is only 1/4-inch thick, made of two laminations of 1/8-inch Western red cedar veneer. Building with laminations gives many advantages: You can orient the wood grain of each layer for maxi-

mum strength, and each can compensate for defects in the other. Veneers dry faster than thicker cuts of wood. They also bend more easily and to a smaller radius, so they can be built up on jigs of just about any shape and curvature.

A 1/4-inch-thick wooden hull may sound delicate, but when the laminations are applied and bonded with epoxy, the hull becomes a solid monocoque structure with surprising strength. It is a process that must be experienced; no description can convey the feeling you get when you lift a bonded hull off the building form.

Wood-epoxy-composite boat

Cold-molded boat is made over a male mold. The mold stations (transverse supports) are cut from plywood according to the plans (see text) and set up on a building form. Stringers are attached over the stations. Drawing 1 shows the transoms and keel ready to drop into cleats on the mold and the first two strips of 1/8-inch veneer being applied. Each veneer strip must be fitted to its neighbor—a simple process done by following the edge of the first strip with a compass and tracing a corresponding line on the mating strip. Trimming can be done with a plane or panel saw. Drawing 2 shows the forward end of the mold, with keel, transoms, and the first two veneer strips in place. The strips are secured with epoxy and stapled (through 40-mil plastic) to the stringers. When the epoxy has set, the staples are removed by pulling off the plastic—staples and all. The second layer of veneer strips is applied (with epoxy and staples) in the direction opposite to the first. In drawing 3 the epoxy has set, and the staples are removed as before. Drawing 4 is a plan view showing the joints at which gunwale and transoms meet. Interior components are added after the hull is sheathed and covered with at least three coats of epoxy.

1

PLANKING: ⅛" VENEER

KEELSON: ⅜" × 4" MARINE PLY

KNEE

CLEATS HOLD TRANSOMS

TRANSOM: ¾" PLY OR LUMBER

STRINGERS: 1" × 1"

WEDGES

FRAME BASE (2 PCS. 2" × 6")

KEELSON

FRAMES

FRAME SUPPORTS

FRAMES: ½" OR ¾" PLY

2

PLANKING: ⅛" VENEER

STRINGERS

WEDGES

TRANSOM

STRINGER HOLDS WEDGES

FRAME SUPPORTS

PLANKING (FIRST LAYER)

PLANKING (SECOND LAYER)

CLEATS

3

STAPLES THROUGH 40-MIL PLASTIC

4

CARRIAGE BOLTS, COUNTERSUNK AND PLUGGED

LAMINATED KNEE

HULL SKINS (PLANKING)

SPACER BLOCKS

GUNWALE (INTERIOR)

GUNWALE (EXTERIOR)

WOOD SUPPORT BLOCK

DRAWINGS BY MARYA BUTLER

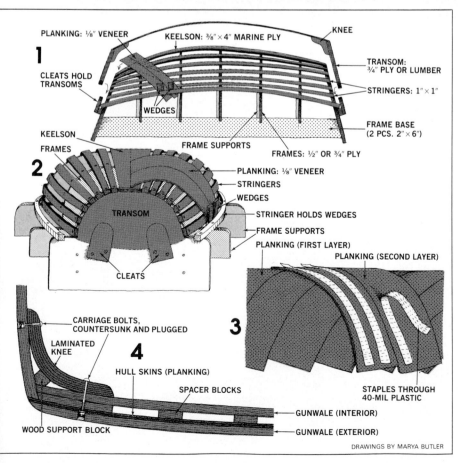

Norwegian pram (top photo) is 8 feet long with a 4-foot beam. Its gently curved hull requires no steam bending: It is made of veneer bonded and sealed with epoxy. Oars (above) were laminated from scraps of molding pine.

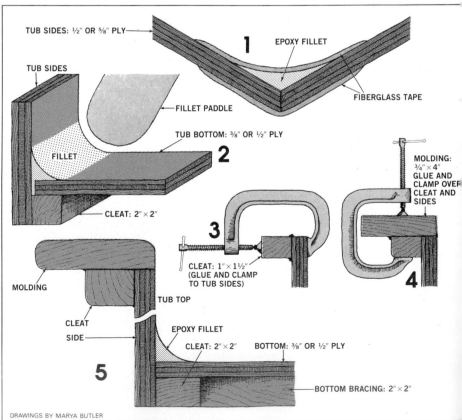

Hot tub (top) is 45 inches across (corner to corner) and 24 inches high. It's made of ½-inch hardwood ply (a larger tub would use ⅝- or ¾-inch ply). Bench (above) is made from scraps of teak laminated with epoxy and finished with oil.

TUB SIDES: ½" OR ⅝" PLY

1

EPOXY FILLET

FIBERGLASS TAPE

TUB SIDES

FILLET PADDLE

TUB BOTTOM: ⅜" OR ½" PLY

FILLET

2

CLEAT: 2" × 2"

MOLDING: ¾" × 4" GLUE AND CLAMP OVER CLEAT AND SIDES

3

CLEAT: 1" × 1½" (GLUE AND CLAMP TO TUB SIDES)

4

MOLDING

CLEAT

SIDE

TUB TOP

EPOXY FILLET

CLEAT: 2" × 2"

BOTTOM: ⅜" OR ½" PLY

5

BOTTOM BRACING: 2" × 2"

DRAWINGS BY MARYA BUTLER

The finished hull has no nails, screws, bolts, or other mechanical fasteners. These would concentrate stress in one local point; a glue joint spreads it out. Metal fasteners are also heavy and expensive, collect moisture, and can leach salts into the wood, which will cause local weakness and eventual degradation of the wood fibers.

We built the pram over a male mold, covering it with heavy plastic to keep from bonding the boat to the mold. The laminations were laid diagonally over a full-length keel of marine plywood and attached to gunwales of vertical-grain Sitka spruce. The bow and transom are spruce, as are the thwarts (transverse components) and laminated knees (reinforcing members shaped to bridge the angle between joining parts) inside the boat. We held the first lamination in place with staples and wedges until the bonding coat of epoxy had set. Then we removed the staples as we applied the second lamination (see drawing)—also with epoxy and staples. Finally we removed those staples and sanded the hull smooth.

Next, we sheathed the hull exterior with a layer of fiberglass cloth imbedded in epoxy. The cloth, invisible when applied properly, provides additional reinforcement, abrasion and puncture resistance, and it ensures

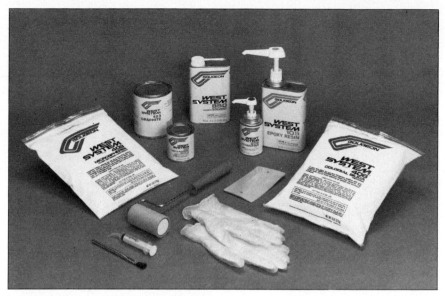

Ingredients for WEST System epoxy-composite technique include epoxy resin and hardener, fillers such as microballoons and coloidal silica to alter viscosity, and graphite powder, added to resin to create a harder surface and reduce friction on rudders, centerboards, and boat bottoms.

low maintenance. Interior sheathing is not essential, but it does add strength and wearability.

A varnished cold-molded wooden boat requires about the same maintenance as a fiberglass boat. It compares favorably, too, in cost, strength-to-weight ratio, and longevity.

Plans for this 8-foot pram (along with other boat designs suited to cold-molded construction) are available from Gougeon Brothers, Inc., 706 Martin St., Bay City, MI 48706. The firm also sells the epoxy, the necessary fillers and additives, and an excellent book on cold-molding (*The Gougeon Brothers on Boat Construction: Wood and WEST System Materials*, Pendell Printing Inc., Midland, Michigan).

Splashy hot tub

One of the most enjoyable projects we've made with the wood-epoxy construction technique is a hot tub. The traditional problems of wooden hot tubs—leakage, rot, and maintenance—are eliminated by encapsulating the wood in epoxy.

Our hot tub has a natural look that complements our deck. And because wood is a pretty good insulator, the water stays hot longer than it would in a fiberglass tub, so we use less energy. The hexagonal tub is our design. It's made of luan mahogany plywood (ordered from Plywood and Door Mfg. Corp., 7701 W. 79th St., Bridgeview, IL 60455) with reinforced corner and bottom joints. The molding is also luan. The tub can be built for a fraction of what commercial hot tubs cost.

The hex configuration is easy to build. You begin by constructing a simple jig to hold the sides together while gluing and sheathing. This small tub—large enough for one adult and a child—can be built from two 4-by-8-foot sheets of ply. Plywood can be any good exterior grade, but marine or hardwood ply is best. The basic design is easily modified and can be enlarged to a family-size tub.

Side joints are reinforced with glass cloth and fillets—cove-shaped beads of thickened epoxy (see drawings). We also used fillets to seal and strengthen the joint where the sides meet the bottom. Fillets spread stress over a larger area and give a finished, organic look. To make a fillet, you thicken the epoxy resin to the appropriate viscosity with microballoons or silica or a mixture of the two. The thickened mix is spread into the corner with a shaped paddle of the proper radius. You pull the paddle along the joint, leaving behind a pleasing concave bead. Then you scrape away any excess along the edges with a putty knife. The fillet can also be sanded if you feel it necessary.

The tub can be fitted with a gas or electric heater, whirlpool, or other standard hot-tub options. Alternative heating systems are available, such as the wood-burning immersible stove made by the Snorkel Stove Co. (108 Elliott Avenue West, Seattle, WA 98119). You can also build a heat-retaining top for the tub. For complete plans, send $10 to Plans, Box 1513, Hamilton, MT 59840—*by Paul and Marya Butler.*

Plywood-epoxy hot tub

Sides for the hot tub are cut at 30-deg. angles so that they will form the hexagonal shape when assembled. If the tub is to be varnished, the plywood for the sides should be measured and cut with the best side out; grain should run in the same direction on all panels. Cut and stack all six sides to be sure they are identical before proceeding further. If the plywood has voids, they should be filled with epoxy thickened with microballoons. If you're building the small-size tub shown, the bottom can be made from one sheet of ply. Larger sizes require a seam with a reinforcing butt block. Side joints (1) are reinforced with fiberglass tape outside and with a shallow fillet (see text) and tape inside. Joint where sides meet bottom is also reinforced with a fillet (2), which is formed with a paddle of the proper radius. The bottom must be supported on cleats that bear on the ground. If a bottom seam is used, it too must be supported from below. Molding around the tub's top rests on cleats (3) that are glued (with epoxy) and clamped to the tub sides. When the epoxy has set, the top molding is glued and clamped in place (4). Section shows the complete assembly of the hot tub (5).

working with the new solid-color laminates

No matter how you cut them, Wilsonart's Solicor and Formica's Colorcore are solid color all the way through. The color you see on the surface of these two new surfacing materials is full-depth. Gone are the dark substrate lines that run along joints made with conventional laminate materials. The solid-color materials retain the toughness you expect from high-pressure laminates, but nicks and scratches have almost no visual impact. In fact, you can use sandpaper to minimize a surface flaw or to smooth a nicked edge. Keep cuts to a reasonable depth, and you can also engrave, rout, or kerf surfaces for unusual effects.

Is all the news about solid-color laminates good? Here's one thing to consider: They cost two-and-a-half to three times as much as conventional laminate materials. My experience has been that they're also not as readily available, although this is sure to change. In any case, if a local supplier doesn't stock them, he can order the color you want.

There are some special bonding and cutting tricks to working with the new laminates. In bonding, the thickness of the glue line is critical; if the line is obvious, you negate

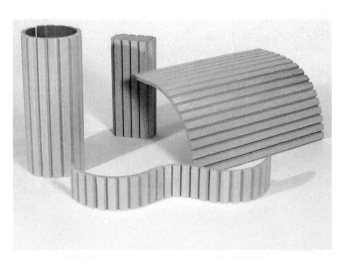

Formica's Colorcore surfacing material gives kitchen and dining-area counters clean, one-color edges. Wilsonart's Tambour-Plus (left) comes in various groove configurations and in solid-wood, laminate, and metallic materials.

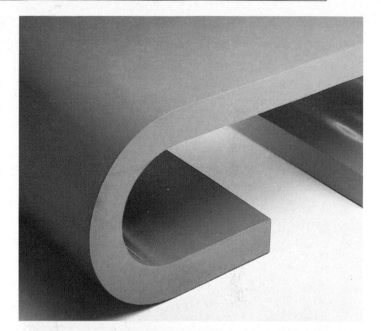

Dazzling effect is achieved by laminating bookcases (above) with three hues of solid-color material. Curved table (above right) is finished with Wilsonart's Color Quest. Sink backsplashes (lower right) are laminated with Solicor.

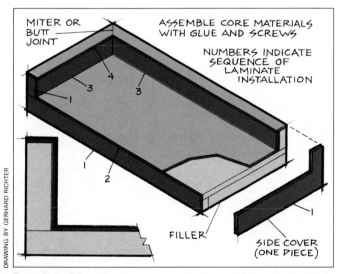

DRAWING BY GERHARD RICHTER

MITER OR BUTT JOINT

ASSEMBLE CORE MATERIALS WITH GLUE AND SCREWS

NUMBERS INDICATE SEQUENCE OF LAMINATE INSTALLATION

FILLER

SIDE COVER (ONE PIECE)

Drawing above shows correct way to laminate a backsplash: Horizontal pieces should overlap the upright piece to keep out water trying to seep underneath.

the solid-color feature of the laminate. Although any non-pigmented contact cement can be used, it's best to work with adhesives recommended by the manufacturer (see table). As these adhesives are highly flammable, it's important to observe the precautions printed on the containers. You apply the cement just as you would for conventional laminates: Working with a wide paintbrush or solvent-resistant roller, quickly and evenly cover both the laminate and the substrate. The laminate is ready for bonding when the adhesive feels tacky but won't transfer to your

PS takes a quick look at solid-color laminates

Colors	Thick.	Price	Handling	Forming	Remarks
SOLICOR[1]					
Available in 10 solid colors, and in all other Wilsonart colors by special order	0.040 ± 0.005	Approx. $3.71 per sq. ft.	Heavier and more brittle than conventional material; use care, especially when handling full sheets	Can be formed to ½-in. radius with professional tools	Work with carbide-tipped tools; glue line is critical; recommended contact cements are Wilsonart's LW801, LW851, and LW806
COLORCORE[2]					
Available in 94 solid colors	0.051 ± 0.005	Approx. $4 per sq. ft.	Same as above	2½-in. strip will follow a 6-in. radius at room temperature; tighter bends require heat	Work with carbide-tipped tools; glue-line is critical; recommended adhesive: Formica 100 or 140 for brushing, 151 for spraying

[1] Ralph Wilson Plastics Co., 600 General Bruce Dr., Temple TX 76501-5199; [2] Formica Corp., Information Center, 114 Mayfield Ave., Edison NJ 08837

Laminate was formed around 8-in. radius to finish top of small table (right)—but only after generous application of heat gun to laminate and core.

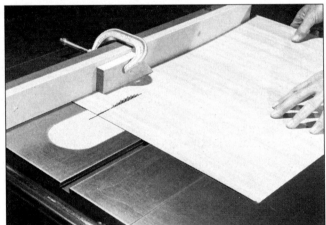

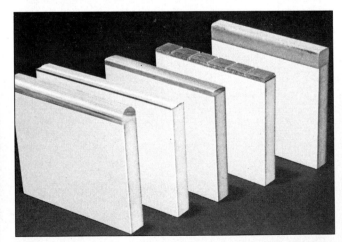

Simultaneous cutting can be done with a router (top). Workpieces are taped face-to-face and clamped with strip that also guides tool. Bit passes through groove in plywood jig. Solid-color edges (above) can be sanded with 400- or 600-grit sandpaper. Use a wooden sanding block when you want square edges. Follow with an application of lemon oil.

Author uses a table saw for all straight cuts (top). Attach a facing to the rip fence for zero clearance between it and the table. Clamped block helps eliminate flutter that can occur when sawing thin sheets. Edges (above) can be finished with materials other than laminate. Attach pieces with glue and a few strategically placed finishing nails.

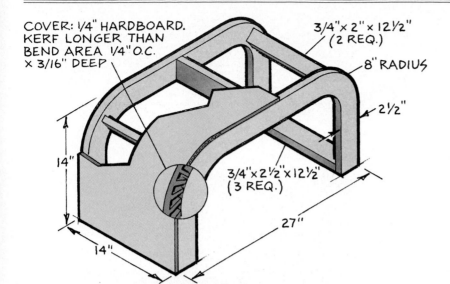

COVER: 1/4" HARDBOARD.
KERF LONGER THAN
BEND AREA 1/4" O.C.
x 3/16" DEEP

3/4" x 2" x 12 1/2"
(2 REQ.)

8" RADIUS

2 1/2"

14"

3/4" x 2 1/2" x 12 1/2"
(3 REQ.)

27"

14"

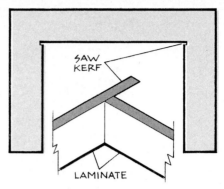

SAW KERF

LAMINATE

When covering edges of a U-shaped top (above), cut a short saw kerf into core, and allow plastic strip to extend into kerf. Butt remaining pieces against it.

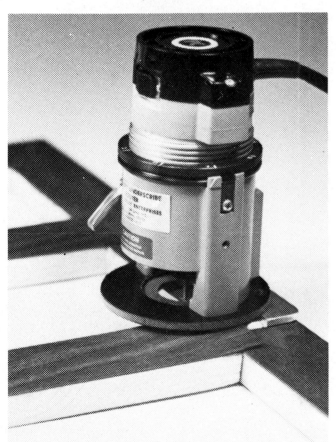

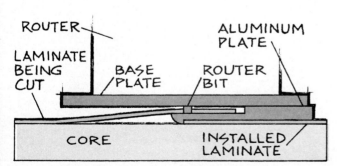

ROUTER

ALUMINUM PLATE

LAMINATE BEING CUT

BASE PLATE

ROUTER BIT

CORE

INSTALLED LAMINATE

Router base (photo above) from Art Betterly Enterprises (1160 Central Ave. N.E., Blaine, MN 55434) makes perfect butt-edge joints on blind cuts.

finger. You can also use white glue; in fact, Formica recommends it for light-colored Colorcore, advising that a 0.001-inch glue-line thickness is ideal. But unlike cement, white glue requires clamping, and this can prove to be a nuisance on some work.

Efficient cutting procedures are essential, and carbide-tipped tools make the job easier. I do all straight sawing on a table saw, getting the best results with either a 60-tooth blade with a triple-chip grind or with Freud's 80-tooth Teflon-coated blade. Keep the good side of the material up, and provide enough support to prevent flutter. Adequate blade projection prevents topside chipping, and slowing the feed at the end of the cut will greatly lessen the chance of breakout.

The score-and-snap method, often used for separating ceramic tile, will work—but use it only if you must. Score deeply, preferably with a carbide-tipped tool, and place the scored line directly over the edge of a wooden block before snapping. It's a good idea to have a second block on the top side clamped to the lower one. There is no guarantee of a clean break, regardless of the care you take, so allow extra material for cleaning up.

Core material should be free of surface voids. Use the A-side of Douglas fir A-D plywood or 45-pound particle-board. Medium-density fiberboard and hardwood-veneered plywoods also make suitable cores. If you want to use a lumber core for a large surface, join the pieces of wood carefully to ensure a flat bonding surface.

A hint: When you need many similar pieces—say for cabinet drawers or drawer bottoms—laminate a full sheet of material, and then cut to necessary sizes on a table saw. You won't have to edge-trim individual pieces. Edge-trimming can be done with a file or block plane or, ideally, with a router. When filing, work down and away from the surface. With a plane, take light longitudinal strokes with the plane angled down and away from the top surface. Trimming with a router and a carbide-tipped bit gets the job done quickest and cleanest. The easiest way to rout is to use an edge-guide attachment and work with a special edge-trimming bit that has a ball-bearing pilot. Other hints: Cover both sides of shelves before installation. If they are set in dadoes, remember to cut dadoes to fit the shelves total thickness with two laminate faces. Saw dadoes in vertical piece after attaching laminate. Lastly, you can avoid trimming by attaching laminate before sizing and shaping—*by R.J. DeCristoforo. Drawings by Gerhard Richter.*

biscuit joinery

The ideal joining system: After more than 30 years of woodworking, I've finally found it. It's fast, easy, strong, and accurate. It produces tight, invisible joints in plywood, particleboard, softwoods, and hardwoods. In fact, it has become just about the only system I like to use anymore. Dowels, dadoes, mortise and tenon, dovetails, splines . . . all can be replaced by this system.

It's called biscuit—or plate—joinery, and, like a lot of good ideas, it comes from Europe. Biscuit joinery isn't new in Europe, but for some reason it has just begun to catch on in the United States.

The system consists of two parts. First, there's a flat, football-shaped biscuit or plate made of compressed beech. This biscuit—made in three different sizes for different-size joints—fits into mating slots cut in the two pieces to be joined. It's sort of a cross between a spline and a dowel.

Second, there's a special tool that uses a small circular saw blade to plunge-cut the mating slots.

30-second frames

The speed and ease of biscuit joinery is astounding. Joining mating frame parts, for example, might take 30 seconds. You simply cut the mating slots in the two parts, squeeze some glue into the slots, insert the biscuit, and press the parts together. The slots are about 1/8 inch longer than the biscuits so you have a little leeway to slide your parts into perfect alignment (try that with dowels!). Then you simply clamp the parts until the glue sets up.

Meanwhile, because the biscuits are compressed somewhat during manufacture, the water content of the glue makes them swell slightly. Thus they expand to fit their slots and produce a joint as strong as the surrounding wood.

That's the good news. The bad news is, the tools used to cut the slots are expensive. Three different tools are currently available, two by Steiner Lamello in Switzerland and one by Elu in Germany. Lamello tools are imported by Colonial Saw (100 Pem-

Biscuit joinery can be used for face joints (top), miters (center), or edge joints (bottom). Biscuits come in three sizes and cost about three cents each. Compressed-wood biscuits are available where you buy plate-joining tools.

broke St., Box A, Kingston, MA 02364). Elu Corp. (9040 Dutton Dr., Twinsburg, OH 44087) imports the Elu cutter.

Of the three, the Lamello Top is clearly the most convenient and the best built. If I ran a production shop every day of the year, it would be my choice. But nearly $600 for what is essentially a miniature circular saw with a plunge-cutting base? You could buy a decent table saw if you wanted to spend that kind of money!

Fortunately the Elu sells for around $400, and Lamello's brand-new Junior is about $350. This is still a lot of money, but it's more in line with what an advanced amateur would be willing to pay. And if you shop around, you can probably find a retailer that offers a discount.

Neither the Elu nor the Junior is quite as convenient to use as the Top. But for over $200 less, I don't care. If I had to choose between the Elu and the Junior, I might lean toward the Junior. It's a bit more convenient to use when you're preparing face and miter joints.

Beat the system

You can do just that—on some joints —by using a ball-bearing slotting cutter in your router. It can't cut panel slots out in the field as a real biscuit tool can, but it will do the job on edge joints—even miters—if you build a simple jig. A 5/32-inch bit with a pilot that allows cuts 1/2 inch deep works well with the largest biscuit size.

The resulting slots are semicircular, not stretched footballs as needed, so you have to move the cutter or your work to lengthen the slots slightly. It's a little extra work, but the bit is a lot less costly than a plate-joining tool. If you can't find one locally, FSM Tools (132 College Ave., Annville, PA 17003) has a three-wing, carbide-tipped bit for about $20—by A.J. Hand.

Three plate-joining tools available in the United States are shown above: the Elu (foreground), Lamello Junior (top left), and Lamello Top. These cost from $350 to $580. At lower right is a $20 bit for routers that also forms joining slots.

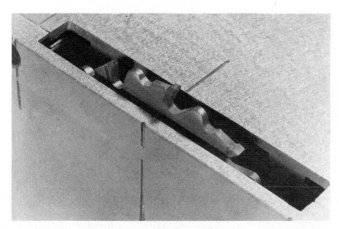

All biscuit tools use a 4-inch circular saw blade (far left, top) to cut 5/32-inch slots. The blades are completely covered in the tool housing until you plunge them into your work. This is the carbide-tipped Elu blade, extended from its housing. To cut slots (far left, bottom), align an index mark on the tool with a pencil line on your work. Then plunge the blade down. A slot is cut to perfect size in a second. For stock thicker than 3/4 inch you can use two biscuits side by side for greater strength. On long joints (on cabinet sides, for example), plates should be centered every 4 to 6 inches. Plate joiners can do more than make fixed joints. They can also cut mortises for special hinges (left, top) or slots for aluminum knock-down fittings (left, bottom). Epoxy the fittings in slots, and you have strong, invisible joints that can be disassembled in seconds. Hank Koelmel (64-30 Ellwell Crescent, Rego Park, NY 11374) sells the knockdown fittings, and Colonial Saw handles the hinges.

14 clever fasteners

Common fasteners—nails, bolts, screws, and blind rivets—handle many fastening jobs with aplomb. But some jobs can be done better with specialized fasteners that are unknown to many home craftsmen. Some of these unusual devices form extra-strength joints in weak materials or allow easy assembly and knockdown. Others make ugly joints more presentable. If you can't find them in your favorite hardware store, contact the mail-order houses listed in the captions.

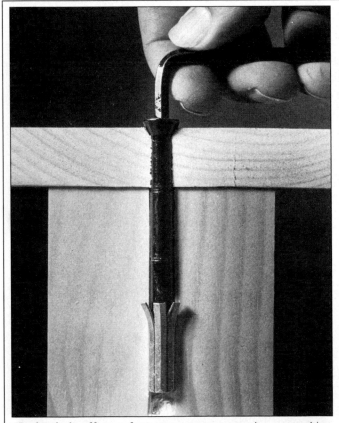

1 **Jawbolt offers a fast,** strong way to anchor a machine screw into nearly any material. It provides extra strength in weak materials such as particleboard and end-grain softwoods. To install, drill pieces to be joined, then hammer the bolt and hexagonal anchor into the hole until bolt head is flush with surface. A few turns with a hex wrench flares out the anchor top, providing a grip with more than 3,300 pounds of pullout strength. Both can be repeatedly removed and replaced. Jawbolts are made by Jaw Mfg. Co. in ¼- and ⁵⁄₁₆-inch diameter and a variety of lengths.

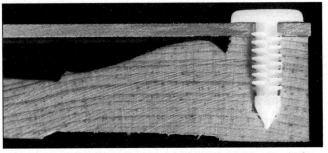

2 **Fin clips** (or Christmas-tree clips) are reusable plastic fasteners with fins that hold them firmly in either blind or through holes. Tap or press them into position, and they'll hold; you can pry them loose if desired. Here, one fastens acrylic glazing to a window casing to create an indoor storm window. Fin clips can be used to secure two panels or attach compressible materials such as cloth or rubber (for inspection covers, for example). Clips are from DRI Industries.

3 **Elite fittings are quick,** clever knockdown fasteners often used by Scandinavian furniture makers. Each has two parts: a long, slender stud and a cammed anchor disc (see inset). To install, drill a small-diameter hole for the stud, intersecting a larger hole for the disc. To assemble a project, slip the mushroom tip of the stud into the slot in the perimeter of the disc, then give the disc a half turn with a screwdriver. The ramplike slot in the disc draws the stud and joint tight. To disassemble, loosen the anchor disc. You can get Elite fittings from The Woodworkers' Store.

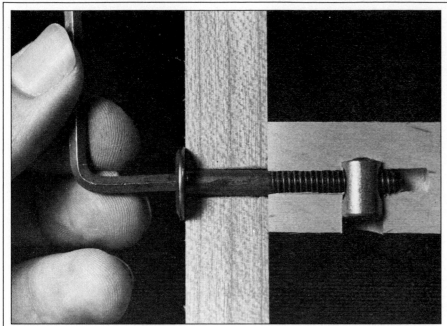

4 **Bolt and cross-dowel fasteners** provide a strong connection in the end of dowels and turnings and in particleboard and other materials with poor screwholding ability. The bolt engages the threaded-steel cross dowel and can be drawn tight without tearing the stock. The cross dowel is slotted and can be turned with a screwdriver to line up with the bolt. To disassemble the joint, unscrew the bolt. They're sold by The Woodworkers' Store and Leichtung.

5 **Push-pull fasteners** are made of high-strength polycarbonate and come in two parts: plunger and grommet. They hold two panels together. Here, one secures a circuit board to a metal chassis. They can also secure automotive trim panels or cover plates on trucks and boats. To use, snap the grommet into a hole in one panel, then slip the plunger through a hole in the other panel and snap it into grommet. Flared mushroom head makes disassembly easy. DRI sells them.

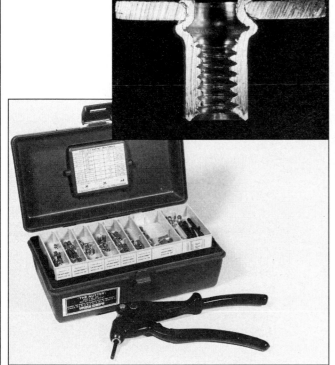

6 **Threaded rivets** use the blind-rivet principle to let you put threaded inserts into through holes in metals, plastics, and fiberglass, and into blind holes in just about any solid material. Rivet kit from DRI includes a rivet-setting tool and assorted threaded rivets. To use, drill a hole into the material to which you want to fasten. Put a threaded rivet in the setting tool, insert the rivet into the hole, and squeeze tool's handles. Base of rivet will flare out (see inset) and provide a firm anchor for bolts and machine screws. (Threaded rivets are also available in Bostik's POP brand.)

7 **Threaded inserts provide a tough,** threaded anchor in softer substances such as wood, plastic, and composition materials. They're ideal in places where you need a strong joint that you can disassemble many times without wear. The inserts have deep, sharply cut threads on the outside to grip firmly into the material. Their internal threads accept bolts and machine screws. The top is notched for driving with a screwdriver. Threaded inserts are made of solid brass and come in a variety of sizes. DRI, Leichtung, and The Woodworkers' Store sell them.

8 **Stem snaps** from DRI are plastic fasteners that can secure cloth, leather, wood, metal, fiberglass, and more. They consist of a pair of discs, each studded with little mushroom-head fingers. Press discs together, and fingers interlock to create a firm but easily disassembled joint. The discs can be attached with nails, screws, and rivets. Here, leather is being fastened to plywood.

9 **Plastic rivets** are medium-strength, nonconducting, noncorroding fasteners from DRI. Like blind rivets, they can be used when only one side of the work is accessible. Drill a hole in the materials to be joined, and insert the split end of the rivet; tap the stem with a hammer. Rivet's legs flare out on the back side of the work to provide a firm, vibration-proof anchor.

10 **Snap Caps** are actually fastener covers. They provide a smooth, attractive cover over screws, nails, and rivets. They also protect fastener heads from corrosive elements. Snap Caps consist of a plastic cover cap that snaps in place over a plastic washer. The washer is made in two types: One (right) fits over countersunk screws, the other (left) will take round or panhead screws plus nails and rivets. DRI sells Snap Caps in black, white, and brown.

11 **Knockdown joining device** (Woodworkers' Store) is designed for assembling cabinets. It can fasten tops, sides, bottoms, and backs, yet comes apart in seconds for disassembly. To use, screw the mating brown plastic parts to adjacent sides. Insert the stub of the top piece shown here into the recess in the piece below it. Then slide the metal locking clip over both pieces to hold them together.

12 **Bulbex is an unusual blind rivet** designed for fastening soft, brittle, and delicate materials such as plastics, fiberglass panels—even glass (right). Slots that are cut into the shell of the rivet allow it to expand easily, forming three separate segments that spread its compressive force over a wide area. Bulbex rivets are made in one diameter (³/₁₆ inch) with a grip range of from 0.032 to 0.250 inch. You install them with an ordinary blind-rivet tool, following standard procedure. Bulbex rivets are made by Avdel.

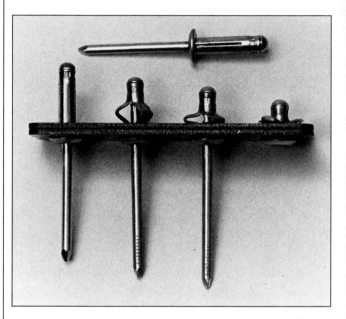

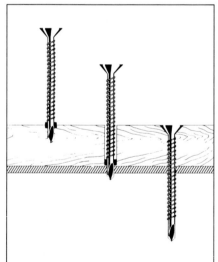

13 Spedec fasteners save time in any cladding job in which wood is joined to metal. Made by SFS Stadler in Switzerland, they have a fluted cutting tip that first drills through the wood. A pair of boring "wings" behind the point enlarge the hole to clear the screw threads. The tip then passes through the metal below with accurate centering and without separating the two materials. The wings shear off when they hit the metal, and the self-tapping threads fix the wood to the metal as the screw is driven home. Screws have a Phillips-head recess and can be driven with a power drill.

14 **"Common Sense Fasteners"** hold down tarps, tents, pack flaps, and other heavy materials. To fasten, you insert the twist-top base through the hole in the oval grommet and twist to lock. Bases come in two types: One has countersunk holes for screw-mount application to wood, metals, fiberglass, etc. The other has twin fold-over prongs for fabric-to-fabric fastening (ovals come with prongs only). Made of chrome-plated steel, they're from DRI—*by A.J. Hand.*

WHERE TO GET UNUSUAL FASTENERS
Avdel Corp., 50 Lackawanna Ave., Parsippany, NJ 07054; **Bostik Consumer Div., Emhart Corp.,** Box 3716, Reading, PA 19605; **DRI Industries,** 11100 Hampshire Ave. S., Bloomington, MN 55438 (special fastener catalog is $1); **Jaw Manufacturing, Co.,** Box 213, Reading, PA 19603; **Leichtung, Inc.,** 4944 Commerce Pkwy., Cleveland, OH 44128; **The Woodworkers' Store,** 21801 Industrial Blvd., Rogers, MN 55374; **Wurth Fastener Corp.,** 3 Pearls Ct., Allendale, NJ 07401

hide peeling paint with inside-out siding

When house paint is peeled and cracked as badly as mine was (see inset), the customary treatment is to scrape off the loose paint then sand a featheredge on the remaining paint. I tried that—for a few square feet—and then sat down to reconsider.

A quick calculation showed that I would be scraping and sanding for 50 hours or more. After that I'd still have to prime the entire house and apply at least one finish coat. And a few years later I'd have to do it all over again.

I hit on a better way. Every clapboard has two sides, and one of these has never been painted. I decided simply to remove the clapboards, turn them over, and nail them back on again inside out. To simplify the job further I stained the unfinished wood instead of painting it. Also, while the siding was off I added fiberglass insulation to the walls.

Here's why I decided to stain instead of paint: The back side of the clapboards is rough sawed. If I had wanted to paint the house—and repaint it every few years—I'd have to sand or plane the boards smooth before reinstalling them. That would have required time and effort, although not as much as scraping and sanding the old paint.

But the decision to stain cut the preparation work to practically nothing. Only the bottom edges of the boards needed sanding. And that went fast with a belt sander and 16-grit paper. I had to replace one short section of clapboard because it was rotted beneath the paint.

Staining was fast and easy. A two-gallon garden sprayer applied the stain evenly. Because of the sprayer's low pressure there was no problem with overspray—even on a windy day.

If your house isn't well insulated, an added attraction of this home-improvement technique is that you can easily add insulation when you reverse the clapboards. Remove the sheathing and staple in fiberglass insulation, keeping the vapor barrier toward the inside of the house. The job doesn't have to be done all at once. I reversed the siding and applied the insulation in small patches, working whenever I felt like it.

There are two tricky parts to the job. First, make sure you number the boards before you remove them so they can be reinstalled in the same place. The clapboards may not fit properly otherwise. Second, where boards are angled at gable ends, with a window in the middle, you'll have to switch the boards with their counterparts on the other side of the window.

I didn't have any trouble with this because my windows are centered in the gables. But if you have an off-center window, you may have to saw off some long boards and add those sections to the shorter boards on the other side of the window. It's simple if you plan the job. Again, the actual work is easy.

The entire operation cost only a few dollars for galvanized siding nails and stain. The insulation was a little more expensive, but fiberglass is one of the cheaper types, and insulation costs are tax-deductible.

To complete the job I painted the trimmings to match the stain. The result is a light, natural finish—an enormous improvement over the peeling siding I started with. Best of all, because stain doesn't peel, blister, or chip, I'll never have to scrape or sand again—*by Donald Maxwell.*

Numbered clapboards (left) removed by the author are easily reinstalled inside out after bottom edges are smoothed (bottom). The siding reversal can proceed in stages, with optional insulation added beneath sheathing (below). The stained finish (above) blends nicely with the surroundings.

Dramatic improvement in weathered siding (inset) was achieved by exposing and staining inside wood surface.

Tiled patio (above), shaded by trees, is a delightful spot for entertaining. Mortar was spread in small sections with ³/₈-inch square-notched trowel (1). Tile was set with rubber mallet (2) to ensure firm bond. Where butting an adjoining surface, an expansion strip of silicone (Dow 790) was added (3). After approximately 30 days, heavy loads can be installed (4).

pave a patio with ceramic tile

Picture a patio laid over a plot of brown grass or bald spot in your backyard. Imagine a crowd of friends partying around the barbecue grill. Is there anything missing? How about the work involved in removing the stains and debris from the floor after an especially active get-together?

Patio cleaning and maintenance are a nuisance, but with a ceramic-tile patio, the work can be minimized. That's what the owner of the house shown here found with his tiled patio. The project was sponsored by American Olean Tile Co. (Lansdale, Pa.), makers of the Primitive Ultra Pavers slip-resistant 8-inch-square tile shown.

The 16-by-26-foot patio covers a steel-reinforced concrete slab. To lay the tile, the slab was covered with a latex-modified dry-set mortar (American Olean sanded floor mortar with an acrylic additive). To ensure that the tile would adhere, the mortar was spread onto small sections of the slab and the tile was laid before the mortar skinned over—within 10 to 15 minutes. One section was finished before moving on to another.

The backs of the tiles were "buttered" with mortar and pounded into place with a rubber mallet, ensuring that there were no voids for water to enter and freeze.

Two days after setting the tile—a minimum length of time—the patio was grouted with American Olean sanded floor grout, a mixture of sand and portland cement. The finished patio was then covered with canvas tarps to ensure even drying and to prevent the latex in the mortar from being reemulsified—*by Charles A. Miller. Drawing by Carl De Groote.*

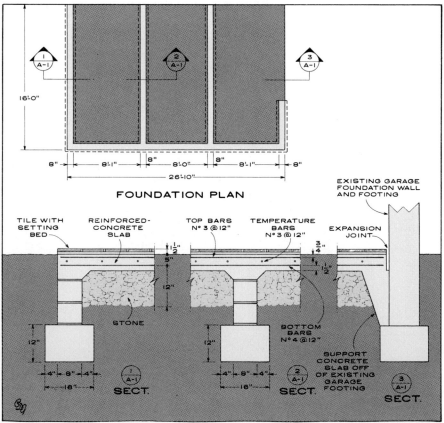

FOUNDATION PLAN

replace your old patio doors

Those old aluminum sliders are light and need little maintenance —but they're terrible for keeping out the cold. The aluminum frame is a thermal conductor, and the age of such doors likely means that they no longer seal properly. Even if they did, the single pane of glass does little to help your fuel bill.

The cure: Replace those old doors with an energy-efficient unit. New patio doors—such as the Andersen Perma-Shield Gliding Door II shown here—are double-glazed and framed in vinyl-covered wood for thermal insulation now and no maintenance worries later.

The new doors come as a kit that

Use glass of old doors for storm panels

Don't throw away your old patio doors. For only about $35, you can convert them into storm doors that cover the new patio doors for triple glazing.

The dimensions shown here are for a five-ft.-two-in.-by-six-ft.-nine-in. opening. Cut each door frame out of 2×4s as shown. Square the four sides, and lay the glass on top. Scribe the pieces to mark the router (or table-saw) depth. Assemble the eight corners of the storm-door unit using nails and plugs.

When completed, nail the stationary panel into the door frame; attach the access panel to the stationary door frame with hinges. Finish by adding door latch.—*Harold Gill*

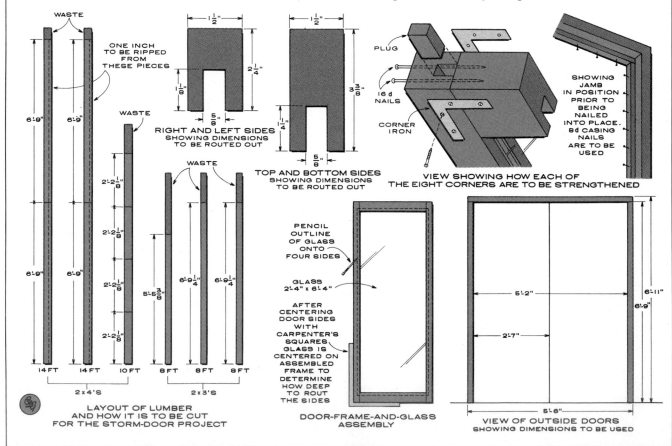

LAYOUT OF LUMBER AND HOW IT IS TO BE CUT FOR THE STORM-DOOR PROJECT

DOOR-FRAME-AND-GLASS ASSEMBLY

VIEW OF OUTSIDE DOORS SHOWING DIMENSIONS TO BE USED

You'll be snug next winter inside a thermally efficient door like the double-glazed Andersen above. If you prefer a multipane look, add snap-in grilles like those at bottom right; they're removable to simplify cleaning the glass. Final step is adding sliding screen (bottom left)—or hinged storm panel (facing page)—for all-weather versatility.

includes all hardware and is designed to fit into a standard opening without extensive carpentry. In fact, with a little help, the job can be done in a day.

What do you do with the old doors? Simple—follow the detailed drawing and use the glass for a storm door that offers even greater protection from the cold.

If you'd like information on patio doors, write to the National Woodwork Manufacturers Assn., c/o Sumner Rider, 355 Lexington Ave., New York, NY 10017, for a free copy of "A Guide to Energy-Saving Doors" —*by William J. Hawkins. Drawing by Carl De Groote.*

Old glass panels are removed by sliding them to the center of the frame, lifting, and pulling out bottom.

Take out the door frame by first removing all screws and old caulking. Tap the door frame loose, and tilt it out.

Assemble the new frame. Use butyl caulking (comes with door) at each corner; screw the frame together.

Apply several beads of caulking to the underside of the sill to form a tight seal between it and the rough sill.

Install the frame from the outside. Apply pressure to the sill to distribute caulking. Check level and plumb.

Secure the frame. If needed, add shims between jambs and rough opening to be sure the frame does not bow.

Install the new stationary door first. Position it in the outer sill run, and then force it into the side-jamb rabbet.

Remove the inside head stop. Tip in operating door, and slide the door closed. Install and secure head stop.

Install handle, and check door movement. If door binds, raise or lower it by turning adjustment screws.

Finish the outside work by caulking between the frame and wall. On a wood home, molding may then be added.

Inside, loosely pack strips of insulation between the door jambs and jack studs for additional weatherproofing.

Finally, cut and install the interior casing trim to cover the joints between the door frame and the inside wall.

installing plastic plumbing

Are you planning a major re-modeling job, complete with plumbing? You can make the job easier—assuming your local codes permit it (as most do)—by using chlorinated polyvinyl chloride (CPVC) tubing. CPVC is ideal for most water-supply plumbing work, and its versatility makes the job easier than it seems. CPVC has revoluntionized home plumbing in recent years, making most jobs possible for the do-it-yourselfer. But to avoid hassles, you still need to know exactly how to plan and install a run in your home. Here's what I've learned from the many plumbing jobs I've tackled.

CPVC tubing generally comes in ½-and ¾-inch nominal sizes and in 10-foot lengths. It can be cut with any fine-toothed saw or with a tubing cutter that has a plastic-cutting wheel. Tubing and fittings are joined by solvent welding—you use an all-purpose solvent cement in a two-step process.

First, plan your system based on the direction of water flow. Position the fixtures first, then the tubing necessary to serve them. Space hot- and cold-water lines a reasonable distance apart so that heat is not transferred to the cold line, and never cross-connect a potable-water line with a source of potentially contaminated water, such as a lawn-sprinkler system. Use an air gap or an approved backflow-prevention device.

Accurate measurement makes for a trouble-free plumbing system. No piping should be installed in unheated spaces unless it can be drained.

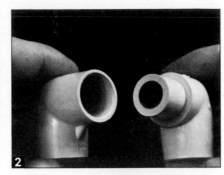

(1) Shown are transition unions (top, left to right): 1/2-inch female and male fittings to adapt CPVC tubes to threads, 1/2-inch special female adapter with running threads—rather than tapered pipe threads, which tend to leak—and a sealing washer. Bottom row: 1/2-inch street (tube-sized) to 5/8-inch OD, 1/2-inch street to 3/8-inch OD, 1/2- to 3/8-inch OD, 1/2- to 3/8-inch angle. (2) One end of street elbow (right) is same size as tubing so that it fits into the socket of another fitting. (3) Because of expansion, space CPVC at least 1 inch from frame. (4) Wing elbow screwed to headers supports stubout pipe for fixture. The temporary cap closes the supply system for pressure testing (CPVC withstands 100 psi at 180 degrees F).

PS pipefitter's guide—CPVC fitting measurements

Fitting*	Fitting gain—in. (mm) (center to tubing end)		Makeup—in. (mm) (socket depth)	
	1/2-in. pipe	3/4-in. pipe	1/2-in. pipe	3/4-in. pipe
90-degree elbow, tee	3/8 (10)	9/16 (15)	1/2 (12)	11/16 (17)
45-degree elbow	5/16 (8)	3/8 (10)	1/2 (12)	11/16 (17)
90-degree street elbow (street side only)	1 (25)	1 3/8 (35)	1/2 (12)	11/16 (17)
Coupling	1/8 (3)	1/8 (3)	1/2 (12)	11/16 (17)
Universal line valve	1 (25)	13/16 (20)	1/2 (12)	11/16 (17)
Union	5/8 (16)	9/16 (15)	1/2 (12)	11/16 (17)
3/4 × 3/4 × 1/2-in. reducing tee	3/4 (19)	1/2 (12)	1/2 (12)	11/16 (17)
3/4 × 1/2 × 1/2-in. reducing tee	1/2 (12)	1/2 (12)	1/2 (12)	11/16 (17)

*Genova brand fittings; for other fittings take actual measurements.

If you use isometric paper to lay out the system, you can plot each pipe direction along a different set of lines, showing the system clearly. I recommend that you simply sketch out the system, but not necessarily to scale. Show all pipes and fittings, and label each one.

Although initially they might seem bewildering, don't allow the characteristics of the material to confuse you. Consider, for instance, tubing sizes. All CPVC materials designed for domestic hot- and cold-water lines are sized the same as copper tubing—that is, they closely follow the nominal sizes of copper for inside diameter. The two sizes of CPVC commonly used for domestic-water supply are: 1/2-inch tubing, which measures about 1/2 inch ID and 5/8 inch OD, and 3/4-inch tubing, which measures about 3/4 inch ID and 7/8 inch OD.

In general, here's how to size your system to avoid flow problems: Use 3/4-inch tubing for the water-service entrance. CPVC may be buried belowground (be sure to test the system for leaks before backfilling).

Use 3/4-inch tubing to supply the water heater, for the hot and cold mains, and to serve the water softener. You should branch to fixtures with 1/2-inch tubing, but bear in mind that a 1/2-inch branch should serve only one fixture.

A shower or tub-shower is the place where plumbing flow problems are most noticeable, so make sure that 1/2-inch hot- and cold-branch tubing run untapped from the 3/4-inch mains to the fixtures. Fittings such as shutoffs are permissible, but no tapoffs. Treat a shower with great deference.

Make 1/2-inch taps from 3/4-inch hot and cold mains with 3/4-inch reducing tees. Two kinds are available—3/4-by-3/4-by-1/2-inch and 3/4-by-1/2-by-1/2-inch. The latter splits a 3/4-inch main into two 1/2-inch branches at its end. [Note: Tees are described with the two run diameters given first, followed by the branch diameter.]

You can fashion other kinds of reducing tees by solvent welding 3/4-by-1/2-inch bushings inside the 3/4-inch tee sockets to be reduced. But remember, once you've reduced the tubing size from 3/4 inch to 1/2 inch, you must not group in size to 3/4 inch again. That is a plumbing misdemeanor.

To keep garden-hose use from stealing too much water pressure from house fixtures, make hose-outlet runs with 1/2-inch tubing. If a branch is to serve two hose bibs, make it with 3/4-inch tubing—but use 1/2-inch tubing for the bib runs. Try to tap hose-bibb runs from near the service entrance. Minimize or, better yet, don't install end-of-main hose takeoffs, which could cut down on water flow through the house cold-water main.

If your house water pressure exceeds 50 psi, install a 3/4-inch pressure-reducing valve after the water meter. Adjust the regulator to about 50 psi. Outdoor water taps may come before or after the pressure reducer, depending on how much pressure you want them to have. Remember, though, that water running at high pressure through house piping creates noticeable sounds.

There are a great many CPVC fittings. They include couplings, caps, 45- and 90-degree elbows and street elbows, reducing bushings, reducing tees, unions, and male and female thread adapters. For secure mounting of faucets and fixture stubouts, there are wing elbows and new wing tees.

Transition unions are also available for adapting threaded metal fixtures and appliances (transition unions are required on pressurized hot-water connections to prevent leaks that can be caused by thermal

Planning your water system and calculating measurements

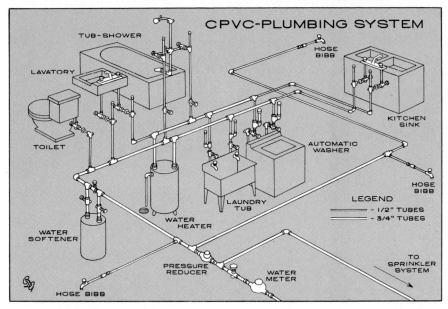

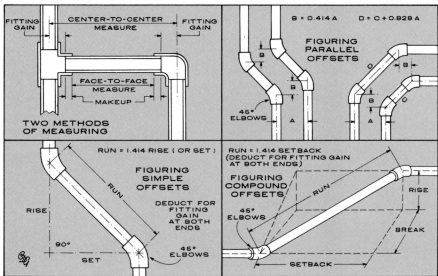

hand-tight, then give a full turn further with a wrench. A correctly sized adapter should have some thread showing when it has been properly tightened.

You can make piping measurements two ways: center-to-center or face-to-face. Center-to-center measurement has the advantage of letting you easily figure piping offsets using trigonometric-based factors (see illustrations). You then simply subtract the fitting makeup (the distance that the tubing extends into the fitting at each end) before you cut the tubing (the lengths vary with the fitting; see accompanying table).

With face-to-face measurement you have to remember only two figures. Add 1 inch to ½-inch tubing, and 1⅜ inch to ¾-inch tubing for fitting makeup at both ends.

Figuring piping offsets in which only 90-degree water-supply fittings are involved is simple. You can determine the length of 90-degree offsets by measuring directly, either face to face or center to center.

If calculations get confusing, simply lay the fittings out on the floor and take actual measurements face to face. Add for makeup, and then cut the tubing.

In any case, it pays to assemble the parts of a subsystem dry (without solvent cement) to see that everything fits. You can then take it apart and solvent weld. If you make a mistake with CPVC tubing—and this is one of the virtues of the material—you can just saw out the incorrect portion and replace it with a correctly made section, using two couplings to join new to old.

CPVC tubing expands and contracts about ¼ inch for every 10 feet of length so don't restrain the tubing. Instead, leave space at the ends of runs. Make foot-long doglegs on runs more than 35 feet long. Taps off mains should be free for at least 8 inches before they are restrained. This lets the main expand and contract. Holes drilled for tubing should be extra large: ⅞ inch for ½-inch tubing, and 1 inch for ¾-inch tubing.

Support CPVC tubing every 32 inches (every other joist) using straps designed for CPVC. The straps hold the tubing firmly to the framing yet permit the pipework to slide with thermal movements —*by Richard Day. Drawings by Carl De Groote.*

Plan your supply system carefully, taking into account the sizes of tubing needed for each branch (top). There are two ways of measuring (upper left). Most plumbers prefer center-to-center measurements because if you forget to deduct for fitting gain, a too-long tube can simply be cut a bit and used. With face-to-face measurements, if you forget to add makeup length, the tube will be too short, i.e., wasted. To make neat parallel 45-degree offsets (upper right), find distance B by multiplying distance between tubes (A) by 0.414. To make a parallel

turn with 45-degree elbows, first figure distance B, as above. Find length of D by multiplying distance between two tubes (A) by 0.828 and adding results to length of C. Fitting gain is not a factor except in positioning the first fitting. You can calculate lengths of 45-degree offsets (lower left) by multiplying distance from center line to center line (rise or set) by 1.414. Deduct for fitting gain before cutting tubing. To find the run in compound or rolled 45-degree offsets, multiply the setback by 1.414.

movements). For instance, use transition unions to connect CPVC to the threads of your water meter, pressure reducer, water softener, water heater, and tub-shower mixing valves. Simpler, lower-cost male adapters may be used at hose bibbs, T and P valves, and for non-pressurized shower risers.

Threaded CPVC male adapters

used to join with female metal fittings should be used for *cold water only*. Be careful not to overtighten, which could strip the threads or crack the fitting. Use a good pipe dope, silicone rubber sealant, Teflon plumber's tape, or Teflon paste on the male threads before making up the joint. When tightening the threaded adapter, turn

how to check for wrong-way polarity

Reverse the hot- and cold-water pipes in your home, and you'll still get water (even though your next shower will be a nuisance). Reverse the hot and neutral lines of your home wiring system, and you'll still get electricity. But now the possibility of a shock hazard exists.

Conventional 120-volt-AC household circuits have two current-carrying conductors. One is neutral; it has about the same electrical potential as the earth. The other is hot; it has a constantly changing potential different from that of the earth. The National Electrical Code (NEC) calls for maintaining hot-neutral wiring continuity throughout the house—from the utility entrance to the lamp in the den. The reason: appliance safety.

All appliances are designed to keep the hot line as far away from the user as possible. For example, in a lamp the center contact of the bulb socket is designed to be hot; it's difficult to touch and is switched off when the lamp is turned off. The shell of the bulb socket is neutral. This keeps the screw base of the bulb—which might be touched while screwing the bulb in or out—at ground potential.

However, if the hot and neutral lines to the socket are reversed, the bulb base becomes connected to the hot side of the circuit. You increase the chance of shock when changing the bulb.

"And unfortunately, it is not unusual to find reverse polarity in a home," says Bill Dall, who teaches electrical wiring to California State

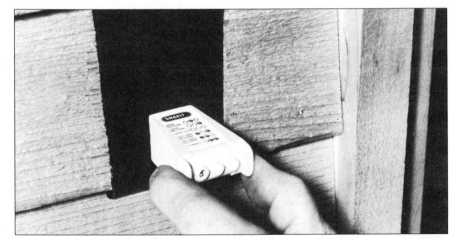

Three LEDS on outlet checker display results of ground and polarity tests.

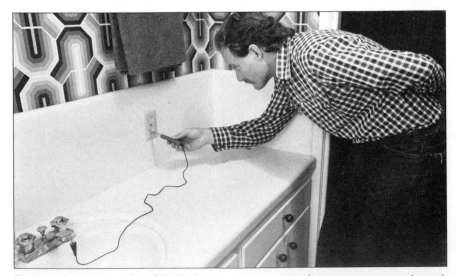

Pro's trick: Place one hand behind your back during all tests. Should something go wrong, voltage cannot pass through your heart to ground.

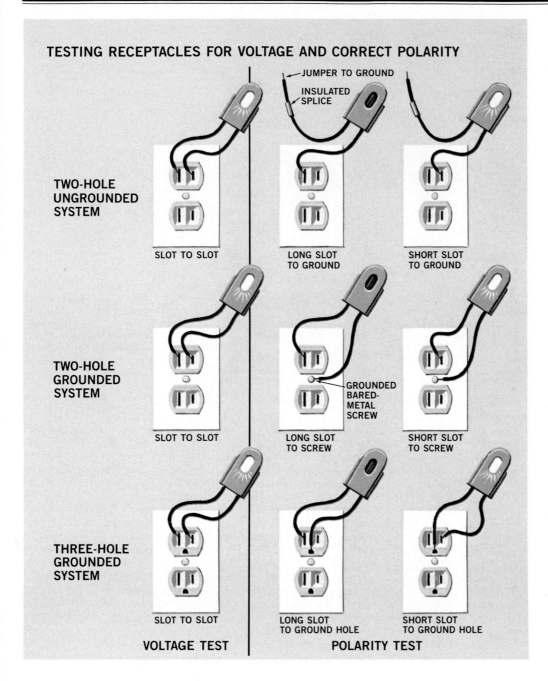

TESTING RECEPTACLES FOR VOLTAGE AND CORRECT POLARITY

JUMPER TO GROUND
INSULATED SPLICE

TWO-HOLE UNGROUNDED SYSTEM

SLOT TO SLOT   LONG SLOT TO GROUND   SHORT SLOT TO GROUND

TWO-HOLE GROUNDED SYSTEM

GROUNDED BARED-METAL SCREW

SLOT TO SLOT   LONG SLOT TO SCREW   SHORT SLOT TO SCREW

THREE-HOLE GROUNDED SYSTEM

SLOT TO SLOT   LONG SLOT TO GROUND HOLE   SHORT SLOT TO GROUND HOLE

VOLTAGE TEST   **POLARITY TEST**

Voltage and polarity checks using neon tester are shown for all three types of wall outlets. If an outlet fails a test, correct the problem or call an electrician before use. Do not use body-capacitance tester (see box).

Department of Parks and Recreation maintenance personnel.

I know of an East Coast homeowner who was electrocuted while working on a plugged-in portable dishwasher. The appliance was connected to a backward-wired receptacle. It proved fatal when the man accidentally touched an exposed live Calrod heating-element terminal that was supposed to have been on the neutral side of the appliance's circuit. The reversed polarity had made it hot.

How can you test for reverse polarity? What can you do to correct it? The tests are simple and so are many of the cures. If you uncover more-seri-ous problems, you should call an electrician. The following is what you need to know:

At the outlet

To maintain the correct polarity to an appliance, all outlets and plugs should be polarized. That means the outlet will accept the plug in only one direction. To do that, the outlet has one slot larger than the other, and one prong on the appliance plug is wider than the other.

Look closely at each electrical outlet in your home. Most manufactured since the 1930s should be polarized. Each should contain one long and one short slot. And, as of 1968, all new installations use polarized outlets with a third D-shaped hole for a ground conductor.

However, if both slots are the same length, the outlet is not polarized and should be replaced, if possible. You can buy polarized two-hole receptacles to replace nonpolarized ones, but use these only if no grounding wire is provided by your house wiring. (For additional safety, the NEC permits a ground-fault circuit-interrupter receptacle to be used for a non-grounding-type receptacle where no means of grounding exists in the outlet box. It has special grounding requirements.

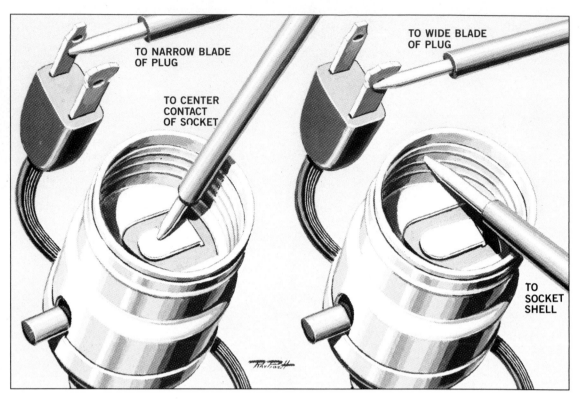

TO NARROW BLADE OF PLUG

TO CENTER CONTACT OF SOCKET

TO WIDE BLADE OF PLUG

TO SOCKET SHELL

Appliance polarity is tested with a continuity checker or ohmmeter. The center contact of a lamp socket should connect to the narrow (hot) blade of the plug; the lamp socket's shell should connect to the wide (neutral) blade.

Check the NEC guidelines.) If there is a grounding wire or if you're willing to provide one for the circuit, you should replace the nonpolarized receptacle with a modern three-hole grounding-type receptacle.

But having polarized outlets in your house and using them with polarized plugs doesn't mean you're automatically protected. Polarity can easily be reversed behind the walls by an incorrect wiring hookup. The short slot should be connected to the hot side of the circuit, and the long slot connected to the neutral side. If they are reversed, using a polarized plug in such an outlet would *guarantee* wrong polarity and its attendant shock hazard.

The polarity test for a modern three-hole grounding outlet is simple. The D-shaped hole in the outlet serves as a handy ground for one tester prod. Moreover, a $5-to-$10 plug-in outlet checker (see photo) like General Electric's TRC1–3C makes this test even simpler: Plug in the tester, and its LEDs show the results.

To make sure your outlets are wired correctly, check them against the tests shown in the drawings. All you need is a neon test light like the GE model 2598–01D or any other 125/250-volt-rated electrical tester. A voltmeter will work, but don't use a low-voltage or continuity tester. The tests will damage these instruments. And for your safety, *do not use a body-capacitance-type neon tester.*

Checking an older two-hole polar-

ized receptacle is also easy, provided its center cover screw is grounded. If your tests show no sign of voltage (light remains off) between the screw and one of the prongs, there is no ground (or no voltage is present). In this case you'll have to supply a ground from another source. How?

You could bring a grounded jumper wire from a metal water pipe or some such good ground. Then you could make the test using a neon test light or voltmeter between the receptacle and the jumper. Trouble is, this method has you holding a grounded wire in one hand and shoving a test prod into a live receptacle slot with the other. The hand-to-hand 120-volt potential with a through-the-heart electrical pathway to ground leaves this popular electrical test open to criticism. *Don't do it.*

The safest way is to use a professional's test light that has an insulated alligator-clip grounding lead. One brand is the Circuitracer Model 100 (Desco Ind., 761 Penarth Ave., Walnut, CA 91789; about $12). The Circuitracer has a test prod at one end and a clip-type pigtail test lead at the other. A 220-kilohm resistor inserted in series with the neon lamp serves as a further current-limiting device for added safety. In use, the Circuitracer's insulated pigtail lead is clipped to a ground. Then, using one hand (a standard procedure is to place your other hand behind your back as shown in the photo), insert Circuitracer's

single test prod into a receptacle slot.

Lacking a professional's tester, the next-best method is to do away with hand-to-hand exposure to electricity by converting an ordinary neon test light or voltmeter. (You're forgoing the Circuitracer's protective in-circuit resistor, however.) Simply splice *and insulate* a short jumper wire to one pigtail of the tester. Then put an alligator clip on the end of the jumper. The result: a 125/250-volt neon test light (or voltmeter) with the usual test prod at one end and a longer grounding-clip lead at the other.

A water pipe usually makes a good test ground unless plastic pipe has been used somewhere in the system. If so, look for another ground. An electric meter box—not a socket—is almost always grounded. Never ground to a gas pipe. It may be leaking small amounts of gas, and your test could create a small spark.

Reversed-polarity cure

If you find an outlet with reversed polarity, it's likely to be wired incorrectly. To check an outlet's wiring, first *turn off the power.* (Always check with a test light to be sure it's off.) Then remove the outlet cover, and possibly the outlet to inspect its wiring.

In most cases, one or more black or red wires are used as hot wires. They are supposed to be connected to the brass (darker-colored) terminal for the short slot. White or gray wires are used as neutrals. They should be connected to the chrome (lighter-colored) terminal for the long slot. With back-wired screwless receptacles, the correct color designations are printed above the push-in terminal holes.

If a white or gray wire wrongly goes to the brass screw and a black or red wire wrongly goes to the chrome screw, you've found the problem. Disconnect the receptacle, and rewire it correctly. But if the wire color-coding proves correct yet the outlet tests with reverse polarity, the hot and neutral wires have been reversed somewhere else in that circuit. The problem could be anywhere, even back inside the main electrical panel. Such a wiring system has major ills. Call an electrician.

Polarized plugs

In 1957 GE produced the first television set to use a polarized plug. Now the plug is required on all Edison-base lamps and flat-wire two-conductor extension cords, and is used on practically all tools and home appliances.

The plug's two blade widths guarantee the correct polarity from the outlet to the appliance. (Three-prong grounding plugs are polarized as well because the prone configuration allows them to be plugged-in only one way.) *Never replace a polarized plug with a nonpolarized one. Similarly, don't file down the wide prong of a polarized plug to make it fit a nonpolarized outlet.* And to maintain the correct polarization to an appliance, always use polarized extension cords and multiple-outlet taps instead of nonpolarized ones.

Of course, a nonpolarized plug will work in a polarized receptacle, but the correct polarity could be lost depending on how the plug is turned when plugged into the outlet. Where possible, replace nonpolarized plugs with polarized ones. On appliances that use cords with color-coded wires, connect the black wire to the narrow (hot) blade of the plug, the white wire to the wide (neutral) blade. Flat lamp cord is not color coded, but usually one of its two wires has a ribbed coating; the other is smooth. Attach the ribbed wire to the wide blade, the smooth wire to the narrow one.

You can also test an appliance for the correct polarity by using a continuity testor or ohmmeter. For example, the tester should show continuity between the socket shell of a lamp and the large prong of its plug (see drawings). Most appliances don't have exposed conductors, but for those that do—toasters, for example—the conductor should show continuity to the wide (neutral) prong, and no continuity to the narrow (hot) blade when the appliance is switched off.

If you suspect that an appliance has reverse polarity but can't accurately test it, call a professional—*by Richard Day. Drawings by Ray Pioch.*

Body-capacitance grounding: Don't risk it

The common neon voltage tester will light when one of its leads is held in your hand and the other is inserted in a receptacle's hot slot. Why? Because it uses body capacitance—*your* body's capacitance—as a ground return.

Some makers recommend this use of the tester for polarity or voltage tests in which a convenient ground is not available. And some makers offer neon testers specifically designed to be used this way. (They often look like a screwdriver: Its blade is inserted in the hot slot, and you touch its pocket clip.) Although the probability of getting a shock may be small, the experts warn against tests that use body capacitance.

The neon bulb and a built-in resistor inside the tester limit the amount of current through your body to extremely low levels. However, as one electrical-safety engineer pointed out, "If your body is well grounded and the tester happens to be defective, dirty, or wet, you could be exposing yourself to a lot more electricity than you bargained for."

How much? "A short circuit in the tester could conceivably give you the full 120 volts," he told me, "and with enough amps to be deadly." That doesn't take much: At 120 volts, only about $3/10$ ampere flowing for $1/10$ second can kill an adult. And the risk becomes greater as the voltage increases. The instructions on one $2 tester I found recommended its use in circuits containing up to 380 volts. "I'm horrified at the idea of making *any* body-capacitance test with that much voltage," the expert said.

Although checking polarity with a body-capacitance tester is quick and simple, you're putting immense faith in the tester. Don't risk it. It's much too easy to find a safe ground.—R. D.

You can install a polarized plug on an older lamp or appliance made without one. After cutting off the old plug, you need to know which wire goes to the center socket contact. This wire should serve the narrow blade of the polarized plug. Testing with a VOM or battery-powered continuity tester will tell you.

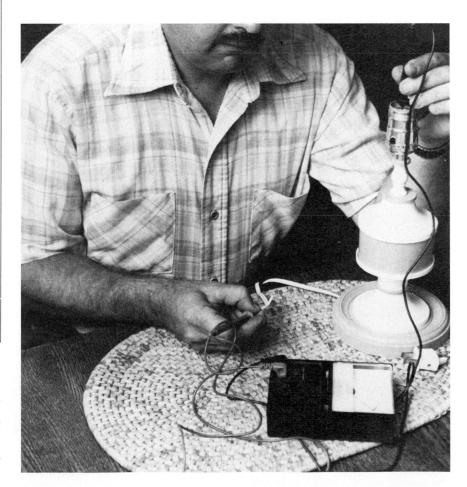

beginner's guide to auto repainting

Repaint my own car? Originally I thought I might have a pro do the job, and I'd simply document the procedure from the sidelines. But after some research I realized that the best insights would be gained by doing the job myself. I already owned a compressor and had previously done minor repainting and body-repair work. Besides, it looked as if it might even be fun.

I found that a beginner can do a competent job provided that: (1) he or she has some previous experience with spray painting and (2) his or her expectations are realistic.

Preparation

First I bumped out all of the dents and dings in my Volkswagen Beetle. Fortunately all of the surface imperfections were easily filled with body putty. But this article isn't on body-pounding, so I won't go into these preparations in any detail. Many auto-supply stores now sell do-it-yourself body-working kits and other material such as tubes of body putty, and local libraries have lots of books on body-working techniques.

Next I applied a wax-and-grease remover (Du Pont Prep-Sol) on all of the painted surfaces. This was to remove contaminants that might have prevented the new paint from adhering properly. If any of your original paint is cracked, bubbled, or peeling, you'll have to sand or strip the area down to a bare, stable surface. I used a large electric disc sander-grinder to help smooth out the really rough spots.

Most of the chrome, antennas, wipers, and badges must be removed before the paint is applied. Sometimes it may be easier to mask these specific pieces of hardware.

Big Sears Craftsman sander-grinder comes in handy for knocking down the cracked and peeling paint to bare metal. Wear safety glasses when sanding or grinding body panels.

Some experts I spoke with insisted that a good paint job can't be executed on anything but bare metal. To remove the paint from an entire vehicle you'd need a liquid paint remover. But unless the original finish is in truly sorry shape, try to stay away from the strippers.

The next big step was removing all of the chrome hardware and bright trim. (You may find that it's easier to mask a particular piece of brightwork rather than remove it.) I then wet-sanded the car with 240-, 360-, and then 400-grit paper to give the primer something to bite. The windows were masked with 3M masking paper and fresh tape. You can use newspaper if you're on a tight budget, but you run the risk of the print bleeding onto your new paint job. Don't try to make do with an aged roll of masking tape. I found that old tape is brittle, won't stick properly, and allows paint to creep underneath and get onto the wrong surface.

I sprayed the entire car with Platinum Gray 30 S primer-surfacer from Du Pont. Primers provide a coarse surface to which the topcoats can adhere. A primer-surfacer not only primes the surface, it also fills minor surface imperfections such as sanding or grinding scratches. My compressor is a small, single-horsepower unit from Sears. Make sure the compressor you use, whether rented or your own, can supply a minimum of three cubic feet per minute (cfm) at 35 pounds per square inch (psi). Also make sure you have enough air hose (35 to 50 feet) to move completely around the car. I didn't. During my second coat I had to move the compressor, and it accidentally became unplugged. I didn't notice the pressure drop until poor paint flow showed up on my car.

Thoroughly clean the work area before you begin. After the body work, sanding, and primer application, I swept carefully, then covered the entire floor with masking paper to keep the dust at bay. (You may want to do all of the body preparation in your driveway to keep the contamination out of your garage or spray area, especially if you intend to shoot enamel.)

Before I started spraying I practiced shooting paint at an old fender and a cardboard box. This gave me a chance to set the air- and fluid-adjustment screws on the back of the spray gun.

When I finally applied the topcoats, I held the gun about 8 to 10 inches from the panel. I was told you shouldn't arc or tilt the gun. If you do, it will deliver too much paint to the center of the panel section and too little at the ends of your stroke. I also made sure each stroke of paint overlapped the previous stroke by 50 percent. Finally, if you're about average height or less, you may want to position a step stool in the work area so you can reach the top of the car or truck.

Painting procedure

Two topcoat paint types are generally considered best for beginners: acrylic lacquer and acrylic enamel. (The solvent for lacquer is referred to as thinner. The solvent for enamel is called a reducer.)

If you repaint a car the original color, as I did, you'll want to check the vehicle-color code on the ID tag. This is usually located somewhere in the engine compartment. My VW's was in the front trunk.

Acrylic lacquer offers some excellent advantages for beginners. It's less complicated to mix and spray, and it dries much more quickly than enamel. That means there's less chance for dust or suicidal bugs to settle into the finished paint. And if you make a mistake, you can sand or buff the problem away much sooner. But there are some negative aspects about lacquer.

Use the compressor and an air nozzle to blow loose dust or water drops out of crevices before the spray gun does. A roll of wide paper and fresh tape make masking easy.

Spray-painting safety

Talk about shop safety usually generates about as much enthusiasm as a long session with an insurance salesman. But if you intend to paint a car, at least a few words of caution are in order. First, because most automotive-type paint products are flammable, you should have a fire extinguisher handy in the work area. Second, wear a good respirator with replaceable filters. If you apply any paint removers, wear Viton or butyl-rubber gloves because the caustic chemicals in most removers will attack your skin. Wear safety glasses or goggles during any mixing, grinding, or power sanding. Finally, proper ventilation is extremely important. I propped a pair of old window fans in the open door and window of my garage.

Lacquer must be rubbed out to get the best-possible results. Rubbing out requires going over the entire car with ultra-fine sandpaper after the car has been painted. In addition, lacquers and some enamel paints don't get along. If you spray lacquer over an original enamel top coat, the lacquer may not adhere or will craze or bleed through the old layer of paint.

How can you tell what type of paint is on your car? Rub some lacquer thinner on the old surface. Lacquer paint will dissolve quickly and acrylic lacquer somewhat more slowly, but the lacquer thinner won't put a dent in alkyd or acrylic enamel.

Still, if you decide to paint over enamel with lacquer, you have a choice. You can take the car down to bare metal with a paint remover, or, if the enamel is in pretty good shape, you can use a primer-sealer. This will not only seal the possibly incompatible original paint from the new but will also act as a primer.

I chose an acrylic enamel for three reasons: It doesn't have to rubbed out like lacquer, it provides a tougher finish, and it covers with fewer coats (I shot three coats). Unfortunately enamel takes much longer to dry than lacquer. Result: Even with all my attention to shop cleanliness, my finish coat picked up some dust and a few minor sags.

Mistakes can be corrected

If a mistake occurs, don't panic. Even big problems can usually be cured without starting the entire job over. The two best ways to avoid mistakes are to read the directions carefully and then to take your time.

One of the most-common problems is a run or sag. Although beginners are usually guilty of applying too much paint, there are other, more-complicated reasons for runs and sags. When you mix your paint and thinner or reducer, make sure the proportions are correct. Although it would seem that too much thinner would be the only cause of runs, too little also will produce runs and sags. That's because the thinner is the evaporative agent in the paint and dries the application. This stabilizes the paint on the panel.

In addition, thinners and reducers are temperature specific. If you've selected a warm-weather thinner or reducer and the mercury drops, your paint will have a much greater tendency to run or sag. Be sure, too, that you're using the proper air pressure. Insufficient pressure won't properly atomize the paint. Beginners may also find themselves holding the spray gun too close. The best distance for most paints is the hand span from the tip of your pinky to the tip of your thumb.

If a sag appears, first try using a fine paintbrush to remove it. Then spray another coat over the brush marks. I let my small runs dry. You'd be surprised how well a 600-grit paper works with plenty of water, rubbing compound, and patience.

"Orange peel" is the second-most-common problem for painters. It looks like its name: The paint develops tiny pits instead of flowing smoothly over the surface. It's generally caused by using a cool-weather thinner or reducer on a hot day, improper mixing, too much air pressure, or holding the gun too far away. Orange peel is actually pretty easy to cure. If it isn't a serious case, apply a second, wetter coat over the problem area. If the problem doesn't appear until after the paint dries, you can still rub it out with wet 600-grit paper and rubbing compound.

Would I attempt the job again? Yes. I learned a lot from doing it myself. And I believe that even a beginner can do a competent job. You're not going to get the perfection of a baked-on, factory-applied finish or the mirror surface that a professional refinisher's dust-free paint booth can provide, but you can get darn close. Would I do anything different? I'd probably use a lacquer next time. The shorter drying time would make corrections quicker and easier. Even so, I'd be hesitant to try a major color change—especially from dark to light—because that requires multiple coats for even coverage. But simply renewing an existing finish is well within the skills of a determined do-it-yourselfer—*by Jack Keebler. Photos by Greg Sharko.*

how to check your emissions systems

If a part in one of your car's emissions-control systems goes bad, the quantity of noxious fumes the engine blows into the atmosphere will increase. That's pretty obvious. But here's a fact that's not as apparent: Malfunctioning emissions-control parts can also cause practically every drivability problem in the book.

"Drivability problem"—that's car-manufacturer lingo for a host of troubles that irk drivers, including hesitation, surging (stumbling), power loss, spark knock (pinging), poor fuel economy, rough idling, hard starting, and run-on after engine shut-off (dieseling). Countless carburetors and ignition-system components have been needlessly replaced in efforts to cure these problems, for which faulty emissions-control components were really to blame.

Car makers are currently waging a campaign urging professional mechanics to test emissions-control parts before plunging into expensive repairs. Here's what one expert at the General Motors Research Center in Warren, Michigan, told me about just two of these parts:

The systems

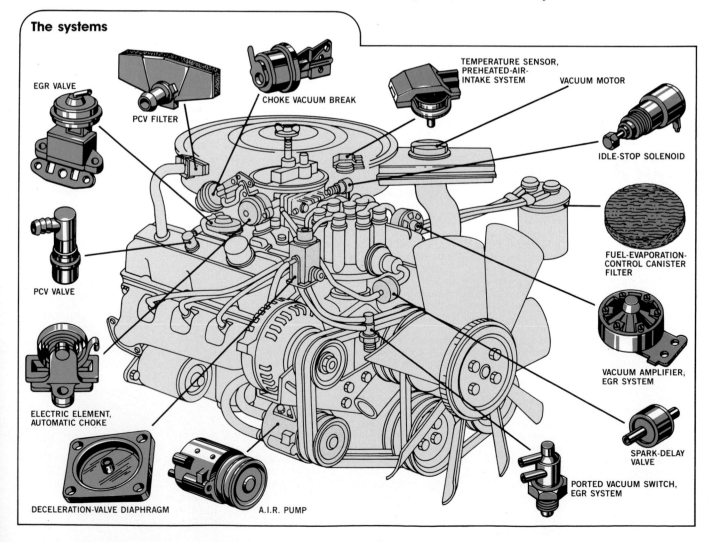

EGR VALVE

PCV FILTER

CHOKE VACUUM BREAK

TEMPERATURE SENSOR, PREHEATED-AIR-INTAKE SYSTEM

VACUUM MOTOR

IDLE-STOP SOLENOID

PCV VALVE

FUEL-EVAPORATION-CONTROL CANISTER FILTER

ELECTRIC ELEMENT, AUTOMATIC CHOKE

VACUUM AMPLIFIER; EGR SYSTEM

SPARK-DELAY VALVE

DECELERATION-VALVE DIAPHRAGM

A.I.R. PUMP

PORTED VACUUM SWITCH, EGR SYSTEM

"If mechanics would make sure that preheated-intake-air cleaners and exhaust-gas-recirculation (EGR) valves were working before doing tuneups, they'd resolve innumerable spark-knock, stalling, and hesitation complaints, save themselves time, and save their customers money."

Your car may have more than a dozen emissions-control parts. If you can't find these emissions parts on your engine (manufacturers locate them differently), tell your mechanic to test those parts first before looking for other reasons for your trouble—*by George Sears. Drawings by Russell von Sauers.*

PCV system

The positive-crankcase-ventilation (PCV) system draws combustion gases that accumulate in the crankcase into the combustion chamber, where they are burned. PCV was the first emissions-control system put on cars—in the early 1960s.

Malfunctioning PCV components can cause excessive oil consumption, hard starting, stalling, rough idling, missing at slow speeds, and power loss. Parts that cause trouble are the PCV valve, PCV air filter, and PCV hoses. Check them this way:

1. Pull the PCV valve from the engine. In most cases, it's located in a rocker-arm cover (see drawing).

2. Shake the valve. If it doesn't rattle, replace it.

3. Start the engine, and hold your thumb over the end of the valve. If you don't feel vacuum, replace the valve and test again. If there is still no vacuum, remove the PCV hoses. Replace any hoses that are cracked. Are the hoses OK? Then clean out any carbon by ramming a dry cloth through them. In most cars there's a PCV hose between the air cleaner and the rocker cover, and another between the PCV valve and the intake manifold or carburetor.

4. Find the PCV filter. In most cars it's inside the air-cleaner housing, as shown. Inspect the filter. If it's dirty, replace it. Instead of a PCV filter in the air-cleaner housing, Chrysler uses a filter in a breather cap located on the rocker-arm cover. To find it, trace the PCV hose from the carburetor air cleaner to the rocker-arm cover. Wash the breather cap in carburetor cleaner, turn upside down to drain solvent, and fill it with SAE 30 oil.

(Note: Many imported and some domestically built engines, such as the Chrysler 2.2-liter and the Ford 1.6-liter, don't have PCV systems of the traditional variety. They use a closed-crankcase-ventilation system with a fixed orifice [instead of a PCV valve] through which crankcase gases enter the intake manifold. The part of this system that clogs and causes engine problems most often is the carburetor air-cleaner filter.)

Carburetor-control parts

Depending on the vehicle, a carburetor may be equipped with an idle-stop (anti-dieseling) solenoid, electrically operated automatic choke, and a vacuum break (choke pull-off). Although these cannot technically be called emissions-control parts, they work closely with the emissions systems to maintain sound engine performance—which the emissions systems working by themselves would tend to disrupt.

The idle-stop solenoid overcomes the tendency of some engines to run on (diesel) after the ignition is shut off. This solenoid allows the throttle to close beyond the normal idle position when the ignition is turned off. Many modern engines require a high idle for efficient operation of emissions controls.

(Note: Many engines use a device resembling an idle-stop solenoid that is activated by the air conditioner. It opens the throttle slightly when the air conditioner is turned on, to prevent stalling that could occur when the load imposed on the engine by the compressor is applied. Refer to the emissions-control information label in the engine compartment to determine whether the solenoid on your car's carburetor is an antidieseling solenoid or an air-conditioner speed-up solenoid.)

The following procedure should be used to determine whether a defective idle-stop solenoid is causing dieseling, or whether a defective air-conditioner speed-up solenoid is causing the engine to stall when the compressor is on:

1. Turn on the ignition switch, but don't start the engine. When testing an air-conditioning speed-up solenoid, also turn on the air conditioner.

2. Watch the plunger of the throttle-lever end of the solenoid as you disconnect the electric wire at the solenoid. The plunger should draw away from the throttle lever. When you reconnect the electric wire, the plunger should extend out and make contact with the lever.

3. If the plunger doesn't move, connect a test light between the solenoid wire terminal and ground. If the light glows, showing that current is reaching the solenoid, the solenoid is defective. Replace it. If the light doesn't glow, there's a problem with the wire or with the circuit feeding the wire. Test the wiring, checking for short circuits.

Other emmissions-control components

The components discussed to this point are the ones you'll find on the majority of engines. However, depending on the make of your car and its engine, there might be other emissions-control parts that can cause drivability problems.

The following is a list of these components, the functions they perform, and the trouble they can cause:

Deceleration valve: It prevents backfiring in the exhaust system during deceleration, when the fuel mixture becomes richer, by allowing more air to bleed into the intake manifold. If the valve fails, an engine idles roughly and may backfire, which can cause engine damage.

Air-injection reactor (AIR), found on six- and eight-cylinder engines, and pulse-air-injection reactor (PAIR), on six- and four-cylinder engines: Both of these systems inject air directly into cylinder exhaust ports to aid in the burning of hydrocarbons and carbon monoxide. The major problem caused by a malfunctioning AIR or PAIR system is a strange and unpleasant noise (rumbling, chirping, knocking, or squealing) from the engine compartment.

Spark-timing controls: There are spark-delay valves, thermostatic vacuum switches, spark-advance vacuum modulators, and vacuum-reducer valves. Which one is used depends on the engine. If a spark-timing-control device is on your engine, it would probably be positioned in the vacuum line between the distributor vacuum advance and the vacuum source.

These emissions components control the vacuum signal to the vacuum advance under various engine conditions, including acceleration, deceleration, idling, and cruising. They can also be responsible for most of the drivability problems outlined.

EGR system

The EGR system recirculates exhaust gas back through the intake manifold into the engine, where it acts as a cooling agent to lower combustion temperatures. This

Preheated-intake-air system

Given different names by different manufacturers—Thermac Air Cleaner system (GM), Inlet Air Temperature system (Ford), and Heated Air Inlet system (Chrysler)—the purpose of this system is to keep warm air flowing into the carburetor at all times, even when the ambient temperature is below zero. Warm intake air curtails emissions by allowing a leaner carburetor setting and shorter choke-on time. Problems caused when a part fails include spark knock, stalling, surging, power loss, hesitation, and a drop in fuel economy.

The parts that can fail (see drawing) are the vacuum motor (normally in the air-cleaner snorkel), temperature sensor (normally in the air cleaner), and ducts. To trouble-shoot the system, do the following:

If there's a duct over the end of the air-cleaner snorkel, unclamp and remove it. Start the engine cold, and look inside the snorkel. As the engine warms up, the valve you see should move (downward in most cases). If the valve moves completely opposite to its cold position as the engine warms up, the system is operating properly.

If the valve doesn't move, shove it with your finger. Is it binding? Shoot compressed air into the snorkel to try to free it. If this doesn't work, replace the valve by replacing the air-cleaner housing. If the valve does move without binding, pull the vacuum hose from the vacuum motor. With the engine running at idle, hold your finger over the hose. If there is no suction (vacuum), check each duct and the hose to make sure they're tightly connected and that they aren't kinked or cracked. If a duct is an accordion type, look closely inside the folds; an unseen tear

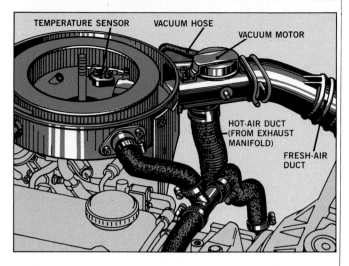

TEMPERATURE SENSOR   VACUUM HOSE   VACUUM MOTOR

HOT-AIR DUCT (FROM EXHAUST MANIFOLD)

FRESH-AIR DUCT

may be allowing cold air into the system. Replace any damaged duct or hose.

If ducts and hose are OK, the cause of an inoperative preheated-intake-air-system valve is a malfunctioning vacuum motor or temperature sensor. Check the motor by attaching a hand vacuum pump to the vacuum-motor hose nipple. Apply 10 inches Hg of vacuum, and watch the vacuum-pump gauge. It should maintain the vacuum for five minutes. If it doesn't, replace the motor. If it does, replace the temperature sensor.

Choke system

Most engines have an electrically operated automatic choke for more-precise choke operation. They also have one or two vacuum breaks to pull open choke valves slightly when the engine is first started cold. When the electrical element or vacuum break is not functioning, stalling and poor fuel economy result. Check these parts as follows:

1. With the engine cold and ambient temperature less than 80 degrees F, remove the carburetor air cleaner to watch the choke valve.

2. Have someone depress and let up the accelerator pedal. The valve should close the carburetor throat.

3. Start the engine. The choke valve should open slightly. If not, suspect a faulty vacuum break.

4. As the engine warms up, the choke valve should open fully. If not, check the electrical choke element.

(Note: Dirt-encrusted choke linkages and choke valves cause many more

choke problems than do the above components. Before proceeding, clean the linkage and choke valve, and test the system again.)

5. To test the electrical choke element, disconnect the wire terminal at the element, connect a voltmeter between the terminal and ground, and run the engine at idle. If the voltage is between 12 and 15 volts, replace the choke element. If the voltage is less than 12 volts, there is an open circuit, so check all wires and connections.

prevents oxides of nitrogen—a type of pollutant—from forming in the engine and being expelled into the atmosphere. A malfunctioning EGR system can cause spark knock (particularly when the engine is cold), hesitation or stalling on acceleration, stalling on deceleration and during quick stops, rough idling, hard starting, lack of power, and engine surge at a steady driving speed.

The heart of the system is the EGR valve, which is on the intake manifold near the carburetor (see drawing). Here's how you can tell whether the system is working properly:

1. With the engine warmed up and running at idle speed, the transmission in "Park," and the parking brake engaged, place your fingers under the EGR valve so they touch the diaphragm. Have an assistant increase engine speed. (Caution: The EGR valve will be hot, so wear soft work gloves.) The diaphragm should move up (open position) as the engine is accelerated, and down (closed position) as the engine returns to idle speed.

2. If the EGR-valve diaphragm doesn't move, pull off the valve nipple, and hold your finger over the hose opening. Accelerate to about 2,000 rpm for six- and eight-cylinder engines, and 3,000 rpm for four-cylinder engines.

3. If you feel a strong pull (vacuum), the EGR valve is faulty. Replace it. A faulty valve is usually the cause of EGR-system failure. If there is no vacuum, trace the hose to its other end. Make sure it isn't kinked. Then pull it free. Check the hose for cracks, and be sure it isn't clogged. If the hose is OK, reconnect it securely, and look to the other EGR parts for the cause of the trouble: They are all involved in making sure that exhaust-gas recirculation takes place at the temperature and time it will do the most good without adversely affecting drivability. These parts include: back-pressure variable transducer, temperature-control valve, vacuum amplifier, ported vacuum switch, temperature vacuum switch, temperature-sensor vacuum valve, engine-heat-sensing valve, and sub-EGR valve.

Fuel-evaporation-control system

This system has as its main element a charcoal-filled canister that you'll find in the engine compartment. Hoses attached to it extend to the carburetor, fuel tank, and intake manifold. The system traps gasoline vapors and diverts them to the engine, where they are burned.

A clogged or damaged fuel-evaporation-control system is a major cause of gasoline odors in cars. The system may also cause hard starting and rough idling when the engine is hot.

To resolve problems caused by the evaporation-control system, first check hoses for cracks. Replace damaged hoses with those specifically manufactured to handle fuel vapors.

The next step is to determine whether the charcoal canister has a replaceable filter, which is usually in the bottom of the unit. Replace the filter. If there is no filter, you'll have to replace the canister. Generally, manufacturers suggest doing this every two years or 30,000 miles.

trouble-shooting electronic ignition

When Chrysler introduced electronic ignition (EI) in 1971, the system's newness and relative scarcity kept it low on the do-it-yourselfer's priority list. Today, with 75 to 85 percent of all cars on the road sporting an EI system, the big question among DIY mechanics is: "Can I trouble-shoot and repair my electronic ignition?" The answer is yes. Furthermore, you can do it with an ordinary voltmeter and ohmmeter.

Rather than trying to skim the surface of every EI system in use today, this chapter tells you in detail how to service Chrysler's basic EI system. That way, you can do the same for, say, a Ford, Chevy, Datsun, or Honda by using these specific instructions as a guide, along with the layout and specs of your car's EI system given in most general auto repair books.

Pinpointing ignition trouble—all cars

Not even the ultra-reliable electronic parts of an EI system last forever. When one of these parts falters, your car engine will be difficult if not impossible to start although it turns over briskly. To determine whether the problem is ignition-caused, start by twisting any spark plug boot off its plug. Then shove a metal paper clip inside the boot so that it makes contact with the cable terminal. Grasp the boot with a pair of insulated spark plug pliers, holding the metal clip 1/4 to 1/2 inch away from a clean, dry metal part of the engine.

Have someone in the car crank the engine. If there's no spark or if a yellow spark jumps the gap between the metal clip and ground, you have an ignition problem. If a bright blue spark jumps that gap, your problem is in the fuel system. *Important:* Keep all sparks away from fuel system components where fuel vapors may form. Do not hold the cable in your hand—you could get a shock.

Secondary circuit problems

Once you've traced the problem to the ignition system, inspect those parts of the secondary circuit that can keep an engine from starting. In most EI systems, the secondary circuit consists of the high voltage cable between ignition coil and distributor cap, the distributor cap, rotor, spark plug cables, and spark plugs. Cables and plugs usually fail one at a time, which will cause an engine to miss rather than not start. On the other hand, a damaged high voltage cable between the coil and distributor cap, a bad cap, or a damaged rotor can prevent engine starting.

Fig. 1. Pickup coil and reluctor are the key elements of the Chrysler EI system in the distributor. They make and break the circuit necessary to step up low voltage to high voltage.

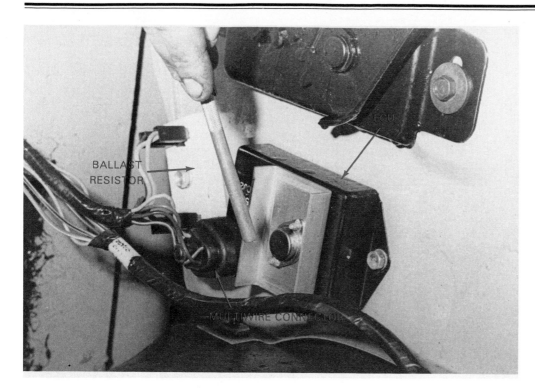

Fig. 2. ECU power transistor that can give you a bad shock is pointed out. Don't touch it. Other EI elements include the multiwire connector, which has to be disconnected from the ECU to test the system.

First be sure the high voltage cable is securely connected at the coil and center distributor tower. Also check tightness of the primary circuit wires flanking the high voltage cable at the coil. Remove the cable and test it with an ohmmeter. It should show a resistance of no more than 25,000 ohms. If the cable shows more, replace it or any of the spark plug cables similarly tested. If you don't have an ohmmeter, just replace the cable; it often fails after 30,000 miles. *Important:* The High Energy Ignition (HEI) system on most GM cars does not have this high tension cable because the ignition coil is inside the distributor cap.

Continue your check of the secondary circuit by taking off the distributor cap and rotor. Examine both for cracks, burned or corroded terminals, and carbon tracks (which indicate hairline cracks).

Primary circuit problems

If the secondary circuit checks out okay, move on to the primary circuit. That is where low voltage supplied by the battery is stepped up to the high voltage carried by the secondary circuit to the plugs, which ignite the fuel mixture. The Chrysler system's primary circuit consists of a ballast resistor, electronic control unit (ECU), ignition coil, reluctor, and pickup coil in the distributor, as well as the ignition switch, battery, and wiring between these units.

Here's a step-by-step test procedure for the Chrysler basic EI system. Similar techniques can be used to uncover problems in other EI systems.

1. Test the battery by connecting a voltmeter between the battery's positive terminal and a ground. Crank the engine. If the reading is below 12 volts, charge battery and retest.

2. With the ignition switch off, disconnect the multiwire connector from the plug of the ECU (figure 2). *Important:* That bright metal button in the ECU near the multiwire connector is a power switching transistor. It's "hot" when the ignition is turned on, so don't touch it.

3. Connect the positive lead of the voltmeter to cavity No. 1 of the multiwire connector and the negative lead of the voltmeter to ground (figure 4). Turn the ignition switch on. The voltmeter should read battery voltage +1 volt. If the reading is not within this range, inspect the wiring connections shown in the diagram. They should be clean and tight.

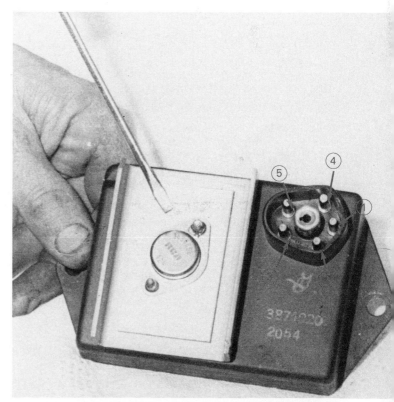

Fig. 3. ECU multiwire plug shows multiwire connector pins to which connector cavities attach. *Note:* Make tests with the ECU mounted in the engine compartment.

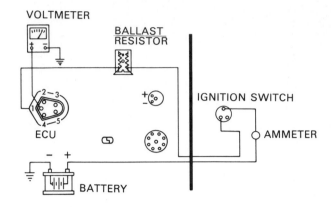

Fig. 4. Voltmeter hookup for multiwire connector cavity No. 1. If the system fails this or subsequent tests, check the wiring between the parts called out.

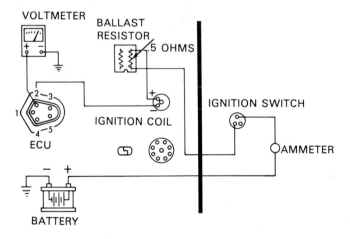

Fig. 5. Voltmeter hookup for cavity No. 2.

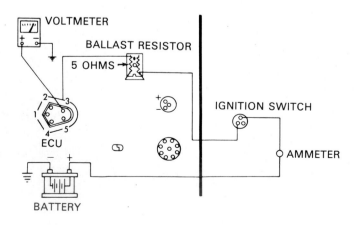

Fig. 6. Voltmeter hookup for cavity No. 3.

4. Repeat the same test for cavity No. 2 and No. 3 of the multiwire connector (figures 5 and 6). *Note that the No. 3 pin and cavity are omitted from Chrysler EI systems of 1980 and newer models.* Remember to turn off the ignition switch when connecting the voltmeter, then turn it on to make the test.

5. If when testing cavity No. 1 you get a voltmeter reading that isn't normal but wire connections are clean and tight, the dual ballast resistor may be defective. As the name implies, the dual ballast resistor is two resistors in one. One side of the unit, called the compensating side, is a 0.5-ohm resistor in models before 1980. Beginning with 1980 models, a 1.2-ohm resistor is used.

The compensating side maintains primary current at a constant level although engine speed varies. When the engine is cranked, current bypasses this part of the ballast resistor so that full battery voltage can be applied to the ignition coil.

The other side of the dual ballast resistor, called the auxiliary side, is a 5-ohm resistor. Its job is to protect the electronic control unit from excessive current.

Before disconnecting wires from the ballast resistor, identify them in relation to the terminals to which they connect. Reconnecting wires incorrectly can damage EI components. Connect an ohmmeter across the two top terminals of the ballast resistor. Record the reading. Then connect the ohmmeter across the two bottom terminals. Record the reading. *Note:* Make sure both ohmmeter leads are connected either to top terminals or bottom terminals only. Keep the ignition switch off during this test.

The compensating resistor should show a reading of 0.5 to 0.6 ohm or 1.2–1.3 ohms, depending on the year of the car. The auxiliary resistor should show a reading of 4.75 to 5.75 ohms. If either of the readings is not within specification, replace the ballast resistor.

6. If necessary, test the pickup coil next. The pickup coil is in the distributor (figure 1).

With the ignition switch off, connect an ohmmeter between cavities No. 4 and No. 5 of the multiwire connector as shown in figure 7. You should get a reading of 150 to 900 ohms. If you don't, pull apart the connector that joins the distributor and multiwire connector. Attach an ohmmeter to the part of the connector on the distributor side as shown in figure 8. Keep the ignition switch off.

If the ohmmeter gives a reading of 150 to 900 ohms, reconnect the two parts of the connector tightly. If the ohmmeter reading still doesn't fall between 150 and 900 ohms, replace the pickup coil in the distributor.

7. If the cause of trouble still hasn't been found, turn your attention to the multiwire connector pins. With the ignition switch off, hook one lead of an ohmmeter to connecting pin 5 and the other lead to ground (figure 9).

If the ohmmeter shows other than zero ohms, remove the electronic control unit. Using a wire brush, clean the back of the unit and the mounting area. Reattach the ECU, making sure bolts are tight. Retest.

If this procedure does not result in an ohmmeter reading of zero ohms, replace the electronic control unit and dual ballast resistor. Since the ballast resistor protects the ECU, a failed ECU may mean the ballast resistor had previously failed.

Inside the distributor

If the cause of ignition failure has not revealed itself at this point, remove the ohmmeter and voltmeter and reconnect the multiwire connector securely to the ECU. Remove the distributor cap and rotor, and adjust the air gap between a reluctor tooth and pickup coil tooth as follows:

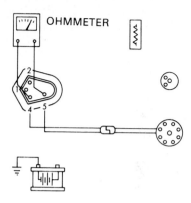

Fig. 7. Ohmmeter hookup to test pickup coil. Note that cavity No. 3 is missing from the multiwire connector, as is the case if the car you're working on is a 1980 or newer model.

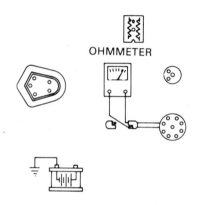

Fig. 8. Ohmmeter hookup to test connector that joins distributor and multiwire connector. Note that the ohmmeter is attached to connector half on the distributor side.

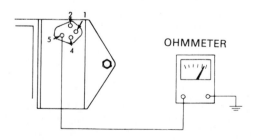

Fig. 9. Ohmmeter hookup to test multiwire connector pins. This test will show whether the ECU is causing ignition failure.

● Engage the large nut of the crankshaft pulley with a wrench and turn the pulley clockwise until a reluctor tooth and pickup coil tooth line up.

● Loosen the pickup coil adjusting screw and insert a plastic (nonmagnetic) feeler gauge between the reluctor tooth and pickup coil tooth (figure 10). In most Chrysler cars, a 0.008-inch feeler gauge is required. For 1978 and 1980 models use a 0.006-inch feeler gauge.

● Move the pickup coil in or out until the tooth of the pickup coil, feeler gauge, and reluctor tooth come in contact. All three elements should touch, but you should be able to move the feeler gauge without having to use force. Tighten the pickup coil adjustment screw.

● Double-check the air gap with a feeler gauge 0.002 inch larger than the one you used to make the adjustment. You should not be able to get this gauge between the reluctor tooth and pickup coil tooth. If you can, the adjustment isn't correct, so do it again.

● Disconnect the vacuum advance hose from the engine and draw in on it with your mouth or a hand-vacuum pump to create a vacuum. Watch the pickup coil plate. If it does not rotate as vacuum is applied, the vacuum advance unit must be replaced. Also, the pickup coil tooth should not strike any tooth of the reluctor. If it does, the gap between the pickup coil and reluctor isn't set properly.

If you still haven't found out why the EI system didn't pass the spark intensity test, the fault lies with a bad reluctor, pickup coil, ignition coil, or ECU. If the reluctor has a broken tooth, replace it. If not, see if you can install a new pickup coil, ignition coil, and ECU, and return those parts that don't solve the trouble—*by George Sears.*

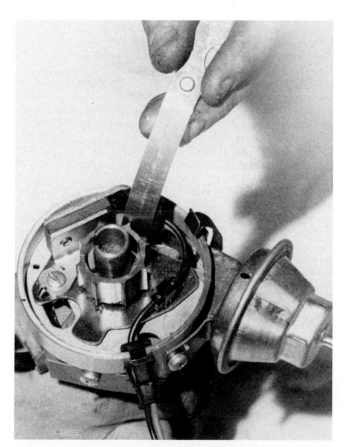

Fig. 10. Use a plastic feeler gauge to adjust the air gap between a reluctor tooth and pickup coil tooth.

trouble-shooting front disc brakes

The car swerved sharply to the right, almost going out of control as the driver pressed down hard on the brake pedal. Baffled, the owner coaxed the car into my shop for attention. He said the brakes should have been working perfectly—he had just finished installing new front brake pads.

Before looking at the car I explained to him that replacing brake pads—generally a simple procedure—can quickly become complicated if you don't have a clear picture of how the brake system works. In the next few pages I'll explain what I did to fix those brakes that pulled to the right, offer some trouble-shooting tips, and review the basic front-disc-brake hydraulic system.

Raising the car slightly on a lift, I invited the customer to help me trouble-shoot the problem. I had him step on the brake pedal while I grasped the left front wheel and tried to rotate it. The wheel turned freely. The right front wheel, by contrast, wouldn't budge when I tried to rotate it. That meant something was wrong with the left brake caliper. Removing the caliper and examining it, I could see the problem: The caliper piston was corroded and had seized in its housing. By seating the calipers when he installed the new pads, the customer had unwittingly caused the corroded piston to freeze tight in its bore, putting the brake completely out of action. Only the right front brake was working, causing sharp swerves to the right.

At this point he recalled that the left brake pads had shown more wear than those on the right side. This made sense. The corroded piston had caused the left brake's calipers to drag, resulting in premature pad wear. I told the customer that when he originally checked the brake pads for wear and noticed the extreme difference between the left and right sides, he also should have tried to rotate the front wheels. This would have revealed the faulty caliper. I solved the problem by installing a rebuilt left front caliper.

Here's another piece of advice I gave my customer: It's a mistake to attempt brake repairs without a shop manual

at hand. Make sure the manual shows a picture of the brake system you're repairing because you'll need it to be sure all the hardware is installed correctly. One of the best brake manuals I've seen can be bought by mail from the manufacturers of Raybestos brakes (Brake Systems, Inc., 5 McKee Place, Cheshire, CT 06410).

Checking brake safety

Start with a road test on a quiet street. Park the car, and shut off the engine. Pump the brake pedal several times to use up the vacuum reserve for the power brake. Press the brake pedal, and start the engine. If the power brake is working properly, you'll feel the pedal drop just a bit. If the pedal doesn't move, look for trouble in the power-brake system. With the engine running, press the brake pedal again. Hold it down for 60 seconds. The pedal should hold steady with no fade.

Next, drive the car with the steering wheel held loosely in your hands. Check for a pull to one side when you brake—a common problem. The pedal should remain firm throughout the stop. Check the parking brake by engaging it and trying to drive the car forward. The car should strongly resist the engine's pull.

Now it's time to make an inspection of all the brake components. First, jack up the car and place it on good-quality jack stands. Release the parking brake, shift the transmission to neutral, and rotate each wheel by hand to check for drag. You should be able to turn the wheels with a minimum of effort. If you can't, there may be a problem.

Now remove the wheels, and check the thickness of the front-disc-brake pads. In general, if the pads are the same thickness or thinner than the metal backing plates, replace them. Look over the surfaces of the front-disc-brake rotors: They must be smooth for efficient operation. Check the parking-brake cable for binding. At the rear wheels, check the lining thickness. Make sure all of the brake hardware is firmly in place. Check the self-adjusting mechanisms. See that the star-wheel adjusters move freely.

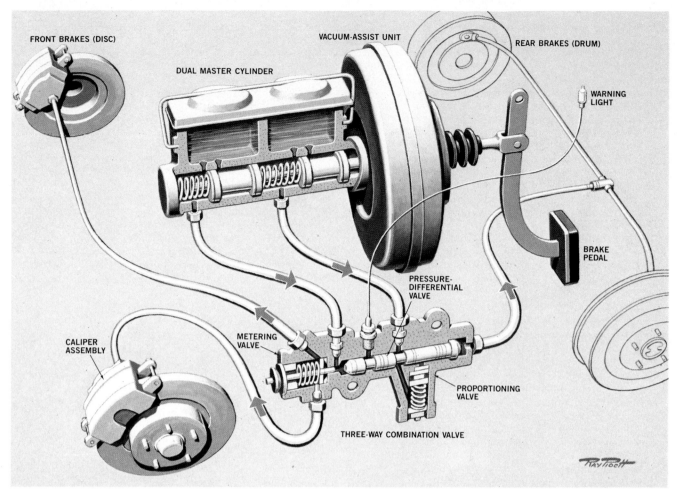

FRONT BRAKES (DISC)

DUAL MASTER CYLINDER

VACUUM-ASSIST UNIT

REAR BRAKES (DRUM)

WARNING LIGHT

BRAKE PEDAL

PRESSURE-DIFFERENTIAL VALVE

CALIPER ASSEMBLY

METERING VALVE

PROPORTIONING VALVE

THREE-WAY COMBINATION VALVE

How brakes work: Foot effort applied to the brake pedal is multiplied by the vacuum-operated power-assist unit (above). Simultaneously, the master cylinder pressurizes fluid in two separate circuits: front disc brakes and rear drum brakes. The combination valve contains a metering valve that controls pressure to the front-disc-brake calipers by restricting the flow of fluid to them until about 125 psi of pressure has developed. This delays front-brake caliper action just long enough for the slower-moving rear drum brakes to engage. The combination valve also houses a self-centering pressure-differential-sensing switch. Should a hydraulic leak develop somewhere in the system, the switch will block off the side of the dual braking system where the leak has occurred. The switch also illuminates a dashboard light warning that one side of the brake's hydraulic system is inoperative. If a leak occurs, it is unlikely that you will experience total brake failure, but you will notice a lower brake pedal. The car will be stopped by either the front brakes alone or by the rear brakes. On cars with diagonally split braking systems, either the right rear and left front brakes or the left rear and right front brakes will stop the car, depending on which circuit has failed. This system is designed to improve braking stability during hydraulic malfunctions. Some systems have a proportioning valve, which balances the hydraulic pressure to the rear drum brakes.

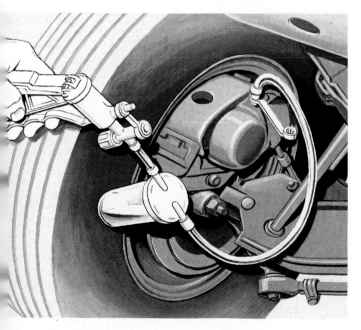

Examine the master cylinder for signs of leakage. Remove the cover, and inspect the gasket. If the gasket is swollen, be suspicious of contaminated brake fluid. Low brake fluid in one section of the master cylinder generally indicates a leak; the brake system itself doesn't consume any fluid. If the level is low, there must be a reason. Check the entire hydraulic system inch by inch until you find the leak. If there is no evidence of brake fluid leaking at the wheels or on the brake lines, disconnect the master cylinder. Check for leaking fluid where the push rod enters the back of the master cylinder. Check the vacuum hose to the power brake for signs of wear. Finally, check the brake warning light by momentarily grounding the wire at the combination valve. The light should flicker.

Brake problems are often indicated by pedal fade: The brake pedal seems to melt away when you keep your foot on it at a traffic light. If there are no brake-fluid leaks, this problem is generally caused by a worn master cylinder. Replace it.

Manual vacuum pump allows you to bleed brakes without an assistant. Reservoir holds fluid drawn from nipple.

163

Trouble-shooting

Air trapped in a newly installed caliper or wheel cylinder will cause the brake pedal to feel spongy. It is important to bleed the brakes whenever the hydraulic system is disturbed. You'll need a helper to pump the brake pedal while you crank open the bleeder screws at each wheel. Many modern auto-repair shops now use a new vacuum brake-bleeding device. This $150 air-powered system sucks the brake fluid and air bubbles through the bleeder screws. An inexpensive hand-operated device is the Mityvac model 6820 brake-bleeding kit (Neward Enterprises Inc., Box 725, Rancho Cucamonga, CA 91730; previous page, bottom). At under $30, it brings one-man operation within reach of most budgets.

Front-disc-brake squeal is usually caused by the pads vibrating. It is important to make sure that the O-rings and caliper-locating hardware are in good shape. Brake-pad-support springs must also be in place and in good condition. On General Motors cars, for example, the tangs on the front-disc-brake outside pads must fit tightly to the caliper. In addition to making sure the pads are secure, you can also apply a toothpaste-like chemical coating to the metal brake-pad backing plate. One that I have found effective is called Disc Brake Quiet, marketed by CRC Chemicals Inc. (885 Louis Dr., Warminster, PA 18974).

If you feel the brake pedal pulsating when you brake, you may have a parallelism problem—which simply means the disc-brake rotor is thicker in some spots. When the thicker part of the rotor passes through the applied caliper, it pushes the piston back into the caliper just a bit. You feel this pulsation in your foot. Machining the rotors generally solves the problem. It may also cure a warped rotor, which causes rough, chattering, or pulsating brakes.

Before you install any new brake parts, carefully compare them with the old parts. If you replace a leaking or corroded brake line, you must use only steel brake tubing. Never substitute copper tubing or use a compression fitting on brake lines. Use only specially designed and flared brake lines and fittings. And don't install a new set of brake pads in a hurry; take the time to inspect the condition of the wheel bearings and other components that make up the brake system.

The condition of the brake fluid is also important for the correct functioning of the hydraulic system. Fluid doesn't last forever. In fact, polyglycol brake fluid is prone to absorbing moisture. Flush out all of the brake fluid when you replace any hydraulic component. Use only top-quality DOT 3 or DOT 4 brake fluid. Or consider changing to the new moisture-resistant silicone brake fluid.

Cut-rate pads don't make the grade

It's incredible how often cars with no history of brake problems suddenly develop difficulties after new brake pads are installed. Very often the trouble can be traced to the quality of the replacement brake pads. You should know what kind of brake pads you need. Newer cars with smaller-diameter disc rotors may require the new semi-metallic disc-brake pads. These pads contain steel fibers and graphite in resins designed to withstand higher braking temperatures than were generated by the brakes on older cars. It's been my experience that good-quality semi-metallic disc-brake pads will last longer than the conventional pads that were originally installed on some cars.

You should also be aware that there are both economy and premium grades of asbestos brake pads. Some disc-brake-pad manufacturers are offering a lifetime limited warranty on their premium brake pads. The pads themselves will be replaced free (you pay the labor) if they wear out during the remaining time you own the car. What this means is that the pad makers are betting the pads will last at least the 40,000 miles their statistics show you are likely to drive before you sell your car. But the new warranties do not mean the brake pads will last indefinitely.

If you are concerned about the hazards of asbestos brake dust, install the new fiberglass brake linings developed by Abex Corp. (Friction Products Div., 30001 Big Beaver Rd., Troy, MI 48084). The Abex EXL friction material contains chopped-strand fiberglass in a heat-setting polymer-resin matrix.

Whichever type of friction material you choose, buy only top-of-the-line pads with a well-known brand name. *Never buy brakes in a plain brown wrapper.* It simply does not make sense to save money on brakes. Poor-quality brake pads or linings may not stand up to the heat and may fade just when you need them most—*by Bob Cerullo. Drawings by Ray Pioch.*

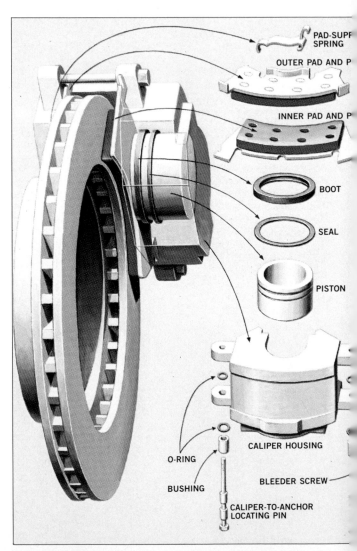

At each front wheel (above), hydraulic pressure causes the disc-brake-caliper piston to move, squeezing the brake pads with a clamp like grip onto the disc-brake rotor. The resulting friction provides braking force to stop the car.

curing preignition and detonation

Known variously as engine spark knock, ping, detonation, and preignition, the rattling sounds emanating from your car's engine can sometimes be perfectly normal. At other times, however, they may signal the impending destruction of major engine parts, so it's important to recognize the difference.

What exactly is spark knock, or detonation? It is the result of two energy forces colliding in a combustion chamber (see drawing, right). The severity of this collision determines whether it threatens to do serious damage to pistons and connecting rods, or whether it is acceptable. As a source at General Motors explains, "Under certain conditions, engines are designed to operate with a faint 'ticking' sound known as trace detonation." But abnormal detonation, over a fairly long period of time, can destroy pistons and piston-related components, leading to huge repair bills.

Preignition is a separate but related problem. It is never normal, and it can cause major engine damage almost immediately. There's no such thing as trace preignition.

When does ping or tick from the engine indicate harmless trace detonation? It's when you hear noise under the following conditions:
● When the throttle is opened or closed rapidly.
● When the engine is cold.
● When the vehicle is climbing a steep hill or in any other situation that requires wide-open throttle.
● When the brake pedal is pressed. This last situation occurs because some cars have an exhaust-gas recirculation (EGR) system cutout switch, which shuts off EGR to the cylinders when the brakes are applied. Because the EGR system normally feeds ex-

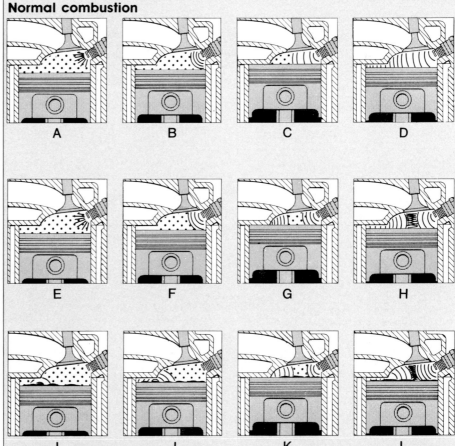

Normal combustion

A B C D

E F G H

I J K L

During normal combustion (top), the spark plug ignites the fuel mixture (A), and the resulting flame front races evenly across the combustion chamber (B and C) until all fuel is burned (D). With the detonation (middle), the spark plug ignites the fuel mixture (E), which begins to burn normally (F). Increasing pressure and temperature then cause an unburned part of the mixture to ignite spontaneously (G). The flame fronts from these two burning pockets of fuel meet violently (H), releasing energy that causes the cylinder head to vibrate with a knocking sound. Power loss usually results. With preignition (above), a red-hot carbon deposit in the combustion chamber (I)—rather than the spark plug—ignites the fuel mixture. The flame front spreads (J), causing a temperature increase that allows the mixture to ignite spontaneously elsewhere (K). Preignition can occur when the piston hasn't reached the top of its upstroke. This will subject both the piston and the connecting rod to destructive mechanical and thermal forces from colliding flame fronts (L).

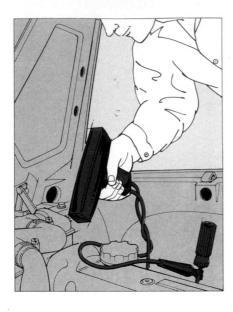

haust gas into the cylinders to lower temperature, the temperature increases when EGR is cut off, causing trace detonation.

You may be able to eliminate trace detonation by using fuel with a higher octane rating than that which you've been burning. The octane rating is an index of gasoline's antiknock properties. It's interesting to note that more and more suppliers of gasoline are beginning to market unleaded regular gas having octane ratings of 88 and 89 (and even higher-rated 91-to-93-octane super unleaded) rather than 87-octane gasoline, which has been the norm since unleaded regular hit the pumps back in the mid-1970s. This is in direct response to the pinging problems affecting so many of today's vehicles originally certified to run on regular unleaded fuel.

Incorrect ignition timing is one of the possible causes for detonation, but the problem often lies elsewhere.

Conditions	How to remedy
Preignition due to overheating of spark-plugs	Remove plugs, and examine tips. If white or blistered, replace plugs with a colder set. Colder plugs, which dissipate heat rapidly, are especially suited for vehicles driven mainly at higher speeds rather than in the city.
Preignition due to deposits inside the engine	Use a carbon-deposit solvent such as GM's Top Engine Cleaner. If three treatments fail to relieve the knock, it's likely that detonation is the real problem.
Detonation due to a vehicle design factor	Call a dealer and ask whether a technical service bulletin involving spark knock has been issued by the manufacturer (see box). If the condition is a result of an emissions-control-component failure, remember that emissions-control systems on many cars are covered by a five-year or 50,000-mile warranty.
Detonation due to engine overheating	A loss of coolant through boiling or a high engine temperature on the gauge or warning light indicates overheating. Tune up the cooling system by testing the radiator cap, checking for leaks, tightening the water-pump drive belt, draining and flushing the system, and checking to see that the fan is working.
Detonation because a high-voltage cable lies too close to a ground or too close to another cable	See that no spark-plug cable is resting on or near an engine bolt. If the engine has a computer control system with electronic spark timing, see that its cable harness isn't near a spark cable or alternator wire. Route cables away from parts that could be causing electrical grounding, which can alter ignition timing and cause detonation.
Detonation due to excessive oil foaming	Check oil level when the engine is cold. If oil level is above the "full" mark on the dipstick, drain excess.
Detonation due to an inoperative heated-air inlet valve that traps hot air in the engine	Remove duct from carburetor snorkel. Start the engine, which should be cold, and see whether valve inside the snorkel moves to close off hot-air opening from exhaust manifold. Replace damaged ducts, hoses, vacuum motor, temperature sensor, or damper valve.
Detonation because a stuck manifold heat-control valve traps hot air in the engine	With the engine cold, see whether you can move the valve, which is on the exhaust manifold. Lubricate the valve shaft with heat-control-valve lubricant. Tap lightly from side to side using small hammer. If

Conditions	How to remedy
	several treatments don't free the valve, replace it. (NOTE: On some cars the valve is controlled by a vacuum valve and a thermal vacuum switch. With the engine running, pull the hose off the vacuum valve, and hold your finger over the end of the hose. Lack of suction indicates a bad hose or thermal vacuum switch. Test the vacuum valve with a vacuum pump.)
Detonation because an air leak at the carburetor-intake manifold joint is producing a lean fuel mixture	Connect a vacuum gauge, and run the engine at idle speed. An air leak is indicated by a vacuum-gauge reading that's below normal but holds steady. Abnormal reading is 17 to 21 inches of mercury (in. Hg). To verify, squirt engine oil around the carburetor-intake manifold joint. The vacuum-gauge reading will rise momentarily. Tighten carburetor bolts. If this doesn't seal the leak, replace the carburetor gasket.
Detonation due to bad head gasket, causing abnormally high cylinder pressure	Connect a vacuum gauge, and run the engine at different speeds. A vacuum-gauge needle that flutters over a range of approximately 10 in. Hg at all speeds indicates a bad head gasket. Replace it.
Detonation due to ignition timing	Use a timing light and tachometer to check ignition timing. Also check vacuum- and centrifugal-advance curves with a timing meter. If at the end of trouble-shooting you haven't found a reason for spark knock, retard timing two degrees to see whether the knock dissipates. You can safely retard timing a total of six degrees from specification.
Detonation caused by a restricted exhaust system	Connect a vacuum gauge, and accelerate the engine. If the gauge needle dips from a normal reading to near zero and then starts to rise, the exhaust system is blocked.
Detonation because of an inoperative EGR system	Warm up the engine. Put on a glove, and reach under the EGR valve to see whether you can feel the valve diaphragm. Open and close the throttle. You should feel the diaphragm moving. If you can't touch the diaphragm, check the system with a vacuum pump. Replace a faulty EGR valve or other EGR-system component.
Detonation caused by failure of a computerized engine-control-system sensor	Use an ohmmeter to find the faulty sensor, which may be the manifold absolute-pressure sensor, differential-pressure sensor, barometric-pressure sensor, vehicle-speed sensor, or throttle-position sensor.

Here's how to recognize abnormal detonation or preignition:
● The knock is constant as the vehicle is cruising, climbing a slight grade, or gradually accelerating.
● The knock is severe but tapers off as the vehicle accelerates.
● The knock is heard only as the vehicle coasts down.

Putting a finger on the reason for an abnormal knock is not easy be-

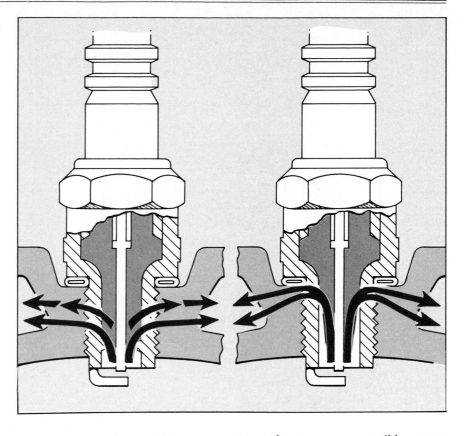

Cold spark plug for high-speed driving (left) has short insulator tip (shaded area) that transfers heat quickly. Hotter plug's long tip (right) retains heat to burn off deposits formed during city driving. Preignition can occur when hot plug is used in place of cold one.

Spark-knock data from Detroit

Here is a list of recently issued Chrysler, Ford, and GM technical service bulletins (TSBs) that concern spark knock. Note that for the GM cars Pontiac TSB numbers are provided. Each GM division has issued the same information—but under a different TSB number. Use the Pontiac number for reference.

Manufacturer	Vehicles and engines involved	TSB No.	Suggested corrective action
Chrysler	1982½–'84 vehicles with 2.2-liter engines and two-barrel carburetors	14-03-84	Install vacuum-reducer valve
Chrysler	1982–'83 cars with 318-cu.-in. engines and two-barrel carburetors	08-14-83	Install vacuum-delay valve
Chrysler	1982–'83 light trucks with 225-cu.-in. engines and four-speed overdrive transmissions	08-12-82 (revision A)	Disconnect computer coolant-temperature switch, and reset basic timing
Chrysler	1981–'82 light-duty trucks and vans with 225-cu.-in. engines	08-18-82	Reset basic timing
Ford	1983½–'84 2.3-liter EFI turbo engines	84-6	Install new oil separator and PCV closure tube
Ford	1984 3.8-liter engines	84-5	Reset timing by installing a retard-octane rod
Ford	1983 2.3-liter engines	83-1	Retard ignition timing
Ford	1982 3.3-liter engines	82-14	Reposition vacuum check valve
GM	1984 2.5-liter engines with automatic transaxles	Pontiac 84-6-32	Install new PROM in engine computer
GM	1983 2.8-liter engines	Pontiac 83-T-61	Retard ignition timing
GM	1983 vehicles with ECM-controlled torque-converter clutch	Pontiac 83-1-51	Clean reflective bars of speedometer head serving as reflective panels for vehicle-speed sensors

cause there are many possible causes. Two of them—carbon deposits in the engine, and overheated spark plugs—cause preignition and should be tackled right away.

Trouble shooting techniques for the other causes of detonation range from simple ones to complex procedures for testing computerized engine-control systems.

Because some of the engine systems that can cause detonation or preignition are not linked to each other—either mechanically or electrically—searching for the problem is something of a hit-or-miss procedure. The table presented here gives you a logical trouble shooting sequence, beginning with the most serious and proceeding through the most common causes for spark knock and how to eliminate them—*by George Sears. Drawings by Russell von Sauers.*

electronic table and radial saws

With the whir of a motor, the blade on the table saw came to life. No, it didn't spin. It tilted. As it did so, red digital readouts flashed on a control panel, racing upward from zero degrees. When the readout hit 45 degrees, the whirring stopped. Then it resumed, but now the blade began to rise from its slot in the table. Again the numbers flashed, this time reading out the height of the blade as it rose. When the motor finally stopped, the blade height read 1.375 inches. The electronic-power-tool revolution had taken another step forward.

The scene was my shop, where I had just spent the better part of a day setting up two brand-new tools from Sears. These tools, the Craftsman electronic table and radial saws, are the first of their kind in the world. And now that I finally had them set up and calibrated, I was anxious to find out just how good these new stationary tools were. I had a lot of questions.

Would the digital readouts be more accurate and easier to read than conventional scales and pointers? Would the motorized controls be faster and more convenient than hand cranks, or are they just another gimmick that could break down? Would the computerized controls really give the precision advertised (depth to 0.005 inch, angles to 0.1 degrees)? If so, would the mechanical parts of the saws have the precision and integrity to match the electronics? And finally, would these tools really be worth their roughly $700 price tags?

After working with both saws for a few weeks and talking with the people who made them, I can report that with a few exceptions, the answers to all of these questions are positive. Let's get specific.

Table saw

The basic guts of this saw are almost identical to those of the Sears saw I have been running in my shop for the past ten years. The big difference? There are no handwheels to adjust blade elevation and tilt. Instead there's a push-button control panel with a digital display (see box). The

panel lets you adjust blade height and tilt in two ways. First, you can punch in the exact settings you want—height in inches, tilt in degrees—and gear motors built into the saw will automatically adjust the blade to those settings. This is the way you'll be working most of the time. Or you can "jog" the blade into any position you want by pressing the JOG buttons on the control panel. Generally you use this feature to adjust the saw for calibration. To

If you take time to set up properly, perfect accuracy is possible from both radial-arm and table saws. Author spent four hours getting table saw ready, two hours on radial-arm.

Controls on radial-arm saw are up front where they're easy to see, easy to work. Here a dado blade has been zeroed, and author calibrates a −0.375 elevation for a ³/₈-inch dado cut.

do this, you jog the blade to its fully raised position. Then, using a square as a reference, you jog the blade over until it is perpendicular to the table. Jog the blade down until it is flush with the table top and press the CAL (calibrate) button. The saw is now set.

How accurate are the settings? Perfect, I found, if your square is square. I proved this by tilting the blade over to 45 degrees and crosscutting a piece of 2-inch stock. When I placed the two miters face to face they produced a perfect right-angle joint.

Part of the secret of this accuracy is that the saw always makes adjustments the same way—it always moves to its depth setting in an upward direction. If the blade is at 2 inches and you set it to drop 1 inch, it will actually run slightly below 1 inch, then reverse and come back up to your setting. This compensates for any "slop" in the mechanical parts of the system and ensures perfect repeatability.

The small gear motors that carry out your instructions work slowly. It takes about 40 seconds to run from zero to 45 degrees, and elevation speeds are around eight seconds per inch. On the surface, that's not as fast as the handwheels on my old saw. But when you punch in 30 degrees on the electronic saw, you get 30 degrees. You don't have to make a test cut, check it, and perhaps readjust as you usually do with mechanical adjustments and scales. And while the blade is tilting, you can turn to other tasks, something you can't do while cranking a handwheel. Speaking of which, after a few years of use, the handwheels on my old saw got pretty tough to turn. The threads in the adjustment screws under the table tend to load up with pitch and dust, and it's not fun going in there to clean them. Would the gear motors be able to cope with that kind of strain?

To find out, I coated the threads with heavy grease, then packed them with sawdust and ran the blade up and down ten times in a row without a rest. The gear motor got warm

but never faltered. Then I talked about the durability of the saw with Burt Wiley, who is product manager for the Sears tools.

My big fear was that one of these motors would give out in the middle of a job, leaving me helpless. "Gear motors have caused no problems on test saws we've run in special boxes designed to trap sawdust," Wiley told me.

What about the electronics? Could dust foul them up? And what about the problem of static electricity that occasionally sends computers into fits? "All these problems have been checked out," said Wiley. "We even ran test saws in humidity chambers to simulate the humid conditions in the typical basement shop."

Personally, I'm impressed. Complaints? The surface of the table is somewhat roughly machined, but you can quickly cure that with a belt sander. And the rip fence on this saw is just not up to the quality of the rest of the tool. Now that my tests are complete, I'm going to junk the stock fence and replace it with the Biesemeyer T Square fence I've been using on my old Sears saw.

Radial-arm saw

This tool is just as impressive as the table saw. It also features a large control panel with an easy-to-read digital display. The readout shows blade elevation to the nearest 0.005 inch and bevel and miter settings to the nearest 0.5 degree. If you've ever tried to read the little protractor-type angle scales on most radial saws, you'll understand how impressive that 0.5-degree capability can be. And what you see is what you get.

To check this out I decided on a severe test: compound miter cuts for a six-sided hopper joint box. This is extremely tricky work in which the geometry of bevels and miters interrelates, and even tiny errors multiply into big ones. This job usually requires a series of test cuts, tedious readjustments, and more test cuts. But with the electronic radial I just looked up the proper miter and bevel settings in a table, set the saw according to those numbers, and made my cuts. The parts fit together almost perfectly.

Most of this accuracy is due to the electronic readouts, but the mechanical integrity of the saw also plays a big part. I've been using a conventional Craftsman radial-arm saw for many years, but no matter how carefully I adjusted it, there was always a bit of side play in the arm. There's none of that in this new saw, however.

Any black marks? While I was torture testing the table

Gear motors under table saw turn pitch and elevation screws; circuitry counts blade height, bevel measurements.

Controlling the electronic table saw

The control panel of the table saw features digital display, control keys directly beneath the display, number keys at right, and master and saw-motor switches at left. Turning on the master switch activates the electronics; turning on both switches activates the saw motor.

Press the ELEV key, and the display shows present blade elevation. Pressing the upper JOG key slowly raises the blade; pressing the lower JOG key lowers it. Tapping either key changes elevation in 0.005-inch increments. To set the blade to a desired elevation, punch in that elevation on the number keys at right, and then press the ACT key.

Press BEVEL, and the display shows the blade's current angle. Pressing the upper JOG key tilts the blade slowly to the left; the lower JOG key tilts it right. Tap these keys, and the blade tilts in 0.5-degree increments. To achieve a desired angle, use the number and ACT keys.

The CAL/ENTER key calibrates the saw when the blade is level with and perpendicular to the table. It's also used for programming the saw to set both bevel and elevation automatically in sequence. The CLEAR/STOP key clears the display and stops any programmed motion.

The electronic circuitry loses its memory if the saw is unplugged or if power is cut off, so it's a good idea to leave the saw at zero elevation and bevel at the end of a day's work. Then if power goes off, you can recalibrate simply by pressing the CAL/ENTER key.

saw's gear motors, I did the same with the single gear motor that raises the radial's arm. I sent it up 4 inches and down 4 inches time after time without rest. The motor got warm, and finally, on the ninth trip up, the overload switch kicked open. That's a lot of raising and lowering, more than you'd ever be likely to need on any job I can think of. And the motor was reset and ready to go in approximately ten minutes. Still, I thought you would like to know.

Conclusions: Both of these saws offer exceptional convenience, accuracy, and precision. Any setup you achieve today you can duplicate exactly, next week or next year. Both saws run smooth and true. If set up properly and used with quality blades, either can produce silky-smooth cuts

in both the rip and crosscut modes. Are they worth the price? That's for you to decide.

The future: Remarkable as these saws are, they are not the final phase of electronic-tool development at Sears. Now engineers are working on expanding the electronic capabilities of both saws. Possible developments in the works include digital readouts for both miter gauge and rip fence on the table saw and digital rip and crosscut readouts on the radial-arm. If and when these improvements become available, will you be able to add them to existing electronic saws?

"The miter gauge could be retrofitted," assured Wiley. "But the other new features would require all-new control panels"—*A.J. Hand.*

Table-saw specifications

Hp	Blade	Rip cap.	Thickness cap. @ 90	@ 45	Table size (with wings)	Arbor
1	10 in.	24 in.	3⅜ in.	2¼ in.	30 by 27 in.	⅝ in.

Radial-arm-saw specifications

Hp	Blade	Rip cap.	Crosscut cap.	Thickness cap. @ 90	@ 45	Table size	Arbor
1½	10 in.	26 in.	15½ in.	3 in.	2¼ in.	27½ by 40 in.	⅝ in.

Controlling the electronic radial-arm saw

The control panel of the radial-arm saw is similar to that of the table saw. Press the ELEV key, and the display shows blade elevation to the nearest 0.005 inch. Pressing the upper JOG key slowly raises the blade; pressing the lower JOG key lowers it.

To set the blade to a desired elevation, punch in that elevation on the number keys, and then press ACT. To cut to a certain depth, jog blade down until it just touches your stock. Press the REF/SET key to zero the display. Then punch in the desired depth of cut and the MINUS key. Finally, press ACT, and the blade will lower to the proper height.

Pressing the BEVEL key displays the blade's current bevel setting. To set bevels, tilt the saw motor by hand while watching the bevel display. Tighten the bevel lock on the motor when you reach the desired bevel angle.

To set miters, press the MITER key. Miter angle will be displayed. Swing the arm right or left until the display shows the desired angle. Then lock the arm.

compact four-in-one tool

If multipurpose tools appeal to you as a way to save space, the Emcostar 2000 from Austria should get your attention. The whole rig takes up about as much space as a Black & Decker Workmate. You get four tools in the base model: table saw, band saw, disc sander, and shaper. How do they work?

As a table saw, the tool has plenty of power. I ripped ash more than 2 inches thick with no problems. The blade arbor runs smooth and true.

On the debit side, the table is small (16 by 27 inches) and awkward for handling large stock. You can add outboard support to handle larger work, but the table—not the arbor— tilts for bevel cuts, and you can't use supports with a tilted table.

As a band saw, the tool, again, has plenty of power; the blade guides are of good quality, so the saw tracks true. But the upper guide assembly can shift out of line when you raise or lower it.

Shaper? Really a chuck that takes 1/4- and 3/8-inch router bits, it works off the table saw's table. Useful table size in the shaper mode is only 5 by 27 inches. Cutting speed is 8,000 rpm, with plenty of torque.

For the disc-sanding mode you simply replace the circular saw blade with a sanding disc. It works fine, but an 8-inch-diameter disc is a bit small for a lot of work.

Overall, the Emcostar is easy to shift from one mode to another. In most cases all it takes is a belt change and a quick flip of the tool. At about 130 pounds, the tool is solidly built, constructed with heavy sheet steel throughout.

Options for the tool include a lathe, mortising machine, drum and 1-inch-belt sander, and flexible-shaft tool. I didn't get a chance to check them out, however. Price of the basic tool is $795. It's imported by Emco Maier Corp. (2050 Fairwood Ave., Columbus, OH 43207)—*by A.J. Hand.*

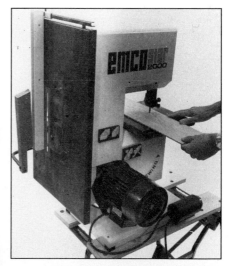

Emcostar 2000 pivots on its base to go into table-saw mode (left) and swivels into an upright position to become a band saw (top). Changing drive belt from one pulley to another completes the transformation. Shaper mode uses router bits and works off the saw table (above). Removable crank raises and lowers table to adjust depth of cut.

glue-gun shoot-out

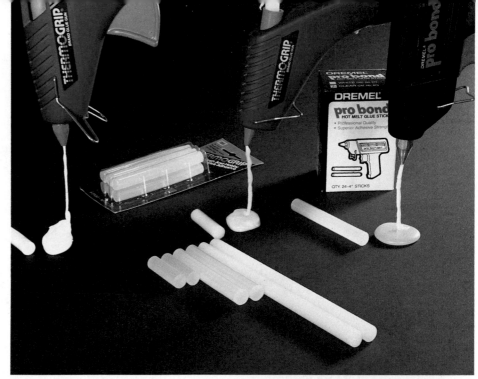

"**Y**ou can pay for one of these glue guns just fixing things on a Saturday afternoon," the enthusiastic clerk at the home center told me as I picked up a sleek-looking model and checked to see how it handled.

Even more enthusiastic was some of the copy on the packing cartons. The German-made Steinel gun's box, for example, boldly proclaimed, "It glues simply everything."

My recollection of the glue guns of a few years ago was of handles that got uncomfortably hot and of hot glue leaking out of the nozzle when I didn't want it to—usually onto something I didn't want glued. And I seem to remember not being able to glue big things because my gun wouldn't melt glue fast enough.

After collecting and trying the latest glue guns, I can tell you that those problems have been pretty much solved. And although you may be able to make a case for paying off a glue gun in one Saturday of repairs, it makes more sense to think of it as a tool you can use every day. Indeed, today's guns are so convenient and so inexpensive that they should be considered basic home and workshop tools.

Do not expect a glue gun to glue "simply everything." (Perhaps that claim gained some meaning in translation from the German.) But it can make quick work of many tasks. And for jobs that require instant holding, where clamping isn't possible and cyanoacrylate (instant glue) won't work, the glue gun may be the *only* way to glue.

Originally, the hot-melt adhesives that glue guns dispense were developed to hold together the soles of shoes. They are petroleum-derived thermoplastic polymers that become fluid when heated. They have particular characteristics. They set up—that is, freeze—very quickly. That's ideal for some applications but disastrous for others. (You wouldn't use a hot-melt to make fine furniture, for example.) Hot-melts are also viscous. That can be great for sealing and gap filling, but you wouldn't use one to mend a delicate vase. Hot-melts cannot tolerate high temperatures, so they're not dishwasher-proof. Nor are they high-strength adhesives. On the

Good-looking new breed of glue guns includes, clockwise from 12 o'clock: Steinel Glue-Matic 3000, Parker GR-66, Thermogrip 208, Swingline 96630, Dremel Pro Bonder 810, Steinel Gluefix 2000, Sears Craftsman 9-80508, Thermogrip 206, Bostik (Thermogrip) 203.

Three hot-melt adhesives (from left) are rubbery white sealer-caulk, neutral-amber all-purpose glue, and clear (for jobs where color would be undesirable). The 1/2-inch-diameter sticks come in 2-, 4-, and 8-inch lengths. Two-inch sticks make thumb-feed guns easiest to handle; 4- and 8-inch sticks work well in trigger-feed guns, particularly when you're using a lot of glue. Two-inch sticks are more economical if you often change from one glue type to another.

Trigger-feed guns (rear) cost half again as much as thumb feeders but are easier to use and give more-precise control. Both types offer similar capacity.

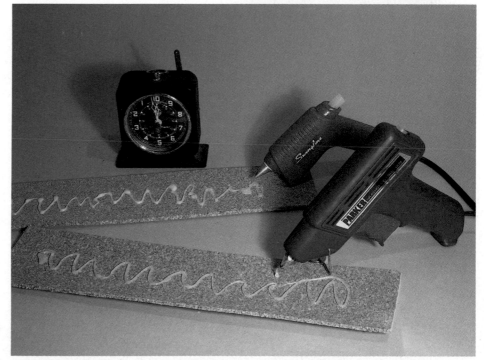

How quickly guns can extrude glue determines how large a project they can handle. The author expected to find some guns lacking in melt capacity, but all performed well in this respect. Photo shows typical 15-second output.

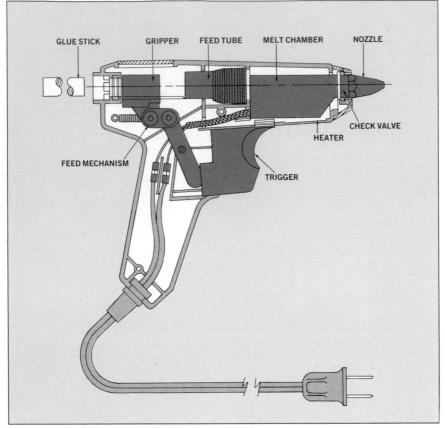

GLUE STICK · GRIPPER · FEED TUBE · MELT CHAMBER · NOZZLE · CHECK VALVE · HEATER · FEED MECHANISM · TRIGGER

Inside a glue gun: Adhesive stick is gripped and guided through feed tube into jacketed melt chamber. Liquid glue is forced through check valve and out nozzle. Check valve, a spring-loaded ball behind the nozzle, shuts off flow when feeding stops. This is a preview drawing of a Parker trigger-feed gun.

PS buyer's guide: how the new hot-melt glue guns compare

Brand	Model	Type	Wattage	Voltage	Price ($)	Warranty (yrs.)	Approx. wt. (oz.)	Comments, special features
Craftsman	9-80508	Trigger	40	100–240 AC	22	1	12	Comes in plastic pouch; 1/8- and 1/4-in. bead nozzles available
	9-80512	Thumb	70	120 AC-DC	14	1	6	Comes in plastic pouch
Dremel	810	Trigger	40	100–240 AC	30	1	12	Includes four glue sticks; hypodermic-extension and 1/4-inch spreader nozzles available
	800	Thumb	40	100–240 AC	17	1	9	
Master Mechanic	203-MM	Thumb	70	120 AC-DC	13	n.s.*	6	Comes in plastic pouch
Parker	GR-60	Trigger	40	100–240 AC	25	n.s.	12	
Steinel	Glue-Matic 3000	Trigger	45	100–240 AC	25	2	12	Includes four eight-in. glue sticks
	Gluefix 2000	Thumb	40	100–240 AC	16	2	9	
Swingline	96630	Thumb	n.a.	120 AC	10	n.s.	9	
Thermogrip	208	Trigger	20	120 AC	25	n.s.	11	1/8- and 1/4-in. long-nose nozzles available
	206	Thumb	20	120 AC	18	n.s.	9	
	203	Thumb	70	120 AC-DC	14	n.s.	6	Comes in plastic pouch

Suppliers' addresses: Bostik Consumer Div., Emhart Corp., Box 3716, Reading, PA 19605 (Thermogrip); **Dremel,** Div. of Emerson Electric Co., 4915 21st St., Racine, WI 53406; **Parker Mfg. Co.,** Box 644, Worcester, MA 01613; **Sears Roebuck & Co.,** Sears Tower, Chicago, IL 60684 (Craftsman); **Swingline, Inc.,** 32-00 Skillman Ave., Long Island City, NY 11101; **True Value Hardware,** Cotter & Co., Chicago, IL 60614 (Master Mechanic); **Woodcraft Supply,** Box 4000, Woburn, MA 01888 (Steinel); **The Woodworkers' Store,** 21801 Industrial Blvd., Rogers, MN 55374 (Steinel).

other hand, there is hardly any shrinkage when the hot-melts cool. And they are resilient, odorless, electrically insulative, waterproof, and resistant to many chemicals.

Performance? About a draw

As the glue-gun suppliers lay their cards on the table, it is obvious that no one gun is very far behind the others in performance or technology. All the new guns have check valves in the nozzles that effectively stop the flow of glue when you stop feeding the glue stick. And they all have solid-state thermostats that do an excellent job of maintaining melt temperature. This control also contributes to keeping the guns acceptably cool when handling.

The heart of the heat control is a reliable, long-life positive temperature coefficient thermistor, or PTC. A thermistor is a heat-sensitive, variable-resistance device. As the temperature of the heating element increases, the thermistor limits current, closely maintaining the desired melt temperature in the gun.

The newest guns generally heat faster than older ones. Depending on the gun, I found that it takes from three to five minutes from a cold start to reach operating temperature—about 340 to 380 degrees F. Even though the new guns are better insulated and their handles stay reasonably cool, the housings can get pretty warm. The nozzles get very hot—hot enough, for example, that Craftsman puts a "hot surface" warning label on its trigger gun. Steinel's trigger gun has a rubber cover on the nozzle to help protect against accidental contact. (You must also avoid touching the hot glue.) The rubber in the feed tubes of the new guns is formulated to last longer. The housings are attractively styled and are designed to be comfortable.

But they're not all alike

Every one of the glue guns I tried worked just fine. But there are features and strong points that may make one model a better choice than another for you. The table sums them up. The black thumb-feed guns sold by Thermogrip, Craftsman, and Master Mechanic are essentially identical. Similarly, the trigger-feed guns sold by Parker, Craftsman, and Dremel are, with some minor differences, the same. These models have neatly engineered feeding systems that automatically control the force applied to the adhesive stick.

Thermogrip's new blue-and-orange guns certainly deserve mention from

What can you do with glue-gun glue?

Hot-melt adhesives work best on porous materials. They can be used in place of staples, nails, tapes, and other glues but should not be used to replace structural fasteners where heavy loads are involved. Nor should they be used where temperatures exceed 140 degrees F.

Instructions on glue-gun packages suggest a host of uses: sealing cartons, making custom cartons, repairing books, repairing shoes and boots, gluing down loose tiles and carpeting, fixing toys, regluing chair rungs and upholstery, gluing craft projects, and making picture frames without clamps.

Here are some of my favorite applications: On the car, I reglued the acoustical material under the hood, fastened down the trunk mat, sealed the empty holes in the fire wall, and reattached weatherstripping. Around the house, I fixed an awning seam, resealed the rain gutters, and fastened a window-screen patch. I installed ceiling molding atop wood paneling without nails by applying glue to the paneling and pushing the molding in place. Then I did the same thing on the floor with quarter-round.

I'm finding a glue gun very handy in the shop. I "tack" parts in place for fitting and for holding while drilling screw holes. Hot-melt fills voids in work, and a few drops hold scrap backing strips so drills and saws don't splinter fussy work. Did you ever want to locate a trammel center without defacing the workpiece? Just put a dab of clear hot-melt in the center to hold the trammel point, and peel it off later. The table at right shows what kind of bonds you can expect with the hot-melts available to consumers.

PVC plastic	Acrylic plastic	Minerals	Cardboard; paper	Glass	Brass	Aluminum	Steel	Concrete	Hardwood	Softwood	
VS	S	S	T	S	P	M	M	S	VS	VS / VS	Softwood
VS	S	S	VS	S	P	M	M	S	VS / VS	VS	Hardwood
S	S	S	S	S	P	M	M	S / S	S	S	Concrete
M	M	M	M	M	P	M	M / VS	S	VS	VS	Steel
M	M	M	M	M	P	M / VS	VS	S	VS	VS	Aluminum
P	P	P	P	P	P / S	S	S	S	S	S	Brass
S	S	S	S	S / M	S	VS	VS	S	VS	VS	Glass
VS	S	S	T / T	VS	VS	VS	VS	S	T	T	Cardboard; paper
S	S	S / S	S	S	S	S	S	S	S	S	Minerals
S	S / T	S	T	S	S	VS	VS	S	VS	T	Acrylic plastic
VS / VS	VS	S	S	VS	S	VS	VS	S	VS	VS	PVC plastic

Key to abbreviations: M, modest-strength joint; P, poor adhesion; S, strong joint; T, material tears before joint; VS, very strong joint. White side of table gives joint strength of white sealer-caulk hot-melt adhesive; shaded side gives joint strength with general-purpose neutral-amber glue.

a styling standpoint. They are comfortable to hold and convenient to use.

The new Swingline gun that I tested was a prototype unit. Production guns will have a rubber accordion tube where the thumb presses the glue into the gun. For a small, inexpensive gun, this one is a good performer. It has good melt capacity and excellent glue shut-off, and the grip stays cool.

All of the glue guns are so light that balance is not a problem. But you'll want to choose one that fits your hand comfortably. I found that the longer guns—ranging from about four to 7½ inches long—are easier to aim. And the longer length will give you more reach in narrow spaces.

If the idea of dispensing hot-melt glue in wider or larger beads appeals to you, note which guns offer accessory nozzles. By the way, never attempt to change nozzles on a hot gun with your bare hands. Be sure to follow instructions.

All but two of the guns have a wire bail on which to rest the device in a nose-down, upright position, like a bird searching for worms. This keeps the heat away from the resting surface while keeping a head of hot adhesive right against the nozzle check

valve, ready to go. The bails have two-position detents: Tilt forward to rest the gun, and tilt back to use it. If you don't tilt the bail back, it can interfere with the work. Sometimes, moving the power cord around can tip a gun off its perch. The Swingline has a built-in rest; the Thermogrip 203 must lie on its side.

The glue guns all have sufficient melt capacity for normal work. But if you're not careful, you can get too eager and try to work a gun either before it is fully heated or faster than it can melt glue. You can force a thumb-feed gun to the point of buck-

ling an extending glue stick. This is unsafe. And you could be dispensing glue that is not as hot as it should be to work properly. You will quickly be able to feel how much pressure to use, however. Trigger-feed guns, because of the way the feed mechanisms are designed, tend to limit the pressure you can put on the stick going through the heating chamber, but a certain amount of acquired "feel" is also necessary. This may be frustrating if you're a slam-banger. My advice: give the gun its own way, and it will work just fine—*by Mack Philips. Photos by the author.*

Glue-gun how-to: Be quick on the draw

Technique is all important when using hot-melt adhesives. First, all parts must be clean. Roughing up smooth surfaces can improve the bond. Because the glues set so quickly (you have about 15 to 20 seconds to get the parts together), you must plan the job before you start applying glue. Know what goes where. Position the parts so there will be no lost motion. Hot-melt glues generally set up enough in 20 to 30 seconds to hold parts without further hand pressure; they're fully set in about 60 seconds and are stressable in about two minutes.

It may be difficult to bond large surfaces because the adhesives may harden before the required amount is extruded. Make the best of this by making sure that the gun is up to temperature and that the loading tube is full. Working time can be extended by puddling the glue in large drops rather than drawing it out in slender beads, and by heating (to slightly above room temperature) the materials to be bonded. This is particularly important when gluing metal; cold metal can chill the hot adhesive quickly. Heating the surfaces can also increase bonding strength.

how to choose and store carbide cutters

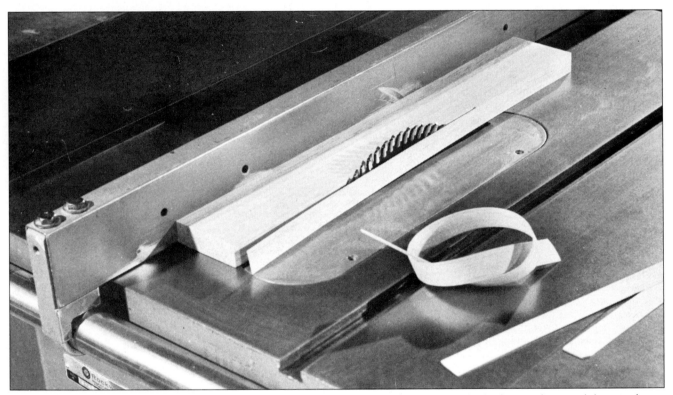

A premium tungsten-carbide saw blade can slice a paper-thin strip and leave a burnished edge on the remaining stock.

You often hear the advice: "Work with a *good* carbide-tipped saw blade." You know that tungsten-carbide teeth are tough and will stay keen longer than those on an all-steel blade. You also know that carbide-tipped saw blades cost much more than all-steel blades. The price of a 10-inch blade can range from $30 to more than $100. But is price the only mark of a good blade?

There are several things to check before you buy even the costliest blade. Some you can see—plate flatness, carbide thickness, tooth attachment, grind quality, blade finish, and even package quality.

But there is more: tooth styles, for instance. Like standard blades, carbides are designed for particular ap-

plications. Is the "all-purpose" blade really the smartest choice? Is the blade that's great on a table saw also good on a radial-arm?

Judging quality

"Cemented carbide" is the technically correct term to describe the tooth material on a carbide-tipped blade. An alloy of powdered tungsten and carbon permanently bonded under high temperatures and extreme pressure (vacuum sintering), tungsten carbide is tough—second only to diamonds in hardness. The final product can contain as much as 94 percent tungsten carbide, with the balance composed of a binder such as cobalt powder.

There are many grades of cemented carbides in the saw-blade industry.

The most common are C1, C2, C3, and C4; the grades refer to the degree of resistance to shock and wear. C4, with the lowest shock resistance and the highest wear resistance, is the proper choice for general-purpose and cross-cut blades. A C2 grade, which is about medium in both areas, is often used on special ripping saws and on blades designed for sawing nonferrous metals. If you don't see the grade marked on the blade, ask what it is.

Another key quality indicator is "runout"—the term for the wobble that occurs when the blade is turning. Runout tolerance affects more than the blade's performance—it determines the accuracy of the initial tooth-grinding phase during manufacture. A teetering blade makes it difficult to achieve precise grinding on both sides of each tooth.

Runout is not something you can check in the store, but you can examine the package to see whether the manufacturer touts his quality control. Or you can ask a knowledgeable salesperson. And you can check the blade's flatness, as I'll explain. The manufacturer that pays careful attention to flatness is also likely to produce a blade with minimum runout. When you get the blade on your saw, you can test for runout with your first cut: If your kerf is wider than the blade's teeth, you've got runout.

Examining the blade

Take two testing tools with you: a short steel straightedge and a hand lens. To test blade flatness, place the straightedge across the body of the blade so it rests between teeth, and then hold the blade up so you can get some backlighting. If the plate resembles an undulating horizon, you know that its flatness received less than expert attention.

Also examine both sides of the blade for concentric rings that run from the bore to close to the teeth. These show the blade was finished by surface grinding instead of being sanded or simply polished. The marks indicate prideful attention to plate flatness. The rings can be quite fine so, to see them, hold the blade at an angle so light will fall across it.

Next, determine whether the manufacturer states maximum rpm —preferably on the blade. Ratings will vary with blade diameter. A six-inch blade may run as high as 12,000 rpm, a 20-inch blade as low as 3,000. Usual maximum rpm for a 10-incher is about 7,000.

An rpm rating also tells you that the plate has been tensioned—hammered to relieve stresses in the metal that might cause hot spots. Tensioning is a critical element because it controls forces that can cause uneven expansion. This in turn can produce wobble, vibration, and excessive noise. Tensioning also affects safety— an untensioned blade can crack and even fly apart.

Use the hand lens to check several teeth about the perimeter of the blade. Check for the quality of the joint between carbide and steel and for the smoothness of the carbide. The joint should be machine-brazed to give automatic control of joint uniformity and the degree of heat used. Uniformity is a sign of machine brazing. Hand brazing or welding of the teeth introduces a human-error factor. Overheating can destroy the tem-

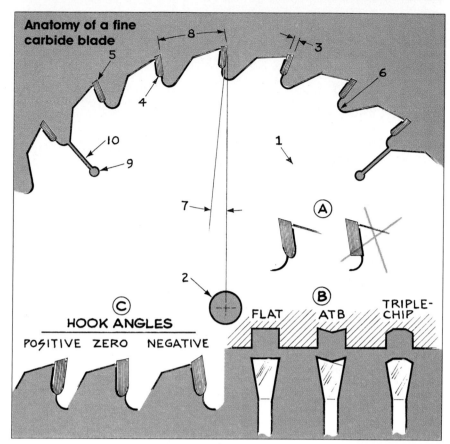

Anatomy of a fine carbide blade

HOOK ANGLES
POSITIVE ZERO NEGATIVE

FLAT ATB TRIPLE-CHIP

The plate (1), or blade body, on premium blades is heat-treated alloy steel that's harder than material used for all-steel blades whose teeth have to be filed and set. The bore (2) or arbor hole is ground instead of being drilled or punched out. The carbide teeth are thick (3) to allow more sharpenings for a longer blade life. Teeth are seated into pockets in the blade body (4) and are not just stuck on the front edge (A). Each tooth face (5) is super-smooth, as are its top and sides.

Teeth are ground in one of three ways (B): flat or "raker," alternate top bevel (ATB), or triple chip. The ATB grind will not last as long as the others because the points on the teeth do maximum work. The pattern above each tooth shows what bottom of kerf cut with that type grind looks like. Kerf must be wider than plate gauge. Commonly, saw blades combine tooth configurations—for example, a bank of ATBs with a single, flat tooth (see photos).

For maximum efficiency, gullets (6),

hook angle (7), and pitch (8) match blade type. The gullets, or waste-clearing channels, between the teeth are deeper on a rip blade than on a cross-cut blade. And pitch, or spacing between the teeth, is greater on the rip blades than on the crosscut blades.

A saw blade has more bite as hook angle increases (C), so a rip blade may have as much as 20 degrees of positive hook (heavy-duty rip saws may have even more). Less hook angle (as little as 5 degrees) is used on combination blades and crosscutting blades. A negative hook angle can be found on metal-cutting blades and often on blades designed for swing saws.

Expansion holes (9) guard against cracking, and expansion slots (10) prevent buckling under heat buildup. Look for a minimum of one slot for every 10 to 15 teeth. On some all-purpose blades, deep gullets between banks of teeth serve the same purpose.

per of the plate and can result in pinholes in the bonding compound. Surface pinholes may not be too critical as far as the bond is concerned, but they can indicate general quality, so be wary of them.

The cutting performance of the blade, its general quality, and how long the initial sharpening will last can be judged by examining the surface texture of the teeth. Tungsten-carbide teeth are shaped by grinding procedures. A quickie method is a sin-

gle rough grinding that leaves ridges you can see and feel. The quality-blade producers will move the product through a second, finishing grind, using a 400-grit (or finer) diamond wheel, and they will boast of it, either on the blade's package or in the catalog listing.

But the difference between single- and multiple-grinding operations is also visible at the shopping place, especially when you use a lens. Study the cutting edge, top, sides, and face of

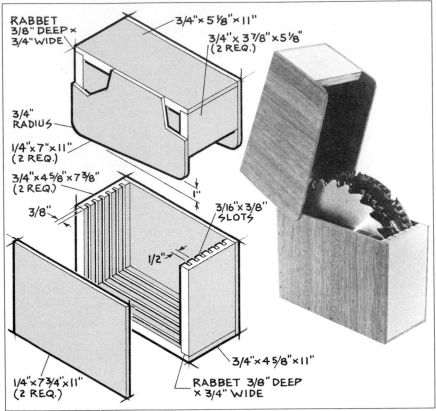

An easy-to-make tote box both stores and transports six 10-inch carbide-tipped blades. A separate slot for each blade gives maximum protection. To make slots in the case sides and bottom, the teeth for smoothness. Grinding marks, if any, should be difficult to see.

What about making the flex test that's often advised? This requires that you try to flex the blade by grasping its perimeter and applying moderate thumb pressure at its center. I've cut 3/16-inch-wide grooves in a 30-inch piece of stock. Saw this into three pieces, assemble as shown, then finish by adding a 2½-inch hinge, handle, and drawer catch (not shown).

tried this on many blades but haven't found one that I'm able to bend, at least not to the point where the flex could be detected without instruments. My feeling is that when all other factors check out in good style, you can assume that the plate and its temper are acceptable. On the other hand, if a blade does have a visible flex, don't buy it.

Choosing blade type

You should expect a lot from an expensive carbide-tipped saw blade, but not everything. The characteristics of wood and the various ways to saw it make it nearly impossible to design the ultimate tooth shape.

There's a clear difference between teeth that are shaped for crosscutting, for example, and those that are best for ripping. Crosscut teeth should have sharp side points that will sever wood fibers cleanly. Ripping teeth have a flat top grind so each tooth will work like a tiny chisel to remove a comparatively large chunk of wood. You can see a difference in the waste produced by the blades; the crosscut's sawdust is much finer.

Combination blades are a compromise—the blades often include both types of teeth in banks separated by a deep waste-clearing channel or gullet (see diagram). I use such blades quite happily, but don't expect one to do the optimum job I demand from a blade designed for a particular application.

Usually, you'll find that the blades that come close to doing a perfect job will have many teeth and comparatively small gullets. They will produce burnished edges on crosscuts and miters. Such high-quality blades will also do clean rip cuts, but the latter application, when overdone, can result in burns on the wood and the blade. The ripping operation generally pulls more amps with this kind of blade, so you'll have to slow the rate of feed.

Does this mean that you should have an assortment of carbide-tipped

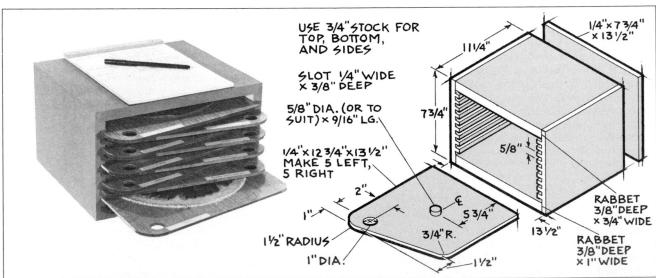

To store test carbide blades, the author uses an open-shelved caddy. Each blade rests on a separate shelf padded with felt or heavy canvas that's been treated with a few drops of oil. Each time the author uses a blade, he makes an entry on the tablet. When there's enough information, he makes a separate record to store on shelf with blade.

The most efficient blade for general use on a radial-arm saw (1) alternates one flat tooth with two beveled ones. A 10-inch blade has 24 teeth, each with a special back clearance and a small 7-degree hook angle that make for easy feeding and little vibration. Deep gullets are an asset when ripping. An all-purpose blade suitable for any saw (2) has banks of four

beveled teeth and one flat raker separated by deep gullets that get rid of waste and dissipate heat. This blade does an acceptable job of crosscutting, ripping, and even mitering. A 10-inch blade has 40 teeth. Best suited for cutoff work on table or radial saws, this toothy blade (3) can be used for general sawing. A 10-incher has 60 teeth, all bevel-

ground with a slight hook angle. A new multitoothed blade (4) favored by the author has 80 teeth on a 10-inch disc—about as many teeth as you can get. To permit minimum tooth clearance, the blade has a baked-on, self-lubricating, antigrip finish. Concave clearance behind the teeth aids both cooling and waste removal.

blades? Ideally, yes; practically, no. Much depends on what type—and how much—woodworking is done.

The expert who produces heirloom-quality furniture will have several carbide blades: a super blade for edge-to-edge and general joinery and for sawing plywood; a special blade for ripping; and a general-use blade for initial sizing cuts.

Others can get by with a single combination blade, one with teeth that make it acceptable for ripping, crosscutting, and mitering in hard or softwoods and in wood products.

If you can buy only one carbide-tipped blade, don't buy the cheapest one. Designed like a typical all-steel, all-purpose blade—but with carbide teeth added—this blade often has a tempting price. It will stay keener longer than its brother all-steel blade. But don't expect the super performance you get from blades created especially to be carbide tipped. Another low-cost blade, the sparsely toothed "economy" carbide blade with only eight or 12 teeth, may be suitable for ripping. But don't expect it to produce ready-to-assemble cuts.

Coddle costly blades

Though tough, tungsten carbide is very brittle. Carbide-tipped saw blades should be handled, used, and stored with exceptional care.

At my local saw-sharpening shop, I've seen expensive carbide blades that were sad examples of blade care. Teeth, gullet, and surrounding areas were coated with wood residue; some teeth were so dull that a lot of carbide had to be removed to resharpen them;

other, chipped teeth required transplants.

Keep the blades clean, and have them sharpened before they start chopping. Don't force cuts. Feeding too fast can cause overheating and won't allow the teeth to work as they should.

Be sure your machine is in correct alignment and that arbor and collars

are in pristine condition. Handle the blade with care when it is off the machine; never place it on a hard surface like the saw's table.

The blades should have special storage facilities; placing them on a hook or peg is not the best solution. Making one of the cases shown is a far better way to go—*by R.J. DeCristoforo. Drawings by Gerhard Richter.*

Carbide-tipped, thin-rim blade (above left) designed for veneers and plywood is also a sensible choice for working on expensive woods because it keeps kerf waste to a minimum. The blade has many crosscut-type teeth—from 60 to 80 on a 10-inch blade—but has limited depth of cut (arrow). Check rpm when buying a

thin-rim blade; its maximum rpm may be less than that of your machine. For sawing abrasive material, the Grit-Edge blade (right) has hundreds of particles permanently bonded to the rim of the plate. Because the blade can be installed in any direction, you can extend cutting life simply by reversing.

index

Acrylic lacquer and enamel, 153–154
Adhesives:
    for laminates, 129. *See also* Glue
        guns
Adjustable pusher, 90
American Solar Energy Society, 10
Appliance polarity, 148–151
Automobile. *See* Car care

Backboard, sports, 106–109
Backsplash, 129
Bandsaw:
    four-in-one tool with, 171
    guard for, 92
    workbench for, 96
Bar stools, butcher-block, 105
Basketball court, 106–109
Bathrooms:
    plastic plumbing for, 146
    remodeling of, 16–18
Battery testing, 159
Beading tool, 78
Beds, folding, 62–64, 72–75
    double-duty room, 62–64
    two-faced bed/wardrobe divider,
        72–75
Belt sander-grinder, 96
Biomass system, 5
Biscuit joinery, 132–133
Blades, 176–179
Board-and-batten fence, 100, 101
Boats:
    homemade catamaran, 121–123
    wood-epoxy construction for, 124–
        127
Body-capacitance grounding, 151
Bolt and cross-dowel fasteners, 135
Bookcases:
    laminates for, 129
    Queen Anne secretary, 76–82
    room-divider, 68–71
Booster fans, 41
Brakes:
    adjusting, 162
    bleeding, 163, 164
    Pads for, 164
Brick-post-serpentine fence, 98, 101
Bulbex rivet, 137
Burner cyclers, 41
Butcher block patio stool, 105

Cabinets:
    double-duty room, 62–64
    swinging-bookcase room divider, 69
    tambour doors for, 83–85
Caradco, 33
Carbide saw blades, 176–179
Carbon-deposit removal, 166

Carburetor-control parts, 156
Car care, 152–167
    auto repainting, 152–154
    disc brake trouble-shooting, 162–
        164
    electronic ignition trouble-shooting,
        158–161
    emissions system checking, 155–
        157
    preignition and detonation service,
        165–167
Catamaran, 121–123
Cemented carbide, 176
Ceramic tiled patio, 140–141
Chlorinated polyvinyl chloride tubing
    145–147
Choke system, automobile, 157
Chrysler electronic ignition system,
    158–161
Clapboard reversal, 138–139
Climate-control system, computerized,
    4–7
Cold spark plug advantages, 167
Combustion, 165–166
"Common Sense Fasteners," 137
Computer carrels, 65–67
    laminated trestle, 67
    veneered stand, 65–66
Computers:
    household function control by, 4–5
    housing design generated by, 4–7
Cutters, carbide,
    176–179. *See also* Saws

Dampers, 39, 41
Day-Star homes, 13
Decks, 22–25, 102–104, 113–114, 115–
    117, 118–120
    elevated, with spa, 115–117
    high-rise planter deck, 102–104
    multilevel outdoor entertainment
        area, 22–25
    parquet, 118–120
    with pool, 22–25
    woodshed addition for, 113–114
Desks:
    Queen Anne secretary, 76–82. *See
        also* Computer carrels
Detonation (spark) service, 165–167
Dining/bedroom, 62–64
Disc brake trouble-shooting, 162–164
Disc sander, 171
Disc sander-grinder, 97
Distributor, automobile, 160–161
Doors:
    patio, 142–144
    tambour, 83–85
Double-duty room, 62–64

Drill press:
    shield for, 89, 91
    workbench for, 96
Dust masks, 91

Eagle's Nest, 11, 12–13
Ear protectors, 91
Easy-access woodshed, 113–114
EGR. *See* Exhaust-gas-recirculation
    (EGR) system
Electricity:
    and body-capacitance grounding,
        150, 151
    and reversed polarity, 148–151
Electronic control unit (ECU), 159
Electronic ignition trouble-shooting,
    158–161
Electronics storage wall, 60–61
Elevated deck with spa, 115–117
Elite fittings, 134
Emcostar 2000, 171
Emissions systems checking, 155–
    157
Enamel, acrylic, 153–154
Energy efficiency, 36–41
    heating-system add-ons, 39–41
    outside insulation, 36–38
    patio door replacement, 142–144
Epoxy. *See* Wood-epoxy construction
Exhaust-gas-recirculation (EGR) sys-
    tem, 155, 156–157. *See also* Emis-
    sion system checking *and* Preig-
    nition service
Exterior insulation, 36–38
Eye protection, 91

Fans, 41
Fasteners, 134–137
Fences, 98–101
Fiberglass brake linings, 164
Fin clips, 134
Fire protection, 7
Folding guest room, 62–64
Four-in-one tool, 171
Freehand shaping shield, 92
Fresh-air intakes, 39
Fuel-evaporation-control system, 157
Furniture-finishing techniques, 49,
    54, 58, 82

Garage waferboard, 86–88
Gazebo, 110–112
General Motors electronic ignition
    systems, 159
Glue guns, 172–175
Goggles, 91, 154
Gooseneck molding, 42, 45, 80–81
Grandfather clock project, 42–49

Handball backboard, 106–109
Heating costs:
 add-ons and, 39–41
 two-faced house and, 8–10
 outside insulation and, 36–38
 patio door replacement and, 142–144
 prefabricated housing and, 3
High Energy Ignition (HEI) system, 159
Hinge-carving, 56, 57, 58, 59
Home repair and maintenance, 138–151
 ceramic tiled patio, 140–141
 patio door replacement, 142–144
 peeling paint, 138–139
 plastic plumbing installation, 145–147
 polarity checking, 148–151. See also House design and construction
Hot spark plug advantages, 167
Hot tubs:
 elevated deck with, 115–117
 wood-epoxy construction for, 126, 127
Hot water controls, 41
Hot water heater, 146
House design and construction, 2–13
 computer house, 4–7
 do-it-yourself projects for, 11–13
 stilt-house construction, 2–3
 two-faced house, 8–10. See also Home repair and maintenance
Humidifiers, 39
Hydraulic pressure, brakes, 163–164

Ignition service, automobile, 165–167
Indoor woodworking projects, 98–123
Insulation:
 advantages of outside, 36–38
 and house-siding replacement, 138
 and patio door replacement, 142–144

Jawbolt fastener, 134
Jigs:
 biscuit-joinery, 133
 power-tool, 89–92

Knockdown joining device, 136

Lacquer (acrylic), 153–154
Laminates, 128–131
Lathe-turning techniques, 44, 50–51, 55–56, 58
Lathe workbench, 95, 97
Lattice-top-board fence, 100, 101

Lighting:
 for swinging-bookcase room divider, 69
 for two-faced bed/wardrobe divider, 73
Lowboy, 50–54
Lung protection, 91, 154

Mirrors, 14–15, 69
 mirrored wall installation, 14–15
 swinging-bookcase room divider, 69
Moore-Tile, 118–120

National Electrical Code (NEC), 148, 149, 150
Neon polarity tester, 149, 151
Norwegian pram, 125

Ogee molding, 47, 53
Ohmmeter, 161
Outdoor decks. See Decks
Outdoor woodworking projects, 98–123
Outside insulation, 36–38. See also Insulation

Paddleball backboard, 106–109
Painting:
 alternative to home, 138–139
 automobile, 152–154
Paneling, solid-wood strip, 26–29
Parquet deck, 118–120. See also Decks
Patios:
 ceramic-tile, 140–141
 sports center with, 106–109
 stool for, 105
PCV. See Positive-crankcase-ventilation system
Peeling paint, 138–139
Pickup coil, 158
Pigeonholes, 78, 80
Ping-pong table, 106–109
Plank paneling, 26–29
Planters, 102–104
Plastic laminates:
 solid color, 128–131
 working with, 64, 128–131
Plastic plumbing installation, 145–147
Plastic rivets, 136
Polarity checking, 148–151
Polystyrene insulation, 36–38. See also Insulation
Positive-crankcase-ventilation (PCV) system, 155, 156
Post-and-beam fence, 100, 101
Power tools:
 general precautions for, 91
 safety devices for, 89–92
 workbench for, 93–97. See also Tools

Prefabricated housing:
 do-it-yourself project, 11–13
 stilt houses, 2–3
Preignition, 165–167
Pusher, adjustable, 90
Push-pull fasteners, 135

Queen Anne drop-leaf table, 55–59
Queen Anne secretary, 76–82

Racquetball backboard, 106–109
Radial-arm saw:
 blades for, 176–179
 electronic, 168–170
 guard for, 92
Radiator valves, thermostatic, 41
Reluctor, 158
Remodeling, 14–35
 bathrooms, 16–18
 mirrored wall installation, 14–15
 multilevel-deck outdoor entertainment area, 22–25
 paneling, 26–29
 passive-solar all-seasons room, 19–21
 skylight installation, 33–35
 window installation, 30–32. See also Home repair and maintenance
Revolutionary lowboy, 50–54
Rivets:
 Bulbex, 137
 plastic, 136
 threaded, 135
Robots, 6, 7
Room divider, 68–71
Routing:
 four-in-one tool for, 171
 laminates, 130
Runout (wobble), 176–177

Safety:
 devices for power tools, 89–92
 from shock hazards, 148–151
 in electronic ignition trouble-shooting, 158, 159
 in spray-painting, 154
Sander-grinder workbench, 96, 97
Sanders, 171
Saws:
 bandsaw, 92, 96, 171
 blades for, 176–179
 electronic table and radial saws, 168–170
 four-in-one tool, 171
 table saw, 90, 95, 96, 130, 168–170, 171
Security, 7
Setback thermostats, 39
Shaper, 171
Shaper-fence shield, 90
Shell-carving (woodworking), 54

Shock hazards, 148–149
Skylights:
  gazebo, 110–112
  installation of, 33–35
Snap caps, 136
Solar Biangle, 8–10
Solar energy, 5, 6, 8–10, 19–21, 33
  all-seasons room addition, 19–21
  energy-saving two-faced house,
    8–10
  skylight installation, 33
Solar-hydrogen-and-wind turbine
    modules, 5, 6
Solid-color laminates, 128–131
Solid-wood strip paneling, 26–29
Sonotubes, 25
Spark knock service, 155, 157, 165–
    167
Spark plugs, 167
Spedec fasteners, 137
Sports center, 106–109
Staggered-box-beam fence, 98, 101
Staining, 138–139
Stem snaps, 136
Stilt houses, 2–3
Storage wall, 60–61
Storm doors, 142–144
Strip-molding jig, 91
Swimming pools. *See* Decks

Table saws:
  choosing blades for, 176–179
  electronic, 168–170
  four-in-one tool, 171
  laminates and, 130
  pusher for, 90
  workbench for, 95, 96. *See also*
    Saws

Tambour doors, 83–85
Tennis backboard, 106–109
Tenoning, 90
Thermal-energy-storage system, 5, 7
Thermostatic radiator valves, 41
Thermostats, 39
Threaded inserts, 135
Threaded rivets, 135
Tiles, 118–120, 140–141
  ceramic tiled patio, 140–141
  parquet deck, 118–120
Tools, 132–179
  biscuit joinery, 132–133
  carbide cutters, 176–179
  compact four-in-one tool, 171
  electronic table and radial saws,
    168–170
  glue guns, 172–175
  power-tool safety devices, 89–92
  workbench for compact tools,
    93–97. *See also* Saws
Trellis-shaded-slat fence, 99, 101
Trestle computer carrel, 67
Truss design, 20–21
Tungsten-carbide saw blades, 176–179
Two-faced bed/wardrobe divider,
    72–75
Two-tiered-louver fence, 98, 101

Vertical table jig, 90
Voltmeter, 159, 160

Waferboard, 86–88
Wardrobe divider, 72–75
Water pressure, 146
WEST System, 124, 127
Window installation, 30–32
Wiring, electrical, 148–151

Wood-epoxy construction, 124–127
Woodshed, 113–114
Woodworking projects, indoor, 42–97
  computer carrels, 65–67
  double-duty room, 62–64
  garage waferboard, 86–88
  grandfather clock, 42–49
  power-tool safety devices, 89–92
  Queen Anne drop-leaf table, 55–59
  Queen Anne secretary, 76–82
  Revolutionary lowboy, 50–54
  storage wall, 60–61
  swinging-bookcase room divider,
    68–71
  tambour doors, 83–85
  two-faced bed/wardrobe divider,
    72–75
  workbench, 93–97
Workworking projects, outdoor, 98–
    123
  butcher-block patio stool, 105
  cocky catamaran, 121–123
  easy-access woodshed, 113–114
  elevated deck with spa, 115–117
  fences, 98–101
  gazebo, 110–112
  parquet deck, 118–120
  patio sports center, 106–109
  planter deck (high-rise), 102–104
Woodworking techniques and ma-
    terials, 124–137
  biscuit joinery, 132–133
  fasteners, 134–137
  laminates, 128–131
  wood-epoxy construction, 124–127
Woodworking tools. *See* Saws *and*
    Tools
Workbench, 93–97